The Man From Ida Grove

A Senator's Personal Story

Harold E. Hughes

The Man
From Ida Grove

A Senator's Personal Story

WITH DICK SCHNEIDER

Published by

√chosen books
Lincoln, Virginia 22078
Distributed by Word Books • Waco, Texas 76703

Names of a few people in this book have been changed.

Unless otherwise indicated, all Scripture quotations are from the King James, or the Authorized Version of the Bible.

Scripture quotations identified RSV are from The Revised Standard Version of the Bible, copyrighted 1946, 1952, © 1971 and 1973.

Scripture quotations marked TLB are taken from *The Living Bible,* Paraphrased (Wheaton: Tyndale House Publishers, 1971) and are used by permission.

Library of Congress Cataloging in Publication Data

Hughes, Harold E
    The man from Ida Grove.

    1. Hughes, Harold E. 2. Legislators—United States—Biography. 3. United States. Congress. Senate—Biography. 4. Christian biography—United States. I. Schneider, Richard, 1922– joint author. II. Title.
E840.8.H83A33   328.73′092′4   [B]   78–31152

ISBN 0–912376–38–4

To Eva—Who shared this pilgrimage in victory and defeat, in sadness and in joy, with quiet strength and constant love; and who always believed in me.

To Connie—Who has helped me always, and whose strength in life's trials, I watch with admiration!

To Carol—Whose gentle spirit, courage, faith, and love amazed us all; and who still lights our way.

To Phyllis—Gentle in heart, strong in her beliefs, and faithful in life; and always my companion.

I LOVE YOU

Contents

Foreword

IN OUR SEARCH for happiness and fulfillment, we frequently go in opposite directions. In striving for excitement, power and even escape from reality, we usually find sadness, disappointment and despair.

In seeking to serve others, we come close to God. But it is in Christ that true meaning comes into one's life.

This is the powerful theme in this book: God's personal intervention in Harold Hughes' life. His search for a relationship with Christ brought to my mind the many men in the Scriptures who struggled with numerous human frailties on their way to becoming God's men. Senator Hughes struggled early in his life but gave in to alcohol. After futilely trying again and again, he found his situation hopeless. Broken and helpless, it was at this point that he called upon God as the only way out.

As you read this book you will learn more about the great work of Alcoholics Anonymous and can follow the transformation of one of God's children from the depths of despair to undreamed of honors and service to mankind.

Harold Hughes frankly reveals his life in this book. His experiences of rural poverty in the 1930s ring true and bring to memory circumstances in my own childhood. His love of outdoor life fills me with nostalgia.

Many of us are confronted by the problems of attempting to keep a semblance of family stability in the face of demands brought on by public life, not to mention retaining integrity in dealing with others in the process of power.

During his many years in public life, Harold Hughes has wrestled with heavy responsibilities. As a servant of Christ, he became a successful and popular governor and then went on to an illustrious career in the United States Senate. But also as a servant of Christ, he left the world's position of power. What wonderful hope this holds for each of us as we rejoice in this vivid demonstration of God's power working among us.

In this work we have the essence of life itself. My hope is that the spirit of this man and, even more, that Jesus Christ, Himself, might flow through this book and join with your spirit.

Albert H. Quie
Governor of Minnesota

1

My First Day
In the Senate

WIPERS SLAPPED AT sleet on my windshield as I drove along the
George Washington Memorial Parkway on a gray Friday morning,
January 3, 1969. White-frosted trees lining the Parkway suddenly
parted on my left to reveal the Washington Monument's pale spire
soaring into the distant mist. My heart quickened. For beyond the
monument was our nation's Capitol. And on this day I was to be
sworn in as a United States Senator.

If I had known what was about to happen to me in the Senate
chamber, my enthusiasm would have frozen like the mush on my
windshield.

Parkway traffic was heavy but once I had crossed Roosevelt
Bridge over the icy Potomac and turned on to Constitution Avenue
which led to the New Senate Office Building, it was even worse. I
was grateful that I did not have to worry about the big U-Haul
trailer that my aides and I had recently pulled from Iowa with our
personal effects.

Even so, as traffic backed up, I became concerned. Though the
Senate didn't convene until noon, there was much to do beforehand.
The building was new to me and I wanted enough time to find my
way around.

As I passed massive gray government buildings—Federal Reserve,
Department of Commerce, Interstate Commerce Commission—I
wondered how I would fit into this pressure cooker. Washington was
a completely new political arena for me. And I had to acknowledge
some apprehension.

To my right loomed the tremendous base of the Washington

11

Monument and to my left I got a quick glimpse, through the mist, of the White House. As I continued past the Internal Revenue, the Department of Justice and Federal Trade Commission, I couldn't help sensing the power centered in this city. Suddenly, the avenue turned and before me loomed the Capitol building.

I threaded my way past it to the gleaming white marble Senate Office Building where, after being cleared by a uniformed guard, I drove uneasily into an underground parking garage. Most of the car spaces had senators' names on little signs suspended over them but I was directed to a temporary spot.

An attendant pointed to a brown steel door and I followed a little passageway into the ground floor hall of the modern building. There I was directed down a long echoing hall lined with gray-swirled marble to my office: a temporary location until everyone had selected their headquarters. Senior senators had first choice and since I was 96th on a roll call of 100, I was at the bottom of the totem pole.

The hall was filled with a muted bustle of men striding purposely and efficient-looking women heel-clicking along the terrazzo floor.

As I checked the room numbers, I noticed that many of the suites had large state seals mounted on the burnished walnut doors. Some were carved of wood in colorful three-dimension. A nice touch, I thought, and mentally made a note to have one made for our Iowa office.

Finally, I found my temporary quarters. The senatorial five-room suites are generally the same: a reception room about 15 by 15 feet flanked by four inner offices, two on each side. Here I met my three aides who had driven to Washington with me: Park Rinard, Ed Campbell and Bill Hedlund. Two others, Martin Jensen and Dwight Jensen had remained temporarily in Des Moines to assist my former lieutenant governor, Robert Fulton, who had been sworn in as governor to fill the interim before the new incoming Iowa governor's inauguration later in January. Most of these men had been with me in Iowa where I had been governor for three terms.

As we stepped into the suite, we wondered how we were going to crowd our staff into such a small space. A senator usually has some thirty-five people working with him, including secretaries, research analysts, plus administrative and legislative assistants.

"It isn't a third as big as your office in the Statehouse, Chief," said one of my aides. He shook his head and muttered, "And no

mansion, servants, limousine, airplane and pilot. I'll take the governorship any day."

He could have added that I would be making about $15,000 less
annually. But that was all behind me now, and I was concerned
about what lay ahead. We freshmen would be sworn in at a ceremony
in the Senate Chamber at noon. Then Gene Kieffer, who handled my
campaign public relations, and his wife would be joining me for
lunch in the Senate dining room. I had no other plans. Many senators, it appeared, were having receptions, as I noticed through open
doors that offices were being set up with white linen-covered tables
for hors d'oeuvres. A festive atmosphere filled the halls and there was
much conviviality with bursts of laughter. But I felt very much alone.
In fact, there was no one in Washington with whom I really felt close
except my three aides. My wife, Eva, and 16-year-old daughter,
Phyllis, had remained in Des Moines to clear our belongings from
the governor's mansion.

At eleven o'clock, a buzzer sounded and a little orange light
glowed on the clock mounted on the office wall. It meant that the
Senate was about to open. An aide had already studied a chart which
explained the various rings and lights. For example, two white lights
indicated a quorum call, one meant a vote coming up, while various
sequences of rings indicated phases of Senate business ranging from
an upcoming "yea or nea" vote to "morning business concluded."

"Well," I said to my aides after the buzzer sounded, "wish me
luck." I stepped out into the hall and followed a group of men into
an elevator which took us down to the basement. There behind a
lighted "Subway Car to Capitol" sign was a miniature subway platform with people stepping into a waiting car. Each car was a separate unit controlled by a motorman, and drawing electric power
through a trolley pylon touching the ceiling. Open at the top with
metal and glass sides, each held twelve people on upholstered bench
seats. As one filled, it would move down a brilliantly illuminated
passageway.

I waited in line and stepped into the next car. The side doors
slid shut and we hummed along at about fifteen miles per hour,
traveling a quarter of a mile under snowy streets and parkways in
almost a minute to a platform underneath the Senate chamber.

An escalator and then an elevator lifted me to the Senate floor
level where I stepped into a small but ornate lobby. Fluted columns
of Italian marble soared to the vaulted ceiling. Busts of statesmen

flanked the Senate chamber door, and down a hall a large marble
Benjamin Franklin smiled benignly down on the milling crowd in
the hall. A sense of excitement filled the air and I was stopped several
times to show my pass.

Finally I reached the etched-glass doors leading into the chamber.
I hesitated inside the door. There was a hubbub of men talking, blue-
suited pages hurrying about and guards busily directing people. I
had seen the chamber before from the visitors' gallery. But this was
the first time I was entering it as a member. And standing on the
figure-carpeted floor I thought how much smaller it seemed.

A guard directed me to the semicircle of desks where the Democrats sat, and told me to look for one with my name written on a
piece of tape. Again, this would be a temporary location until the
final desk selections were made on the basis of seniority.

Vice President Hubert Humphrey, presiding officer of the Senate,
was talking with someone up at the black-marble rostrum. I recognized scholarly-looking Bill Fulbright from Arkansas, white-haired
Albert Gore of Tennessee and slender Mike Mansfield from Montana, the Majority Leader. On the other side of the room was silver-
maned Everett Dirksen from my neighboring state of Illinois. Near
him Barry Goldwater in his black horn-rimmed glasses waved at
someone in the visitors' gallery.

All of them seemed very much at ease, while I was awed and
hoped that I wouldn't make a fool of myself. As I glanced up to
the gallery overflowing with wives, children and friends waving to
the new senators being sworn in, I felt even more alone. My heart
panged as I thought about my family still back in Iowa; I missed them
terribly.

When I found the cherry-wood pedestal desk which bore my name,
I stood beside it for a long moment. It dated back to 1819 when it
was made to replace the equipment destroyed when the British
burned the Capitol in 1814.

A strange sense of destiny filled me as I stood there. For a moment I was a boy again, standing beside a cottonwood tree on an
Iowa hillside looking at the stars. It seemed then that God had
something important for me to do. Was this the calling to which He
had been leading me all my forty-seven tumultuous years?

I became aware of the bustle of fellow legislators taking their
seats. I looked across the aisle to see a silver-haired senator whom

I recognized from newspaper pictures. At that moment, we were the only two men in our area. I turned, reached out my hand and greeted him: "Hello, I'm Harold Hughes of Iowa."

The man stared at me through cold glassy eyes and snapped: "I don't like you, you s—— of a b——!"

I was stunned. The man continued glaring at me.

"Senator," I gulped, "you don't even *know* me."

He leaned forward. "I know everything about you, you s—— of a b——, and I don't like you."

I leaned back in shock. I had been told that in the Senate everyone treated each other like gentlemen regardless of their opinions, even in the intense heat of fiery debate.

I tried to smile. "Well, Senator, maybe if you'll give me a little time, you might get to like me."

He thrust his face into mine. I could catch the reek of alcohol and see the dissipation around his eyes.

"Anybody who would nominate Gene McCarthy for president has to be some sort of a g—— d—— nut," he spat.

I tried to be conciliatory: "So that is what's bothering you?"

He leaned back, still scowling. "That, among other things."

The sharp rapping of the gavel called the chamber to order and the room hushed. The chaplain, the Reverend Frederick Harris, and presiding officer, Hubert Humphrey, walked to the podium together and Humphrey announced that the chaplain would open the session with a prayer.

I hardly heard the prayer, as I was still in shock from my fellow senator's greeting. I do remember hearing the chaplain ask that we senators "rise to greatness of vision and soul as the anxious eyes of all nations are fixed upon this chamber."

After the rituals, some twenty of us freshmen senators went forward to the podium in groups of four where we were given the oath of office by Humphrey. As a traditional courtesy, Jack Miller, my fellow senator from Iowa and a Republican, escorted me to the podium. It was particularly comforting to have someone with me after what had just happened.

After taking the oath of office, ending with "So help me God," I and the other new senators signed a scroll, and photos were taken. Finally it was over and the Senate recessed for the day. But I was still in a daze as I walked out the chamber door. My aides met me and I mentioned the incident. They tried to jolly me out of it.

"C'mon, Chief, forget it," said Ed. "This is your day and you should make the most of it."

But a pall had been cast. The balance of the day was a haze of luncheon, visits and office detail decisions.

I drove home still suffering the verbal impact of my fellow senator. When I pulled into our driveway in McLean, I was tired and after calling home to find out how my family was, looked forward to a quiet evening and early bed.

My wife, Eva, had not seen the house as yet. I had bought it in a suburb southwest of Washington on an earlier trip after telling her about it on the phone. There just wasn't enough time in those hectic days to do anything else.

Eva and Phyllis would join me in three weeks. In the meantime, my aides were staying with me until they could find houses or apartments.

Sometime after dinner, Martin Jensen, who had come to Washington for a quick visit, suggested we all try out the sauna he had found in the basement. Soon we were relaxing on the wooden benches, breathing in the dry hot air. I almost fell asleep, though I could still hear the bitter words of my fellow senator.

As we finished, one of the fellows suggested: "Let's finish this up like the Finns do."

"You mean go outside?"

"Yeah. I tried it once in Finland. It really invigorates you."

"You've got to be kidding. It's below freezing out there."

"But that's what the Finns do and look how healthy they are."

So, wrapping towels around us, we all trotted out into the icy night.

The house sat on a semi-wooded acre with a creek behind it. Lights of other houses glimmered through the trees. An icy wind knifed me to the bone.

"Hey," one of the fellows said, "don't the Finns roll in the snow?"

"Y-y-y-you kidding?" another quavered. "I'm going to die as it is."

The wind picked up and the icy ground stung our feet. Instead of "doing like the Finns," all we five tired Americans wanted to do was get back to where it was warm.

Simultaneously we turned and rushed back to the house. Martin Jensen was first to the door. Then he stopped, turned and in a horrified whisper announced: "It's locked!"

One by one we went forward and tried it, each wanting to see the

awful truth for himself. Martin was certainly right. Evidently we
had let it lock behind us.

"What are we going to do?" asked one man, hugging himself.

"We sure can't go to the neighbors," shivered another as he began
to dance, holding his towel around him.

"Yeah," grunted another, "how would that look in the *Post* tomorrow: "NUDE SENATOR CALLS ON NEIGHBORS.""

"Hey," said Martin, "what about the front door?"

"I'm sure it's locked," I said, "but let's find out."

At that moment a door opened in the house across the street. As
the shaft of light spread across the ground, we jumped back. But it
was just someone calling a dog.

"Who's going to the front door?"

Finally, Ed Campbell agreed to be the sacrificial victim. We held
our breaths as he crept through the bushes to the front of the house.
Some minutes later he crawled back, shaking his head.

"The windows?"

We tried them all; they were locked.

"Well," I said, "I guess we'll have to break one."

"But the noise," said another. "I'd hate to have a police squad
get nosy."

By now all of us were shaking mightily. A brisk night breeze had
picked up and the damp towels had become icy.

"W-w-h-hat a-a-are w-we g-g-g-going to do?" one man quavered.

Then someone asked: "What about the door to the sun deck?"

"Yeah, maybe we can get someone up there!"

Ed Campbell, being the lightest of the bunch, said: "Well, guess
I'm it again."

The four of us boosted him to the railing; he grabbed it and
hoisted himself over. We heard his feet on the deck and then a
beautiful sound of a door creaking back.

"It's open!" he almost shouted.

"Hurry!" we screamed in whispers.

Soon the door to the ground-level recreation room opened and
we crowded in, making a beeline to the fireplace where logs still
glowed.

It was midnight by the time I gratefully crawled between the
sheets. It had been a most unusual day and I was completely fatigued.
I lay my head on the pillow and soon drifted off into that delicious
state of nothingness when . . .

Bzzzzzzzzzzzzzz.

I floated to near consciousness. It was the phone. Finally, I struggled up and grabbed the buzzing instrument.

A strange voice greeted me: "Hello, Senator Hughes?"

"Yes?"

"Well, I'm an aide to Senator —— and he'd like to talk to you."

Inwardly I groaned. He had named the man who had tongue-lashed me on the Senate floor. Now what?

Soon the same voice was on the phone.

"Hell," he slurred, "I don't even know why I'm calling you."

"Senator," I said wearily, "I know why you're calling me and so do you."

"Well if you're so g—— d—— smart, *why* am I calling you?"

"Because you've got a hell of a drinking problem and I think you want to ask for help and don't know how to go about it. As far as what happened today, let's forget it and start over again."

The phone was quiet for a moment. "Look," I continued, "let's quit shooting the bull and lay it on the table. You're in trouble. You've got a problem. If you want to do something about it, I'm willing to talk to you. If you don't, then quit bothering me; we'll just forget it."

Again, silence on the other end, finally an aggressive: "Boy, you really know it all, don't you!"

"No," I said. "I really know very little. I don't know much about the Senate. But I do know something about alcohol because, Senator, I am an alcoholic. And you know that or you wouldn't be calling me."

For a while there was just the hum of the telephone transmission lines. Then: "Senator," he said, "it's not going to make any difference. I have a bottle of pills here in my drawer; I'm going to take them and it's all going to be ended."

A chill entered me. I knew what he meant.

"No, Senator," I said, my voice tightening. I got out of bed and stood up holding the phone. "No, Senator, you're not going to take those pills or you wouldn't be telling me about it."

I continued speaking firmly: "You don't want to take them. You may wish you were dead right now but you don't want to do it that way. Why don't we get together and talk about it? You can quit drinking if you want to try. You can make it and I'm willing to help you."

Suddenly I had a chilling vision of myself in a similar phone conversation at another time, and an urgency surged within me.

"Senator," I said, "I'll come right down to where you are now if you want me to."

"No . . . ," he said, "I wouldn't do that."

"Well, I'm not doing much good on the phone," I answered. "I'll get dressed and come down to your office if that's where you are."

He protested a while longer. Finally, he said he'd send his driver for me. I got up and dressed, told my aides where I was going and then sat in the living room until I saw the headlights pull up into the driveway.

I stepped outside to a long black limousine and the driver, a young man in a dark business suit, held the door open for me. "So glad you're coming, Senator," he said.

I got into the back seat, and settled into the plush cushions. It would be a 25-minute trip to the Senate Office Building where a lonely desperate man sat drinking at midnight.

As the limousine purred through the night, I remembered how I had reached the desperation state in my own alcoholism only fifteen years before, and how a miracle had prevented me from taking my own life. I ran my hand across the soft rich upholstery of the limousine and thought back on my life. Could anything ahead possibly surpass the extraordinary happenings which had brought me to the nation's capital?

2

Storm Warning

THE FACT THAT life was dangerous and unpredictable was borne in on me as a five-year-old one hot muggy afternoon in the dusty yard of our little frame farmhouse in northwestern Iowa.

I was pulling my pet black hen in a wagon. I could hear Mother singing as she scrubbed clothes in the washtub in the kitchen. My eight-year-old brother Jesse was in the garden hoeing sweet potatoes.

Suddenly a sharp wind swirled dust devils across the yard. I looked up. I will never forget that sky, snapping-turtle green with white veins of lightning flickering across it. Thunder rumbled over the hills.

"Jesse! Harold! Help me get the chickens in!"

The screen door shrieked and Mother, her hands dripping soap suds, thumped across the wooden porch down the sagging steps into the yard. She was a large, heavy woman and her ruddy face was flushed with exertion. Sweat glued strands of auburn hair to her forehead and fear filled her gray eyes.

The whole world had turned green and a gale ruffled the chickens into feather balls.

"We must get them into the coop!" she cried. I scooped up my pet hen, ran to the chicken house, and threw it through the door. Jesse frantically shooed the flock with his hoe and a wild cackling rose with the screaming of the wind.

Mother looked up and gasped. Our cottonwood tree bent way over. A roar like a Chicago & Northwestern freight train thundering over the Maple River trestle filled the air.

"Boys, the root cellar!" Mother screamed. I looked again to the southwest and for the first time in my life saw the funnel of a tornado, weaving crazily across the hills toward us like a rearing black snake.

We struggled against the slashing wind and rain to the cellar; Mother yanked up the wooden door and shooed Jesse and me down the steps. The door banged shut above, leaving us gasping heavily in the moist coolness of the dark.

Suddenly an earsplitting explosion surrounded us; I knew the terrible funnel now clawed at our house. A hideous crying filled our ears as the old frame house screamed in agony; rafters convulsed, boards twisted, handwrought nails loosened from ancient bonds, and hundreds of Mason jars full of Mother's canning clattered on the wooden shelves.

I started to scream but something stopped me. Out of the dark I could hear the soft words of Mother: "Oh, Father, in You we trust . . . we know You will protect us."

The horrible thing attacking our house left and only the roar of rain remained. Jesse and I huddled under Mother's plump arms like chicks under a hen.

Then a different sound, as if a giant wagon were dumping tons of gravel on the house. "Hail," Mother whispered. Finally, it became quiet. Mother got up and we followed as she carefully pushed up the cellar door. Hail cascaded down the boards. We stepped into a cold soggy atmosphere.

Mother looked up at the house. "Thank God!" she breathed. "It skipped us." But the entire top of the cottonwood was gone; the funnel had dipped that close. The yard was littered with hailstones, shingles and strange-looking pale yellow objects.

"Oh no!" Mother cried. She bent down and picked up a naked chicken. Every feather had been plucked from it by the tornado. There were many small bodies in pools of rain water, looking like dressed chickens in the butcher shop. Some still lurched wildly about.

Mother sank onto the steps and cried. The chickens were vital to our family. In the winter, Mother would dress and cut them up. Dad would take her into Ida Grove in our old Model T and she would walk from house to house selling them for 75 cents each. The money was a vital addition to what Dad earned on road gangs and construction work.

But even so, that night as we all sat around the dinner table, Dad gave particular thanks for the day and for us and the house being spared.

Dad prayed as if God was sitting right at our table. His closeness with the Almighty seemed to run in the family. And I thought about all the uncles and cousins in my family who were Southern Baptist preachers back in Kentucky where Mother and Dad had been raised. Mother always hoped that one of us boys would become a preacher but I had a feeling the preaching strain of the family ended in those Kentucky hills. Instead, by the age of five I had determined to become a hunter and trapper. I came by that ambition naturally. Back in Pulaski County where my parents came from it was both sport and sustenance for the Hugheses and Kellys. It had been that way for two hundred years, ever since the Hugheses migrated to the New Land from Wales and the Kellys from Northern Ireland. Along with other pioneers, they had worked their way by wagon and flatboat down the Cumberland River to the hills of Kentucky.

There in 1910 a shy young auburn-haired mountain girl and a strapping black-haired youth noticed each other over the oaken pews in the little Cabin Holler Baptist Church. Etta Kelly, who was to become my mother, came from a medium-sized family but my father-to-be Lewis Hughes had 17 great-aunts and uncles. The size of his family never ceased to amaze me. His grandfather had two wives; the first had ten children before she died and the second had eight. Dad said we had blood kin by the name of Hughes living all over the country.

On a cold February 4th in 1912, Dad and Mother were married in her family's cabin by her uncle, a Baptist minister. Dad was also celebrating his 21st birthday that day. He was rather old for a groom of his time, but the two didn't have a dime to their name. They traveled up to McLean County in Illinois where Dad found work as a foreman on the County Poor Farm.

Often as I'd sit by the wood stove in the kitchen chunking the butter churn while Mother kneaded bread dough, she would tell me stories of their life on that farm.

I always liked to hear her tell about the little boy after whom I was named. He belonged to the Joneses, a couple who supervised the farm, and mother as yet without children, loved the baby dearly. When she'd clean the dining room she'd put little Harold Everett Jones up on the sideboard where he'd chortle gleefully.

She kept in touch with his parents and eight years later when I came along she named me Harold Everett.

There were sad stories, too. It was common, said Mother, for young unmarried girls to go there to have their babies. Sometimes the baby would die and Dad would have to build a little box, carry it out to the grave and say words over it.

Mother would tell of old people being brought to the county farm because no one wanted them. "They would sit on the porch all day, vacant eyes looking out on the prairie," she sighed. "Sometimes, when the supper bell would ring, one would still be sitting there, never to arise again." She told of finding a cracked and faded photograph clutched in the hand of one old man who had died.

Tears would fill my eyes and I would look up at Mother, the butter churn quiet: "Didn't they have any family at all?"

"No, Harold." Her gray eyes looked down softly at me. "There are lots of folks who don't have anyone at all."

"And they just go someplace to die?"

"They do . . . they do," she said quietly, again leaning into her bread dough.

As I pounded the butter I would think how blessed we were. I had a dad and mother and brother whom I dearly loved. Big six-foot Dad had taught Jesse and me all about the wild life that roamed the hills and valleys grooved in this area by glaciers thousands of years ago. Built like an oak, Dad was crowned with a mane of heavy curly black hair. Grandpa said I'd look like my father when I grew up, except that his eyes were gray-green and mine were brown. Those gray-green eyes seemed to see everything.

While we were chugging along a dirt road in the Model T one afternoon, he pulled the brake lever. "Look!" he pointed his pipe at a fence row. Finally I saw what his keen eye had spotted: a skunk slowly picking his way through the bluestem prairie grass. Dad accelerated the car a hundred feet, stopped, slid his 200-pound frame from under the wheel and led me to the fence. "Now stand here quietly, Son, and watch him walk by you."

I didn't believe the skunk would do it. But I stood there, still as a tree. Slowly the little fellow approached; suddenly, he scented me and stood frozen, one front paw poised in the air. After a breathless minute, I watched him put it down and amble toward me. He circled me twice—to see who I was, I guessed—and continued on down the fence.

As I leaped back into the car, my heart pounding with excitement,

Dad put his big hand on my shoulder. "See, Harold, animals can get along with us, and we with them. God gave them to sustain us; and we have to take care of them, too."

Dad did this by leaving wild areas for shelter between our fields, spreading grain for ducks and bringing home hurt creatures for Jesse and me to nurse.

In turn, the wildlife helped support us. For without the extra money earned from running trap lines, we could not have existed. A skunk pelt brought two dollars, a muskrat a dollar. On rare occasions we'd get a mink which was cause for celebration; its pelt meant as much as ten dollars.

Each morning at three o'clock Jesse and I would awake in the straw-tick bed we shared on the second floor of the farmhouse. Teeth chattering, we'd dress quickly and soon be out under the bright stars to tend our lines along the Maple River, the snow crunching under our boots. By five we'd be home for breakfast and at eight we'd be in school.

Trapping was why Jesse and I never got our photographs taken with the high school football team on which we both played. The trapping season opened on the same date the pictures were taken and Jesse and I skipped school that day to set out our lines.

We'd go separate ways. I loved to be out in the fields alone, particularly when I had a heavy problem to think about. In winter I'd cozy up in a hollow behind a hill with snow blowing and feel perfectly at peace. Often I would stand on a hillside looking up into a dark sky ablaze with stars and sense a strong impression that the One Who created them had something special for me to do. And then at other times I'd wonder if I was just a speck in the vast universe. What was life? I wondered. Scratching out a living like my parents or reaching for one of those stars?

As the eastern hills began to form against the sky, a morning breeze sighed through the maples and I remembered some words Mother read from the Bible about the wind blowing where it listeth.

And then I'd hear a whistling above the wind and my heart quickened. That would be Jesse. My brother whistled wherever he went. You could hear him coming a half mile away whistling "Red Wing." Three years older than I, Jesse took after Mother. He had the same auburn hair, freckled face and cheerful Irish humor. I admired his hair, so much handsomer than my own black strands which I felt I inherited from the mysterious Cherokee Indian girl who had been my great-great-grandmother on my mother's side. Jesse's red hair was so curly he'd sometimes explode in the mirror as he tried to comb it. But these verbal explosions were about the extent of Jesse's aggressiveness.

Jesse played right tackle on the football team. He was good but did not have the brutal streak so vital to success in the game. He was a gentle, loving person and I could see him holding back from hurting an opponent in the rough and tumble.

As right guard, I always fought to win. But oh, how I wished Jesse was better than I; I wanted him to win at everything. We were about equal in size. And people who watched us play said we looked like two big elephants on the field. "Yes," cracked one sportswriter in his column, "like two pachyderms." From then on folks started calling Jesse "Big Pack" and me "Little Pack."

Linked in name, we tried to do everything together. Some days the two of us would step into that strange world of the country club. I could never relate our sparse life to its rolling greens, parking lot of glistening autos, and the well-dressed people who seemed so light-hearted and debonair as they stepped into the mysterious interior of the clubhouse.

But the golf course was a vital source of money to Jesse and me. For we entered its world as caddies. Odebolt Creek meandered through the links. And occasionally a windfall would come our way when someone would slice a ball into it and we could retrieve it.

One chilly morning I was standing near this creek when I heard a gruff "Hey boy!" I looked up to see a heavyset man in bright yellow knickers staring down at me; a caddy supported his golf bag of glowing leather.

"Yes, you!" he barked, pointing to the creek. "Two of my balls went in there." He named an expensive brand, adding that they were new.

I looked at the creek and hesitated for a moment. It had just rained and the waters were muddy and cold. But it was a job offer. Stripping to my underwear, I waded in to where he pointed. Either he had been mistaken in direction or the roiling waters had carried the balls downstream, but it took some time as I explored the slimy stream bottom. Finally I found the balls and emerged sputtering and coughing.

Pleased with my success I scrambled up the hill to my benefactor proudly holding the balls aloft. He grunted, fished in his pocket and handed me two nickels.

I stared at them for a moment, speechless. It wasn't so much the amount of money that mattered as what my efforts meant to him. As he reached for the balls, I looked at his expensive woven shirt and his complacent face and felt that he probably showed more response to his dog for fetching a stick.

Indignation flooded me. Thrusting the two nickels back at him, I turned and flung the balls back into the creek.

Then I glared at him and walked away. Behind me an explosion of obscenities mounted. I turned and looked back at the man. "Boy!" he screamed, his face flushed, "I'm going to have you banned from this club forever!"

Fear rose in me. The money I made caddying was vital to our family. Then I saw the faces of the three other men in his group. All were laughing. "C'mon," one joshed, "it serves you right, you old skinflint." The four walked off, the other three still laughing and clapping him on the back.

I ran home feeling degraded; mother soothed me and then tried to tell me why I should love this man. I was having an increasingly difficult time understanding her theology of loving others, no matter what, especially when those who had so much seemed to take advantage of those who didn't. But I could understand something of the love she meant when she and Dad took homeless children into our home. They would be waifs whose parents had died, or were too ill to care for them. Mother's big heart would take them in for months at a time. She started doing this before Jesse and I were born and continued it after we came along. I remember two sisters and their brother who spent a whole winter with us. When it got too cold to sleep upstairs, we'd all bed down on pallets in the parlor, like spokes in a wheel, our heads toward the Round Oak wood stove with the nickel-rimmed top and bottom.

Mother's compassion for homeless children came from her parents, I'm sure. Though they both died while I was young, I can still remember Grandpa Kelly, a tall, stately man with red curly hair and mustache, gently ushering me into Grandma's bedroom where she lay ill with cancer, her long black hair wreathing her pale face. Despite her pain, Grandma talked long and kindly with me, and in her melodious voice I could sense that she was a woman used to laughing much. Mother had this same inner joy and even when she rose at four in the morning to bake biscuits and cornbread for the day she'd be singing.

Her hands were red and rough from scrubbing clothes in the old wood tub which she filled from the hand pump in our kitchen. And sweat usually plastered her hair to her ruddy forehead. Then when we'd visit Grandpa and Grandma Hughes, who lived in a little frame house in Ida Grove, I would see another side of her.

She would plump down at Grandma's parlor organ, pull out all the stops, and pump out "The Old Rugged Cross," "Bringing in the Sheaves," and other hymns. I'd stand by the organ and marvel at what Mother must have been like as a young girl. The lines vanished from her creamy freckled face and she looked like an angel as she threw her head back and sang.

After the singing, Grandpa would grab me, and make me sit on his knee while we had a prayer together. I fretted and squirmed and couldn't wait to get down. He seemed a hundred years old and I was in awe of him. A big powerful man who worked as a lumberjack and on road gangs, he never swore or acted like most other men. Sometimes I'd accompany him with the rough men who helped build the timber bridges and handled the blasting and horse-drawn pile-drivers. They called him "Mr. Hughes" and I noticed at noon they all waited for Grandpa to open his lunchbox first, for they knew he was going to pray.

Grandma Hughes was just as devout and exceptionally frugal. She always wore dresses down to the floor and had a habit of drying out her teabags and using them over again.

My grandparents' strict homelife was emulated at our house where Mother persuaded my father to ban alcoholic beverages. Dad did get away with a pipe and snuff, keeping the little round tins of Copenhagen in the sidedoor pocket of the Model T.

One soft summer's morning, I discovered the remnants of another sin. I had been in the outhouse with the door half open for light as I studied the shotguns in the Sears & Roebuck catalog that hung on the wall. As I hitched up my coveralls, a glint in the corner caught my eye. Investigating behind a loose board, I pulled out a dust-covered bottle half full of amber liquid. I knew immediately what "Schenley" meant and to whom it belonged.

I remembered one night a year before when Dad had come home late wearing a silly grin. Mother had really lit into him while Jesse and I shivered in our room. In the morning I had noticed a fender of the Model T had been banged in where he had caught a fence post. Dad laid off the drinking after that, though from time to time I'd find some forgotten bottles he had stashed away earlier in the shed or an old boot. Even so, Mother continued to talk to us about the evils of liquor and those who consorted with drinkers. I also heard this preached often from the pulpit of our Methodist church and by the time I was ten I was convinced drinking was as bad as robbing a bank.

I'd heard a lot about that sin, too. Whenever we'd all be sitting around the fire on a cold winter's night, I'd ask Mother to tell us again about the outlaw who, according to family legend, was a distant relative.

Continuing to peel her apples, she would tell about the one called Jesse James while my brother and I sat wide-eyed, hugging ourselves in excitement. Dad pooh-poohed the family connection. But as the popcorn sputtered on top of the stove, he would lean his huge frame back and tell how Jesse felt the railroads had cheated his family and neighbors.

"But," he would add, "that was no reason for Jesse to go out and do what he did. Look where it got him." We shivered, remembering the words of the song: "He was shot in the back by Mr. Howard, that dirty little coward."

That was something Dad would not tolerate—taking things for which he had not paid. During the Depression, many schoolmates whose families were "on relief" seemed to eat and dress better than we did. But Dad would load up the old Stevens 12-gauge and if he couldn't find a rabbit we didn't have meat with our corn meal. He didn't believe in wasting anything, either. And that included the shotgun shell "seconds" we bought. When I'd go out with ten shells and come back with two rabbits, Dad would say that if one went out with ten shells, he should come back with ten rabbits. It wasn't too long before Jesse and I could do that.

If there was anything that came to us beyond the vital needs of meager everyday living, it came from Uncle Oscar and Aunt Esther. I'll never forget Jesse's and my amazement at the bright new scooters we found waiting for us one Christmas morning, thanks to this younger brother of Dad's. Tall sandy-haired Uncle Oscar and his gracious wife lived in Des Moines where he worked for the city and she was a librarian. They had no children and were like second parents, Uncle Oscar often telling Jesse and me stories about when he was with the Rainbow Division in World War I.

Sometimes Dad felt they indulged us. But there was one time in particular when he was in no position to refuse any kind of help. That was when his face was white as flour and his hair looked even blacker as he lay in his bed hemorrhaging rectally from ulcers. His long underwear was stained red. Jesse and I tried to help Mother get rubber sheets under him but the blood still collected on the floor.

Our family physician, Dr. Morehead, did everything he could, even though we owed him for the last several visits when Jesse had scarlet fever. But there was nothing more he could do.

Then some town doctors came and examined Dad. I remember one looking up at Mother and asking if she could afford to send him to the hospital. I knew we didn't have a cent in the house; Jesse and I had been picking up coal along the railroad tracks to keep the cooking stove going.

At the doctor's question, Mother's face blanched and she asked if she could pay later. The man's lips tightened and he shook his head. "Well," he said, snapping shut his bag, "there's not much use bringing him in anyway; he isn't going to live."

Then Neil Nelson, a straw-haired Scandinavian, roared up to the door. He was the boss of Dad's county work crew. He had removed the right front seat from his beat-up old Pontiac and made a pallet. He had shoulders like the haunches of a bull and in ten minutes he had Dad stretched out in his car.

He ruffled my hair as he told Mother he had called Uncle Oscar who said to get him into a hospital. He'd pay the bills.

Mother got into the Pontiac's back seat to hold Dad's head and the three drove off into the dusk toward Sioux City.

Jesse and I sat at the kitchen table crying. We had never been alone before. Finally we got some of the squirrel stew Mother had made for us and tried to eat. I broke off a big piece of homemade bread, but couldn't swallow. I kept hearing what the doctor had said about my father.

It was midsummer and a hot night breeze rattled the corn stalks. When Jesse had to go to the outhouse, I took the lantern and went along with him for company.

That night we huddled together in our bed. Above the whine of locusts, a dog's lonesome wail rose and fell, and my spine chilled. I lay there staring at the ceiling.

"Jess?"

"Yes?"

"They say a dog howls when someone dies."

Jesse turned over. His voice was choked. "Yeah, I heard something like that."

"What are we going to do if Dad dies?"

The room was silent for a moment.

"Well, I've been thinking about the C's."

That was the Civilian Conservation Corps in which young men could earn money for their families while working on government projects like parks and forestry work. Being 15 years old, Jesse felt he could get in.

But we never had to find out. In a few days Mother came home and excitedly told us that Dad was going to get well. In the meantime our high school coach, Sylvester Vickerstaff would come over with his wife bearing steaming dishes of baked beans and escalloped potatoes. I remember going out at night then to try to tell God thanks. But I had a difficult time picturing Him standing there.

So I just sat looking up at the stars, feeling grateful and thinking about people like Uncle Oscar, Neil Nelson, and the Vickerstaffs who came along when no one else seemed to want to help.

It wasn't long before all of us were around the table again after supper, singing. Perhaps it was our Welsh ancestry, but we never had more fun than when we'd turn up the coal oil lamps and Dad would play his mouth harp, or harmonica, and we'd all sing "My Old Kentucky Home," "Red Wing" or "Way Down South in Dixie." Dad would whoop, slap his hand on his overalls and say that maybe we should start a family singing group and try out for the Barn Dance on radio station WHO.

"Yes," Mother laughed, "this year, the next and then the fireworks!" That was her favorite expression and I always wondered if she said it because she was born on the Fourth of July.

We celebrated her birthday with eating and singing and sat up late watching Dad shoot off Roman candles and a few skyrockets he picked up in town. Then, when bedtime came and not wanting to go to our hot upstairs room, Jesse and I slept on the open porch to be awakened by the flies in the morning.

We left that little place in the country when Dad borrowed $600 from Grandpa and bought a house on the edge of Ida Grove. It was a small one-story frame building with yellow paint curling from weathered boards. There was a living room, two bedrooms, kitchen and storeroom with the usual root cellar. The big difference was town water.

"No more pumping!" Mother exclaimed. To her it was a gift from heaven. We did have a garden, so Mother was able to continue canning her 500 quarts of vegetables each season. I hated shelling peas, stringing beans and hoeing the sweet potato ridges. Why, I wondered, did we have to grow sweet potatoes when no one else in town did?

One good thing about moving into town for me was that it was a shorter walk to school. I liked school because the best things seemed to happen there. When I was ten I had won my family's first Christmas tree at school. We had never been able to afford one, but one year my teacher let the class draw for the schoolroom tree. I won it and proudly carried it home where we decorated it with strung popcorn and cranberries.

Another reason I liked school was because I was active in athletics and music; I sang bass baritone and played the Sousaphone. It was a dented old horn and the keys were loose but I had won some district contests. My most embarrassing moment at one such contest happened when I stepped out on the stage, lifted the Sousaphone and began to blow. But instead of music, out came a low Bronx cheer.

Dumbfounded, I stopped and shook the bell of the instrument. Out popped a butter carton that some jokester had dropped down the horn's throat while it rested on the instrument rack.

But my real problem at such state meets came when both our track team and band would compete simultaneously. I'd race back and forth between the music finals and track events. Often I'd find myself throwing the shot put and discus in street shoes and band uniform trousers.

"Pack," yelled my exasperated coach, "you've got to quit playing that damn horn!"

I didn't, but I more than made up for it at a state high school track meet in Ames at Iowa State University. I had won local meets with the discus but at Ames I felt there were many fellows who would outdo me.

After the first round, one of the visiting coaches, a stranger to me, took me aside. "Son," he said, "you just settle down and you'll win this meet."

I looked at him wonderingly.

He put his hand on my shoulder. "I can tell that you're better than the other guys here. So don't be nervous; just forget them and do your best."

His words gave me heart. On the next round I went out and threw the discus with the same freedom I felt when throwing it behind our shed. I won the meet, becoming state discus champion.

This was a breakthrough, to realize that I was as good as anyone else in the state and not just some kid from down a back alley. It didn't make any difference what kind of clothes I wore or how much money my family had, I could compete with anybody.

But school wasn't all good times. I'll never forget the night Jesse graduated from high school. Our house was very quiet that evening after Jesse left for the ceremonies. Mother sat by the kitchen window, watching the sun sink in the west. Dad was nailing some rubber soles he had gotten at the dime store on the bottoms of his shoes.

As I was preparing to leave for the exercises, I stopped and asked Dad: "How come you all aren't going to Jesse's graduation?"

Pain crossed his face. He sighed, put down his hammer. "Guess I better tell you the truth, Son." He looked toward the room where Mother sat and dropped his voice. "It's because your mother has no decent clothes to wear," he said. "She knows all the town ladies will be there in their fine clothes and she's just too embarrassed to go."

He wiped sweat from his forehead. The May night was hot and June bugs rattled against the screen. "And Son, I rightly can't go and leave her sitting here all alone."

I walked out into the yard, leaned against the side of the house, and wondered why some folks had to live poor and others didn't seem to have any trouble. Outside of people like those who used the golf course and a few of the local merchants, the poor seemed to be in the majority these years. And many of them seemed to be on the move. Husbands, fathers, single men who couldn't get jobs would take to the roads hunting work. Perhaps Omaha had something to offer. So, some night they would catch a freight leaving town, hunched behind the coal on the engine tender, or riding the rods underneath the box cars. In a never-ending search for work, they traveled for weeks, months. They were called hobos, men of the road. Not bums, but good men looking for honest labor.

By the tracks not far from our house was a hobo jungle. Sometimes Jesse and I would go there during the day. There'd be a fire ring of stones, gallon cans in which they heated soup, sheetmetal propped up against the fence under which they slept.

Often these men would come to our door for something to eat. I'd see compassion in Mother's gray eyes as she'd give them a sandwich and coffee. Usually they would chop wood or hoe the garden for their meal.

Dad would talk with them, finding out where they hailed from. Chicago, St. Louis, Cleveland. Yes, they had heard there was work further west: Sioux City? Lincoln? Maybe Denver?

But for the grace of God Jesse felt he would be traveling too. He was fortunate, however, and got a job as a mechanic in Baxter's Garage in Ida Grove. He earned $12 for six days' work, which included the late hours on Saturday when the farmers came into town and had their cars fixed while their wives shopped. I remember Jessee proudly putting his first week's pay on the kitchen table, grease still under his fingernails. "See Mom," he said, "$11.88. They took 12 cents out for Social Security. That's for my old age!" he laughed.

A strange chill pricked my heart when Jesse said those words and I felt a deep sadness. Why? I wondered. I shuddered and then shook it off.

I missed seeing my brother in the high school halls. I also found myself suffering increasingly from one big problem. I was interested in girls but felt tongue-tied and inadequate around them.

Undoubtedly, it stemmed from Mother teaching us that all women were to be placed on a pedestal and not be offended in any way. From time to time we heard of the terrible things that awaited boys who got girls "in trouble." Mother meant well, but in my subconscious mind I began to associate warm thoughts about girls with hellfire and damnation. Thus, at high school dances I found it exceedingly difficult to make small talk with the girls the way my friends seemed to do so easily. Afraid to put my arm around a girl and not really knowing how to dance, I'd stand at the wall and talk football with the fellows.

It was at one of these dances that I found a new freedom. Two fellow sophomores approached me with a gleam in their eyes. "Pack," they asked, "do you have two bucks?"

"For what?" I asked. I still had some money left from a lifeguard job I had at the town swimming pool.

They drew me around the corner. "Look, we've found a guy who'll buy us a bottle at the state liquor store. All we have to do is give him the money and one swig."

Anything seemed better than hungrily watching others enjoy themselves on the dance floor. I quickly handed over the money and they stepped outside.

In twenty minutes, an elderly man sidled up to the door and motioned to us. We stepped out into the hot cricket-chirping night. From under his shirt he pulled out a bottle. The contents glinted in the light from the door.

"First mine," he said, and held it to his mouth.

"Okay! Okay!" shouted one of my friends, grabbing for the bottle. "That's enough. Leave some for us."

He handed the bottle to me. I wiped off the top with my shirtsleeve and lifted it to my lips. I wasn't prepared for the searing fire. I doubled up coughing and choking. My friends laughed so hard they had to slump down on the wooden steps.

One took the bottle and the two of them drank their share, then handed it back. By the time it was almost gone, I felt as if I were walking two feet off the ground. Strains of "Red Sails in the Sunset" flowed from within the hall.

"C'mon, let's go in!" urged my friends.

"Yeah!" I said in a new burst of freedom.

A mellow glow filled me; strangely, I was no longer bothered by inhibitions. I spotted the girl I had been watching all evening and walked up to her. It was easy to ask her to dance, even easier to slip my arm around her waist and glide off onto the floor. Swaying to the music came naturally, and I found myself in an exhilarating whirl of melody and the perfume of this lovely soft-bodied creature in my arms.

"So you're the great Pack Hughes," she smiled, looking up at me. "I've watched you play football; you're pretty good out there."

"Honey," I said, drawing her close, "you ain't seen nothin' yet."

3

The Girl
I Left Behind

WHEN I TOOK a drink I never wanted to stop. Some sort of a chemical process took place in my body making me want to drink three for every one someone else drank.

I never really liked the taste of the burning stuff. Nor did I drink for the glow that most people seemed to crave. I drank because it lifted my inhibitions and made me relaxed and easygoing at dances and social affairs. Whenever a bottle was passed around, whether it was outside a country dance hall or in the rest room at a high school social, it stayed the longest with me.

Some Saturday nights we'd drive up to Storm Lake where there was a big dance pavilion off the highway. On one of these nights I was elected to get the bottle.

Our source was the usual place at the end of the parking lot. I picked my way among silent dark cars, a few of them occupied, until I got to the old Buick Roadmaster. A man under a grease-stained straw fedora was slumped behind the wheel.

"Hey," I whispered.

He lifted the brim of his hat and stared coldly at me, then at the bills in my hand.

"C'mon," I urged, "you know what I want." Finally he passed out a bottle of whiskey and I gave him the five singles my buddies and I had collected.

This was one of those nights that I simply could not stop drinking. Finally, my friends brought me home early in the morning. Struggling to maintain consciousness, I lurched into chairs as I felt my way into Jesse's and my bedroom.

I collapsed on the edge of the bed and the sickness within welled into a torrent that I threw up on the floor. Stomach strained and throat burning, I fell backwards on the bed.

Sometime later I dimly heard someone working around me. I opened an eye to see Jesse mopping the floor. I tried to sit up; he put down the mop and sat on the bed.

"Brother, I'm sure worried about you."

"Aw, mind your own business," I groaned. He rose and finished cleaning the floor. As he squeezed out the mop, a pale light glowed through the box elder trees outside the bedroom window. I could hear my dad snoring in the other room. The bed sagged as Jesse climbed back in it. His feet were cold. Guilt filled me. Jesse didn't drink, yet he never condemned me.

He was quiet, but I knew he was not sleeping. Rising on one elbow, he said in a low voice: "You know you're killing Mother and Dad by doing this."

I turned to the wall. I knew it. I could see the pain in Mother's eyes every time I announced I was going out with the fellows. As yet, she found it difficult to talk to me about it. Instead, she would remind me, "Harold, I believe God has something special for you. You must keep yourself fit for it."

The next morning I swore to myself that I would never drink again. It was an easy promise to make with aching head and nauseated stomach.

The opportunity to break it came shortly. I got summer work with the county road construction crew. Most of the men were older than me. On rainy days, we'd sit in the construction shed. Someone always had a bottle to pass around and I tried to prove that I was as much a man as any one of them.

However, my drinking never seemed to bother my school work or athletics. Early one December morning in my high school senior year, Jesse, Dad and I were taking off before dawn in the Model A to hunt mallards on the Missouri River. Before leaving town, Dad ducked into the Tavern Cafe for a newspaper and as we pulled away Jesse, who was sitting in the back seat, opened it.

"Hey, Little Pack!" he pummeled me on the back. "Look at you!" He pointed to the sports page where I was pictured with a number of other seniors. I had made the Iowa All-State Football Team as a right guard.

That and my other athletic records, plus the help of an attorney friend, Arthur Johnson, earned me a scholarship to the University of Iowa where I planned to study aeronautical engineering. What the scholarship actually amounted to was the promise of a job on campus; half of my wages would go toward paying my tuition.

My graduation suit was ordered from the Sears & Roebuck catalog; it was the first suit I ever owned. I put it on early the evening of the graduation exercises to give Dad and Mother an opportunity to see me in it. Again, Mother or Dad wouldn't make their son's graduation because they lacked the proper clothes.

Before leaving the bedroom, I glanced into the mirror and hesitated in surprise. The suit accentuated the maturity I had gained in my senior year. What had happened to the youth in dusty overalls on the sun-baked bank of Maple River?

That hot May night as I sat among the other perspiring graduates in the Ida Grove High School auditorium, a deep poignancy overcame me. My mind drifted from the drone of the speaker out through the open window into the warm dusk where cicadas hummed. What waited, I wondered, beyond the bright green of the emerging corn and the sun-softened asphalt highway that stretched to the horizon? As the clergyman gave the prayer, I thought about God and wondered if I really believed in Him. He seemed so remote now from my feelings and desires.

After the flurry of congratulations and last-minute signing of high school annuals, I hurried home and packed my suitcase. I was leaving for the University of Iowa to start working through the summer toward my fall tuition. A fellow graduate's father was driving him to Illinois and they offered to drop me off at Iowa City.

Mother, Dad, Jesse and I stood awkwardly in the kitchen that night as we said goodby. Jess gripped my hand, laughing, and saying it was good there was one intelligent guy in the family; Dad struggled to find the right words; Mother cried, hugging me to her great bosom and reminding me to study hard to prepare myself for the work God had for me to do.

I took one last look at the oilcloth-covered table around which we had all sat so many nights, then turning my head so they wouldn't see the tears, I walked out into the night where the car waited.

Iowa City turned out to be a pleasant town with tree-shaded streets and friendly people. I shared a room in a private home with a boy who had graduated from Ida Grove High School a year before. He was away when I arrived, but his clothes were hanging in the closet. I didn't need much room for my work clothes, two pair of slacks and two shirts. After hanging them up, I sat on the bed thinking of home. This was the first time in my life I was away for an extended time; I felt as if I were perched on some lonely star.

I worked all summer at the university as a steamfitter's helper. They paid me eighteen dollars a week, out of which they kept half to apply toward my tuition. My meals were provided by the Downtowner Cafe where I worked each night after eight o'clock closing, mopping the floor and scrubbing tables.

As I wanted to stay in shape for the athletic season, I tried not to drink much. When fall came, students surged onto the campus and I found myself completely engrossed in studying, working and training on the university football team. Before I knew it, Christmas came and I was fortunate to get a ride back to Ida Grove. It was a wonderful vacation, though I missed seeing a number of my friends. The local National Guard ambulance unit to which they belonged had been called up for active duty in late 1940. However, their parents all expected them to be home in a few months when the "alert" was over.

Of the usual holiday parties, one will forever stand out in my memory. I was chatting with someone when I happened to look into the living room. A girl stood next to the Christmas tree; her creamy complexion glowed in the holiday lights and her deep brown eyes sparkled as she laughed in response to someone's remark. I was mesmerized. I never did get the opportunity to talk with the petite girl with the lilting voice that evening but learned that her name was Eva Mercer and she had just moved to Ida Grove from Holstein, a town about ten miles away.

Back at college I still found myself thinking of this slim elfin-like girl with the lustrous black hair.

In May I returned home for the summer. Ida Grove had not changed, I thought, as the bus moved down Second Street. I spotted some friends coming out of the tavern and noticed that the paint was beginning to peel off the old wooden sign that hung in front of the Baxter Hotel.

Mother and Dad had been getting along fairly well and my red-headed brother was happy in his work at the garage. He also had a girl.

There was a carnival in town that week and some friends and I walked down the midway one hot June night. We met another group near the ferris wheel and stood laughing and joking when, suddenly, the lights seemed to shimmer together and the merry-go-round music faded. There she was, the petite raven-haired girl from the Christmas party, Eva Mercer.

We ended up walking down the midway together hand-in-hand, the dazzling lights sparkling in her dark brown eyes. Strange, I thought, I had had nothing to drink and yet it was so easy to talk with this little girl whose head came up to my shoulder.

I learned that Eva lived with her sister and mother. She had a brother living away from home. Her father had died when she was very young. I was pleased to discover that she, her mother and sister liked Ida Grove and planned to stay.

We saw each other constantly that summer, going to picnics, dances, swimming parties. By the time I returned to college that August of 1941, Eva and I had decided we didn't want to wait any longer and we were married in a quiet little ceremony.

Perhaps that is why I found college so dull that fall; my thoughts kept drifting back to Eva, her sparkling eyes, the scent of her hair, her voice rippling like a meadow brook in spring. The more I thought of Eva, the more I wanted to be with her. At night, after finishing my clean-up work at the cafe, I'd walk under the quiet dark maples back to my little room and find myself thinking: Why stay here when I could just as well work at home and be with Eva? The more I pondered this, the less important playing football and becoming an aeronautical engineer seemed to be.

By the end of September I had decided I wanted to live as a married man and not a college student. So I hitchhiked back to Ida Grove. Mother's gray eyes filled with tears after I walked into the house that afternoon. "You're not going back?" she asked in disbelief, pushing back a whisp of hair.

"No Mom, I've had it," I said. "I think I can do just as well without college."

"But how could you?" she cried. "You're only 19; you have to prepare for . . ." She stopped, turned her head and fled into the bedroom sobbing.

When Dad came home he was startled to find me. When I told him, he didn't say anything, just stared at the table, clasping and unclasping his work-gnarled hands. He never again said anything about it.

But Eva and I were ecstatic. That night we spread a blanket on the grass in the backyard of her mother's house and lay there, Eva nestled in the crook of my arm as we looked up at the stars, talking about our future. All we wanted we decided, was a place of our own in which to raise children.

In 1941 there were no jobs to be had in Ida Grove. So I went to Des Moines where I lived with Uncle Oscar until I found a furnished room and kitchenette for $6 a week. I also found a job washing cars in a garage.

Eva joined me in Des Moines and laughed in delight over the "apartment," even though the bathroom was one flight up in a common hall. The only thing we lacked was money. That afternoon Eva came home from shopping and proudly showed me her purchases—two plates, two forks, two spoons, one frying pan and a kettle. Then she sank at the table, tears filling her brown eyes. "But I didn't have enough money left for food!"

I put my arms around her, and leaning down, kissed her neck. "That's all right, Honey," I comforted her, "we have the potatoes." For some reason I had bought a sack of these when I rented the room.

We ate those potatoes for two weeks until I got my next paycheck. A few weeks later I was able to get construction work on a defense plant being built outside of Des Moines and we were able to get more kitchenware so our families could visit us.

Early in December we visited Eva's brother who lived in Knoxville, Iowa. It was a large family gathering in which, as usual, good food and conversation provided recreation and entertainment. On Saturday night most of us slept on pallets on the floor. The next afternoon, after a large dinner, the women were doing the dishes and we men sat around the living room smoking and talking.

Someone had just told a joke and while we were guffawing, one of the women, her face white, stepped out of the kitchen and "shsssed" us. In the hush I could hear an announcer's anxious voice coming from the little table radio in the kitchen. Someone turned up the volume.

"We repeat . . . war planes of the Imperial Japanese Navy have bombed U.S. naval installations at Pearl Harbor . . ."

The room became dead silent and I had a strange feeling that all of our lives would be forever changed.

It was also about this time that I was given earthshaking news of a personal nature. Eva was pregnant. As I held her small form close to me, her dark ringlets resting on my chest, I seemed to stare into the future. All I knew for certain was that I would be entering service. When, I did not know. Would I have the opportunity to see my child before I left?

Eva used to meet me at the streetcar on which I returned from work. As her girth expanded, I'd joke. "You'd better not be meeting me anymore," I laughed, "or folks will think there's something going on between us!"

However, all my homecomings were not that joyful. Perhaps it was because I was anxious about what Eva and the baby would do when I entered service. It took my mind off things to go to a nearby bar where I'd spend hours playing cribbage with friends. Often I'd drink too much and reel home in a stupor.

Eva would meet me at the door, her eyes red from weeping. "Pack, I can't understand why you do this," she'd cry.

In the morning I would apologize and promise to stop. But all I ended up doing was to hide some of my drinking from Eva. Then I'd think of Dad's hidden liquor bottle I found in the outhouse as a youngster.

But we had many good times, too. As warm weather came, we would walk up the hill in the evening to the expansive grounds of the big gold-domed state capitol only a few blocks from the apartment. We'd spread a blanket on the grass and lie there looking at the sky, talking about our future.

"Do you think we'll ever own a house, Pack?" Eva would ask.

"Sure, Honey," I would assure her. "It won't be like the governor's mansion," I laughed, "but some day we'll have a house we'll be proud to have the family visit."

"Oh, Harold Everett Jones," she exclaimed hugging me. I had told her about the boy for whom I had been named. She liked the story and whenever she felt really happy this was her nickname for me.

My brother, Jesse, then 23, visited us occasionally and he looked forward to the baby's coming as much as we did. "I hope it will have red hair," he'd laugh, his bright blue eyes shining. His big worry was that he would leave for service before the baby was born. It looked as if he would. Our baby was due in mid-July and the draft board informed Jesse he would be entering the army in mid-June.

"Nuts!" he said during one of his visits to us. "Here I'm going to be an uncle and won't be able to see my niece or nephew."

By then I had gotten a job with the Des Moines Department of Public Works. Most of my duties were mowing lawns in parks and I appreciated being in the city where I could be close to Eva if she needed me.

There was a big thunderstorm the night of June 1st. And when I started mowing in Greenwood Park the next morning the grass was still wet. I stopped for lunch and was sitting under a tree unwrapping one of Eva's meatloaf sandwiches when a city pickup truck skidded to a stop. The driver leaned out his window and yelled, "Call your uncle right away!"

He accelerated away and worry clutched me. Was Eva having trouble with the baby? I ran to a phone booth and dialed her. No, she was all right, she said. She hadn't heard anything about my uncle.

Somewhat relieved I called him. "Uncle Oscar? Is there anything wrong?"

His voice was strained. "Yes, your brother was in an auto accident."

"How is he?"

"It's bad."

My heart caught. Not Jess, not my big fun-loving brother Jess!

"He's dead?"

"Yes, Harold. He's gone."

I don't remember hanging up the phone. All I knew was that I had to get home. I called the Park Department to get me and the mower. Then, Uncle Oscar came by the apartment and picked up Eva and me for the trip home.

We had to first get Dad in Coon Rapids where he was working as a construction foreman. It was on the way to Ida Grove, about 70 miles from Des Moines.

The car was silent as we drove up route 141 to Coon Rapids. All of us were numb. Uncle Oscar then explained that Jesse, his friend Ozzie, and their girl friends had started to drive up to Storm Lake Monday night to attend a dance. Before reaching Storm Lake they were caught in a terrible thunderstorm. Their car had struck a bridge abutment and was flung sideways into a flooded stream.

The car lay submerged all night until the next morning when a conductor on a passing Chicago & Northwestern train noticed the car roof protruding above the receding waters and phoned the sheriff in the next town. All four in the car were dead.

It was late evening when we pulled in front of Dad's rooming house. I forced myself to get out of the car and walk up the side steps. I knocked on the door and Dad opened it. He had just been ready to go to bed.

"What are you doing here?" he gasped.

"Well, Dad . . ." Struggling for words, I glanced about the tiny room, looking at the rumpled bed, the little bureau in the corner. "Dad, there's a big problem."

His blue-gray eyes bored into mine. "What happened?"

"Jesse has been in a car accident."

He looked startled. "Well," he said, "I'd better come right with you."

I put my hand on his shoulder. "Dad, there's no reason to be in a hurry."

He stood looking at me a long time. Finally, he sagged onto his bed. Tears streamed down my face.

He sat quietly for several minutes, staring into the flowered wallpaper. The overhead bulb highlighted the gray in his hair.

Finally, as if he had aged 20 years in those few minutes, he slowly lifted himself from the bed. "Well," he said, "we'd better get home to Mother; she'll need us." He reached under the bed and pulled out his battered cardboard suitcase.

When we got home we discovered how desperately Mother needed us. The night before she had lain awake wondering why Jesse had not come home. Jesse had always phoned if he were detained.

When the phone rang in the morning she rushed for it.

"Mrs. Hughes," said a man who identified himself as the local funeral director, "do you want me to get your son's body when I go up to Storm Lake after Ozzie's?" The funeral director, who had been contacted by the Storm Lake sheriff, thought Mother had already been informed.

"What are you talking about?" she gasped.

The director realized his mistake, but it was too late. Mother kept pressing him and finally he had to tell her. She screamed and fell unconscious on the floor. The director sent a doctor to our house who found Mother in shock and near death herself.

Fortunately, he was able to treat her in time, but she was still shattered when we arrived home that night.

I went over to the funeral home alone to decide whether Jesse's body should be placed on view or not. They said he had been badly mangled, his chest crushed and head cut.

The undertaker took me into a side room where Jesse's casket rested; the lid was up. Somewhat hesitantly, I approached it. When I saw Jesse I could not believe he was dead. The mortician had done his work well; the only evidence of the accident was a welt running down his forehead. I stood there a long time. I reached out to touch his shoulder. If I could just awaken him, I thought, he'd look up at me with that twinkle in his merry blue eyes, asking: "What's up, Little Pack?"

At the funeral, as I stood by my brother's casket, townspeople came up offering sympathy. Gazing sorrowfully at my brother, they would say: "Well, it was God's will." Inwardly I stiffened.

Finally, when our pastor said the same thing, I replied, "I can't believe that, Pastor," trying to keep the anger out of my voice. "There's no way God means for people to be killed like this!"

Despite the pastor's attempts at consolation, to me Jesse's death was just a horrible accident. Was he in heaven? I wondered. I believed there was some kind of continuation of life. But what was it actually? Would Jesse awake into another life a thousand years from now? A million? I didn't know. All I knew was that Jesse's accident could not be God's will. In fact, I began to question: What kind of a God would allow that to happen to a kind and thoughtful person like Jesse?

Mother was a different person after Jesse's death. Gone was the fun-loving, joking woman who always had a happy remark or a laugh. Dad sank within his grief, but didn't say much.

After the funeral, Dad had to return to his construction job in Coon Rapids. Eva and I prepared to take Mother back to Des Moines to stay with us.

As they all waited out in the car with Uncle Oscar, I walked through the empty house to close it up. I stopped at the door of the bedroom Jesse and I had shared, looked at the little lumpy bed and remembered how we used to laugh at each other in our long underwear. A beaver skin we thought too beautiful to sell hung on the wall, along with a newspaper picture of us in our football uniforms. "Big Pack and Little Pack," the caption said.

I turned and headed for the front door, my throat tight. And then . . . was someone whistling? I listened for a moment, but it was only a morning breeze catching a corner of the house.

Seven weeks later on a hot July night I was awakened by Eva nudging me. "I'm having pains, Pack," she said. I leaped out of bed and called the doctor. "Get her to the hospital," he ordered. Dad and Mother happened to be visiting Uncle Oscar's. I called them and Dad drove right over. We got Eva to the hospital at 5:00 A.M. and at eight o'clock that morning the doctor walked out to me in the waiting room where I was almost prostrate with nervousness. "Mr. Hughes," he smiled, "you have a little girl."

We named her Connie, a name Eva picked out. She had wanted a little girl and I didn't care one way or the other, just as long as she was healthy.

With the baby here, and my mother still not fully recovered from Jesse's death, Eva and I felt it would be best to move back to Ida Grove. Besides, I expected to be drafted in a few months and I felt Eva should be living near our families. In September we returned home. Mother and Dad were happy to have us live with them, and now Eva, the baby and I shared Jesse's and my old bedroom. I got a job helping build bridges on a construction crew but it was not to last long. Then I received notice that I would be leaving for military service on December 28th.

It was a sad Christmas. The prospect of my leaving made Mother even more depressed. Dad tried to get us singing together around the table but we just didn't have the heart. Every once in a while Jesse's name came up and we'd find ourselves silent for a few minutes. Only little Connie, five months old, her bright eyes fastened on the Christmas tree, seemed to be joyful.

The night before I was to leave, Eva and I sat up quite late talking. We draftees had been instructed to meet downtown in front of the Baxter Hotel at 7:45 A.M. I asked Eva not to go with me to the hotel. I couldn't stand saying goodby to her on a windswept street in front of a bunch of other guys. Moreover, she was pregnant again and I didn't want her standing out in the cold.

It was a fitful night; I dreamed of Jesse and me hunting, of sitting on the state capitol lawn with Eva on a hot summer's night . . . suddenly the alarm clock was ringing.

As I crawled out from under the blanket, I wondered how long it would be before Eva and I would share a bed again. Although it was dark outside, Mother had breakfast ready in the kitchen. I was sure she had not slept at all. Dad was sitting with her. Eva joined us at the table. We made small talk. Then I looked at the clock; it was 7:30. "Well," I said, "I had better go." Mother and Dad got up and stood self-consciously. Dad's eyes were glistening and he wiped them with a big hand.

"I'll drive you downtown, Son," he said.

I looked down at Mother, her auburn hair glowing in the hall light. My heart caught; I was reminded so much of Jesse. I took Mother's hands in mine, feeling all the callouses from years spent in the kitchen, the garden and over the washtub. I remembered that she never sang over the washtub anymore.

I reached my arms around her plump waist and pulled her close. She still smelled of the breakfast bacon she had fried. As I held her, her shoulders quivered and I pushed her back. "Now, Mother," I tried to grin, "I'm almost 21, remember? Is that any way to send a man off?"

She pulled me close and memories of my boyhood filled me, of being held in her lap when I had whooping cough and couldn't sleep.

She wiped her face. "I want to give you something," she said. From her apron pocket she pulled out a little package and handed it to me. I unwrapped it. It was a little pocket-sized Bible with a gold-colored metal cover.

"It's supposed to be bulletproof," she said. "You should keep it over your heart, in your shirt pocket. But more important," she added, "I want you to read it, Harold, every night if you can. The words in it will protect you more than any bulletproof shield." She broke into sobs and held me again.

I went into the bedroom and kissed little Connie who was sleeping. Eva followed me into the bedroom and I pulled her to me, breathing in her fragrance.

"Look," I said, "I understand everybody gets a two-week furlough after basic training. That means I ought to be home in May."

Eva smiled, blinking back tears. I kissed her again and picked up the little zipper bag that I had used to carry my gym clothes at school. It held a toothbrush, razor, socks and a sewing kit. Eva had handed me the sewing kit the night before. It was made out of khaki-colored cloth, fitted with needles and little skeins of thread.

She smiled sheepishly. "I thought you'd need it, seeing as I won't be able to sew for you anymore." Then she paused a moment. "Pack, promise me something?"

"Sure, anything."

"Please, please don't drink when you're gone."

I pulled her back to me and laughed: "Honey, on my salary, I can't afford to!" It was true, I thought. With my allotment going to

Eva and the baby, I'd end up getting five dollars a month. That would hardly keep me in toothpaste.

As I looked at her in the doorway of our bedroom, the bed lamp cast a halo around her. Something deep welled up within me and I wanted to go back, take her in my arms and never let go.

Again, I kissed Connie who cooed sleepily; then I turned back into the hall and stepped out the door into the early morning dark.

Dad started up the Model A and as we headed down Forrest Avenue lined with quiet dark houses, neither of us spoke. A cold dawn wind blew down from the snow-shrouded hills and I was alone in my thoughts.

This was the familiar street where Jesse and I used to race to school. A light glowed in the Catholic rectory across the field; the good Father must be on a sick call, I thought. My heart warmed at the thought of the genial black frocked man who used to greet me as I walked home from school. I had hardly attended my own church for several years.

A few house lights winked on here and there as men prepared to get up and go to work. But they'd be coming home that night. I thought about the work for which I was headed and a vague fear trickled into my heart. Then I quenched it; I had handled guns all my life; I knew the outdoors. Surely I was well prepared for what lay ahead.

Then we pulled up to the Baxter Hotel and I stepped out of the car. "Goodby Son," said Dad. "God go with you."

I wanted to put my arms around him but we were both too shy for that. A knot of men was already waiting at the hotel. I recognized most of them and we muttered hellos. No one talked much; each was busy with his own thoughts. A few families had come with their sons and they stood apart in quiet little groups.

An icy December wind swept down the street and I pulled my jacket closer around my neck. Above us the old wooden hotel sign creaked on rusted hinges.

The man from the draft board, Elwood Porter, counted us again, calling off names. He had already done this twice. "What's the matter Elwood," I wanted to say, "do you think we're going to run away?"

There was a murmur in the group and I glanced down the block to see the headlights of the Greyhound bus sweep on to Second Street. It pulled up in front of the hotel, brakes groaning. We boarded and I found a seat near the back. Finally, our group was all aboard, checked once again by the draft board man, and he stepped back, holding his clipboard. The door slammed shut and the Diesel engine roared. Slowly, Second Street began passing before me: Skaglund's Drugstore where I had my first soda, the King Cinema where I watched Hoot Gibson. All of them were dark now. Finally, Ken's Conoco Station at the edge of town slid by; I saw Ken unlocking the door and I beat on the bus window. But he didn't hear me.

A few houses flashed by and then corn-stubbled fields. I looked out the back window and could see the high school on the hill highlighted by the rising sun. I watched it until it, too, melted into the horizon. And all that I could see were telephone poles and a concrete pavement receding behind the window.

I turned and slumped in my seat. The man beside me was sleeping. But I couldn't doze. I began counting the weeks before I would be home in May to see Eva, the baby, Mother and Dad.

4

Holocaust

CAMP SIEBERT IN Alabama was a typical World War II army training base. Bleak, white-frame barracks clustered on red mud fields where civilian-soft men were transitioned into toughened soldiers.

I found the training almost enjoyable, having loved the out-of-doors since I started following trap lines and hunting game in the hills of Iowa. The target range was fun. And though many recruits complained about being awakened at 5:00 A.M., it was a fairly normal hour to me.

What did hurt was the separation from Eva and the family. I wrote every day, asking Eva to share my letters with Mother and Dad.

What sustained me was anticipating the furlough I had coming when our eighteen weeks' basic training was completed. Nights were the roughest. After lights out and the loudspeaker on the parade ground had played taps, I'd lie on my bunk looking up in the dark thinking about Eva, my hands clutching the steel bed rails. Often I'd study my photo of Eva and Connie under the blanket in the light of my flashlight. Connie didn't look like much then, but I could see she had Eva's deep brown eyes.

Whenever someone would walk through the barracks whistling, my head would lift and I'd half-expect to see my red-haired big brother striding by. But of course it wasn't, and I'd lean down and polish my GI shoes harder.

Occasionally, we'd get a night out in a nearby town. On five dollars a month I couldn't drink much. So I became quite good at

49

poker and shooting dice. Many a night's drinking was financed on
a GI blanket pulled tightly over a lower bunk on which I coaxed
the rolling dice into sevens or elevens.

One day while a game was on, a chaplain walked into the barracks
to talk with the men. Some of the fellows left the game, but a few,
including me, kept right at it. My conscience must have bothered me
because that night I found the little Bible my mother had given me
and tried to read a few lines. But before I could get through the
"begats" I wearily closed it.

I held it for a moment before putting it back into my footlocker.
The gold-colored metal was beginning to tarnish and I wondered
how much my mother had given up to buy it for me. I smiled at the
"bulletproof" cover; a 30-caliber rifle slug would go straight through
Genesis to Revelation to Hughes. Maybe then I would find out
about God.

One late March afternoon as I was checking train schedules for
my approaching furlough, I was called into company headquarters.

"Hughes," said the sergeant holding my file, "you're being transferred to the 83rd Chemical Battalion in Camp Gordon, Georgia."

I stood transfixed. Finally I found my voice. "But what about my
furlough?"

"Don't worry about it," he said. "You'll get it. The 83rd Chemical
just needs some replacements."

Two days later I was in Camp Gordon where I found myself
training as a BAR man. Probably because of my size, I was given
a Browning Automatic Rifle, which weighs twenty-one pounds and
is actually a portable machine gun. A partner would carry the ammunition and hand me cartridge magazines as I fired. With it I would
support my comrades who fired the heavy-caliber cannon-like mortars
which lobbed exploding shells on the enemy.

But along with the BAR I was given a surprise. The 83rd was on
its way overseas!

It was April 1943; U.S. troops were still fighting in Africa to help
prepare for the invasion of southern Europe. My company was
leaving under sealed orders for embarkation in ten days.

My furlough? Certainly I wouldn't be shipped into combat without
getting to see my family? I frantically raced from one sergeant to
another.

"No go, soldier," was the answer, "it just can't be done."

Maybe the family could scrape up money for Eva's train fare to Georgia for a quick visit.

My heart soared. Even *one* day and night with Eva would be heaven, I thought, as I hurried to find the right noncom to get permission.

On the sergeant's desk was a photo of his wife and two children; I felt he would understand my plea. He sat there for a moment, toying with a miniature bayonet letter-opener as I pleaded my case: "Just let my wife come for one day, Sergeant . . . one day."

He put the little bayonet down, looked up at me wearily and placed his hands flat on the desk. "I'm sorry, soldier," he said, "but it can't be done; security forbids it."

I thought of a thousand things to say but knew not one of them would make any difference. I turned and walked out into a warm rain slickening the red clay.

In three days we were on a troop train chugging through the Appalachian Mountains. I leaned against the window seeing visions of Eva and Connie in the mist rising from the valleys.

Finally, with unshowered bodies sour with perspiration and coal soot, we pulled into Fort Stanton, Massachusetts. I expected something like a prison because of all the security regulations. But Fort Stanton was very similar to any other army post with barracks, movie theatres and service clubs.

The second evening some buddies and I happened to pass the officers' club. A group of our officers were coming across the road, each with a smiling woman on his arm. I stared at them as the men gallantly held the door open and ushered the women into the club.

I turned to a buddy. "Who were *they?*" I asked.

"Oh," he shrugged, "you know the brass; they all had their wives come up and meet them here."

Rage filled me. The image of the arrogant golfer haughtily handing me two nickels flashed before me.

The beer sold at the army post exchanges in World War II was popularly referred to by GIs as "3.2," indicating the minuscule percentage of alcohol in it. However, that night I was able to drink enough of it to get roaring drunk.

My head still throbbed as we reached New York City where we would board ship. At the dock, Red Cross women handed out doughnuts and a brass band played "Over There" and "Give My Regards to Broadway." But nothing eased the deep sense of loss as I looked up the huge gray side of the ship that would take me so far from my family.

It was late evening when the last of ten thousand men struggled up the gangplank under his duffel bag. Soon we could feel the dull throb of engines under our feet. They let us up onto the deck in shifts. I got up in time to see the New York skyline disappear into the darkness. As I leaned on the rail, watching the vague whiteness of the bow wave curl away into the mist, I wondered how many of us would return.

By now we knew we were going to Oran, North Africa, where American troops were being prepared for a landing on Sicily. I had heard that the National Guard ambulance company that had left Ida Grove over a year before was somewhere in that area. All of us would help begin the Allies' attack on the "soft underbelly of Europe," as Winston Churchill put it.

At Oran we were taken by trucks to our bivouac area. One afternoon word spread that German soldiers were being sent through on their way to prison camp.

We watched in silence as they marched past in their tan desert uniforms, everyone in step, calling out cadence. We had expected to see beaten, bedraggled men. But they didn't look like they were defeated. I then realized nothing would be easy.

Standing among us were the men who had beaten them, the GIs of the 1st Division who had been through the desert war. I was awed by their casualness, the easy way they wore their rifles slung over their shoulders.

But the newness was soon taken out of us in further training. For days we struggled down rope netting with full pack and weapons, then rode in landing craft to hit the beach and rush out and attack an imaginary army.

It was hot, tiring work. And in the evening we'd try to find some enjoyment in Oran. It seemed to be the hell hole of Algeria; the liquor was terrible but we still got drunk on everything from warm beer to a foul-tasting concoction called annisette.

And I had good buddies to drink with. One was Scott, a slender six-footer from western Virginia, who had done a lot of trapping around his home; we had some good talks. One night we decided to tattoo each other. Sitting on G.I. blankets outside our pup tent, we broke open a flashlight battery, made carbon dust from the insides and mixed it with ink. Using a sharp needle, we punched holes through the skin, then tamped in the carbon-ink mixture with the end of a pencil.

When finished, Scott proudly wore a big heart with MOTHER on it. I had him make a cross on my arm with JESSE tattooed under it. I didn't really know why the cross but it seemed nice there with my brother's name.

Toward the end of our training, Scott and I went into Oran with some friends and ended up overstaying. We staggered out into the street to find we had missed the last truck back to camp.

"Oh, what the hell," slurred Scott, "that gives us a chance to drink some more." We lurched into another bar. A uniformed man with bars on his shoulder turned and barked at us. "You men are off limits."

"So are you, buddy," I retorted.

"Don't you sass an officer!"

The light over the bar seemed to blur and all the resentment boiled up within me. The next thing I knew I was in the middle of a flurry of fighting men.

I awoke staring into bright lights. Next to me lay Scott with cut face and blackened eyes.

"Where are we?" I groaned.

"In the stockade," he moaned. I sat up and recognized the guys who had walked into the bar with me the night before. All were nursing bruises.

Soon a military policeman ordered us out. We were lined up for a quick court martial. An adjutant advised each of us to plead guilty.

Slowly the line shuffled along. Finally I stood before an officer who read the charges: "Drunk and disorderly; attacking an officer. Guilty or not guilty?" he asked, his eyes on the list before him.

"Guilty," I said. My sentence was forfeiture of two-thirds of my pay for six months. What really hurt was the remark the judge made as I turned to go. "You can go back to regular duty. Where you're going you'll probably get killed anyway."

On July 10, 1943, our troop transport hove to in morning darkness off the beach town of Gela on the southern coast of Sicily. The smoky shoreline was ablaze with burning ships and buildings. Fighter planes screamed through the blackness above and foaming geysers erupted in the ocean around us. Other American troops would land on both sides of us. British forces would land to the east. Our goal was to invade and capture Sicily. Once this island at the toe of the Italian boot became ours, it would become the jumping off site for the long-awaited attack on Italy itself.

But the Nazis were a determined foe and nature seemed to side with them. The seas were mountainous. Sagging under our heavy equipment, we waited on rain-slick decks for our turn to scramble down the side of the ship. The gray landing craft waiting below us reared and plunged with each gigantic wave. Two cartridge belts, each loaded with 250 rounds of ammunition, bit into my shoulders along with the sling of my automatic rifle. Other men carried heavy mortar shells on their backs.

The disembark signal was given. As I swung my leg over the rail, I looked down to see the landing barge on the foaming ocean leap at me, and quickly drop. I knew I must step onto the barge just at the peak of its surge. As I scrambled down the sagging net, I heard a hoarse scream and looked to see a soldier fall between the side of the ship and a barge. Loaded with mortar shells and rifle, he disappeared into the raging waters like a stone.

I shut my eyes and hung for a moment clutching the net; the hellish roar of shell fire and strafing planes intensified. A boot crunched my hand and I continued down, gasping in relief when I timed my jump and landed on the barge.

Its engine roared and we swung away from the heaving side of the ship. As we headed toward the beach, I tried to pray but could only hunch lower in the bucking, wallowing barge. Shells tore overhead like the sound of cardboard ripping.

Finally, I could feel us grate on the sand. The steel front shield of our landing craft fell forward sending up billows of spray. All we could see were orange shell bursts and thick rolling smoke.

The Nazis' 16th Panzer Division was waiting for us.

Weapons high, we plunged into the heavy surf. Our orders were to rally at a point three miles inland to help secure the beachhead.

It was a nightmare of fiery explosions, screaming shells and crack of bullets. Bending low, my assistant gunner and I ran across the soft sand to escape the brilliant light from burning ships and buildings. Another man running before me staggered, then fell backwards. I knew he was dead, but as we were instructed to do, we pushed on;

the ground exploded near me and I fell flat, my face buried in the sand. Shrapnel rattled off my helmet. Then I crawled forward on my elbows and knees.

Get off the beach! Ahead was a grassy hill. Barbed wire blocked me, but I finally found a space blown open in the coils. Cradling my Browning, I scrambled through it. A man screamed next to me; I glanced to see him face down, the sand dark red under his helmet.

Rifle fire rattled from the hill; I pulled the trigger of my BAR. Nothing. It was jammed with sand. Half crawling another hundred feet, I slipped into a shell crater, my assistant gunner tumbling in after me. A dead G.I. lay hunched in it. I took his M1 rifle, and we scrambled on through the beach grass. Someone shouted for a BAR to knock out a machine gun. Trained to reassemble my weapon in the dark, I laid my handkerchief on the sand and began taking the BAR apart. Most of the trigger mechanism was spread out on the handkerchief when, "WHOOOMPH." A mortar shell exploded nearby. I flattened against the churning earth. When sand stopped raining, my gun parts had disappeared. I grabbed a belt of 30-caliber M1 ammunition from another dead G.I. and with my assistant gunner raced on.

Dawn now lightened the area. We reached our rally point atop a hill to find no officers with us; a buck sergeant gave orders. I found another BAR next to a dead gunner. My assistant and I moved down the hill and began digging in. The ground was flinty but the whine of bullets made our entrenching tools fly.

Sometime later my assistant pointed to a distant copse of trees. Behind them, gray-green trucks unloaded German infantry. Our four mortars zeroed in on the trucks and we heard screams. Then a metallic groaning rose behind the smoke. "Tanks!" someone shouted. In fearful fascination I watched the squat monsters lumber toward us, their machine guns pounding and 88-millimeter cannons flashing. My assistant yelled he was going back.

"Stay put!" I called, but he scrambled out of his foxhole and began running. A burst of machine-gun fire cut him in half.

A tank loomed over my foxhole and I crouched deep. As it roared over, I was choked by acrid exhaust fumes. When I emerged, oddly enough no German infantry followed. That fact saved many of us.

When night fell, I slipped back across the hills to find my outfit. Finally I heard low conversation. I froze, hugging the ground until I caught an American accent.

They were GIs, also separated from their units. We burrowed into a haystack and waited for the gray light of dawn. Finally, I found my outfit. I learned that the German tanks had been clobbered by our Navy guns when they reached the coast.

The burial detail was hard at work picking up bodies. And it was then I saw my friend, Scott, from Virginia. He had been hit by an 88. Sand-encrusted entrails protruded from his torso. However on one arm I could still make out the tatooed heart and the word MOTHER. I stood there, torn with grief and nausea. But we did own the beach at Gela.

Again we dug in. Nightfall brought a new tragedy. Out of the black sky came a deafening roar. Hundreds of planes filled the air; the next thing we saw were paratroopers coming down. Germans! We let loose with everything we had. But as bodies flopped onto the ground, we saw to our horror they were men from the U.S. 82nd Airborne Division. The wind velocity was high, scattering them out of their drop zone.

Now our battalion transferred from the 16th Infantry to the 1st Battalion of the American Rangers. Together we began a 90-mile forced march toward the western end of Sicily, below Palermo. From Palermo allied forces would invade Italy. What we didn't know was that we were part of a race between General George Patton and Field Marshal Viscount Montgomery, both fighting to reach the top of Sicily first.

In long dusty lines, faces drawn with fatigue, we clumped along the sun-baked road, pausing only to snatch a bite of field rations, and then push on.

Heat waves shimmered ahead and rivulets of sweat streamed down my legs. Then a wave of horror swept the long line of men ahead of us. I could smell it before I saw it, the sickly sweet odor of decaying flesh.

As the Germans retreated, they kept the Italian troops at their rear, taking the brunt of the Allied advance. Under the hot Sicilian sun, we marched for hours through smouldering columns of blackened tanks, scout cars and trucks filled with fly-covered masses of putrifying flesh, uniforms bloated to a paper smoothness. We tied handkerchiefs around our faces, but couldn't stem the nausea.

The scene still haunted me as we marched into a town called Castelvetrano, having made the 90-mile trek from Gela Beach in three days. All of us in Company D gratefully fell to the ground in a cool orchard area.

Perhaps it was the beautiful rolling land so like Iowa, but I felt a deep kinship with the farming people there. As I saw silent hay wagons standing in the fields, I couldn't help thinking of the sun-tanned young men who once laughingly threw pitchforks of hay onto these wagons. Now they rotted under the same sun, down the road. I knew we were here to save the world from madmen like Hitler and Mussolini. But why did God allow men to butcher each other?

My thoughts darkened and I found myself steeping them in local wine. But late August brought a break in my depression. A cablegram came from Eva that our second child had been born August 20th; it was a girl but as yet she hadn't been named. Both Eva and the baby were doing well.

I sat for a long time holding the cablegram, not knowing this would be the last piece of mail I'd get for a very long time.

Allied forces on Sicily now gathered strength for the grand invasion of Italy. As a British commando unit needed our cannon-like mortar weapons, a detachment from my Company D was transferred to them and I went along to support them with my Browning Automatic Rifle. Somehow, my mail never followed me.

Early in September, the Allies launched the attack. The main Anglo-American assault force steamed toward Salerno on the Italian west coast below Naples. Meanwhile, our smaller group of some 1,500 men headed toward Vietri, a little seaside town just southwest of Salerno. Our job would be to secure the coastal highway and railroad, cutting off German reinforcements.

Our five landing-craft infantry left Sicily in stormy seas. When we were able to get up on deck, we could see the main invasion fleet on the horizon. It was under a bombing attack. Black puffs of anti-aircraft fire dotted the sky above it and the sky glowed from burning ships.

The enemy fighter-bombers then turned on us. We huddled below decks, flinching at the heavy "whumph" of explosions in the sea. As our deck guns roared, and shell casings rattled onto the thin metal deck above us, I found myself pleading with God to protect me.

But when the attack was over and I climbed into the bright sunlight with the fresh sea wind in my face, I quickly forgot Him. It took five days to reach Vietri. There were some peaceful hours when we watched the sun set in the indigo blue Mediterranean. During these times my new assistant gunner, Steve, a nice fellow from Illinois, and I would talk about home. He was taking pre-law when drafted. Steve had an ivory-handled revolver which I admired and tried to buy.

"No," he'd say, patting it lovingly, "it's the one thing General Patton and I have in common." We had all heard about the general's famous ivory-handled gun.

Early in the morning our five craft nosed up to the quiet beach of Vietri. Evidently the enemy had not considered the seaside resort worth defending.

The ships' side ramps plunged down and we filed off into the knee-deep gentle waves that surged softly onto the sand. It was still dark as we walked through the narrow cobblestone lanes of the town. The building shutters were closed. Suddenly the streets blazed white under a German parachute flare. I froze against a rough stone wall. But there was no follow-up resistance. We set up battle stations outside town.

In the morning the shutters swung open and local people streamed out onto the streets. Shops were opened and it seemed like business as usual. That afternoon, while buddies and I dickered with a man over a bottle of wine, a powerful explosion slammed me against a wall.

Shell fire! The Germans were counterattacking. As we dashed for our battle stations, machine-gun fire hammered from the hills as mortar shells exploded among us.

We found ourselves being pushed back to the sea. Our mortar platoon lobbed shells over the houses onto enemy soldiers in the next street. We finally drove the Germans back, but they kept up the incessant shelling.

Could we hold out until the Fifth Army in Salerno fought their way to Vietri?

The question was discussed that evening as our platoon gathered under a railroad trestle for ration distributions. I was relaxing on an empty ammunition crate and the other fellows were joking about the British rations.

"Think we'll be getting some real food when the Fifth gets here?" asked one.

"Yeah, and I'll be . . ." There was a whistle, an incandescent blue flash of flame and an overwhelming emptiness. I found myself on the ground, my head bursting. We had been bracketed by several mortar shells. I rolled over and found myself looking into a man's head whose skull had been blown open. His brains glistened gray and I began retching.

Medics rushed about and I staggered out of their way. I hadn't been hit, but was still dazed. And then I saw Steve, the boy from Illinois, on the ground. He looked as if he were resting, bright blue eyes staring into the Italian sky, blond hair hardly mussed. The ivory-handled .32 was still in his belt. I turned away and began vomiting again. He and six other men died in that one mortar attack.

Because of the losses, we started going out on outpost alone that night instead of in pairs. My outpost was far forward where I'd watch for four hours. I started up the steep mountain path in pitch darkness, feeling the thin communications wire for guidance. As I crept along, my heart leaped at every falling pebble. I neared the outpost and whispered the first half of the password, "Trafalgar," and waited for the answer, "Square." Not a sound. I called out again: "Trafalgar!" Deadly quiet.

My insides congealed and I lay there, fingers gripping the dirt. Finally, I inched forward to the hole and reached in, expecting to find a body. But it was empty. I dropped into the pit, picked up the telephone, which worked, and settled down with my rifle and waited.

The hours crawled by as I waited. Would the sun never rise? "Let me live through this night," I continued to plead until daylight when I was relieved. We never learned what happened to the sentry I was to replace.

Back in an empty building I had hardly fallen asleep when the Germans attacked again.

All of Vietri became a battleground. One man reported on his walkie-talkie: "We're holding the kitchen; the Germans are in the living room and the bathroom is unoccupied!"

Several days had passed since we landed; the Fifth Army was still tied up at Salerno and could not relieve us. We were short on rations. For water we'd creep down at night to the small fountain in the town square and fill our canteens; the Germans would do the same.

Then we began fighting apartment to apartment. None of us knew if the footsteps heard in the hall were friend or enemy. My assistant gunner and I tore a steel bathtub from a wall, upended it near the balcony and for four nights hunched in it, his gun aimed at the door, mine down at the street.

Finally, we drove the enemy back into the mountains. This time we were able to blow up the railroad and secure the highway. The Fifth Army advanced out of Salerno and our siege in Vietri was over.

We filed out of Vietri seventeen days after we landed, a decimated, dazed bunch of men. After marching eight miles we finally were given permission to sleep. Someone pointed out a small stone church that had been hit by shell fire. It looked like heaven and we straggled into it. One man hauled his sleeping buddy into the building by the heels.

But I couldn't sleep. A headache that had been nagging me for days intensified; I came down with chills and began shaking. When the sun rose, the enemy counterattacked. We fought all day, and that night when I collapsed I didn't wake up. They said I had become delirious.

All I knew was that I was on a stretcher on a beach, for I could hear waves breaking in the distance. A British medic was bending over me.

"What happened to me?" I croaked.

"You're in trouble, bloke," he said. "You've a temperature of 106.6."

I awoke again to find myself in ice packs aboard a British hospital ship headed for North Africa. Despair surged through me; when I asked an attendant if there were any mail for me he shook his head. I turned to the wall; three months without a letter from home. What was wrong? Then the screaming began; it was the teen-ager next to me. Full of tubes from plasma bottles, he was crying that his legs hurt him. But both of them were gone at the hip. I slipped back into unconsciousness.

I came to in a British hospital in North Africa. I had malaria and jaundice. For the next several days I slipped in and out of consciousness. I wondered what had happened to my family. Our second baby girl was two months old and I still did not know her name. Did she have black hair like mine?

After several weeks I was able to go to the latrine. I looked into the mirror and blanched. My face was cadaverous and my bones stood out; I had lost forty pounds in a month.

Finally, I was well enough to be shipped to a combat reconditoning battalion where I would be given a month's build-up before returning to the front. I had little to pack in the way of personal possessions, just the Bible in which were snapshots of Eva and our first little daughter, Connie; the pictures were cracked and stained. But they comforted me as I studied them in the light of the naked bulb that hung over my hospital bunk.

The best way I knew to remedy the loneliness was to drink. But despite brawls and heavy liquor consumption in the reconditioning camp, I was finally considered sufficiently rehabilitated in February 1944 to rejoin my old outfit. I learned the 83rd Chemical Battalion was now stationed outside Bagnolia, awaiting replacements.

It took fifteen days for our ship to zigzag across the Mediterranean. A jeep picked me up at the harbor and sped me to the battalion area where I looked forward to seeing my old friends. The driver left me off at my old Company D, but as I walked between the crowded tents I couldn't find a familiar face.

I got to my assigned tent, threw my duffle bag on a cot and then recognized an old buddy sleeping on the other bunk. I shook him awake.

When he quit blinking, he stared, jumped up and pounded my back.

"Hughes!" he shouted, "where did you come from? We all thought you were dead."

He ran out of the tent and returned with three other men. "C'mon," he said, rummaging in his duffle bag. "I got something here to help us celebrate."

As we all sat on the cots, passing around the bottle, my friend told a horror story. Most of the men I knew in Company D were dead.

"It was terrible," said my friend, head down, his canteen cup of cognac untouched on the floor. "The LST taking us in hit a mine in Anzio Bay." He looked up with haunted eyes. "The whole thing went up . . . loaded with white phosphorus and ammunition. The poor bastards below never had a chance."

He sat quietly for a long moment, then lifted his cup and drank deeply. "C'mon, Hughes," he brightened, "let's celebrate *your* return from the dead!"

But I couldn't get drunk that night. The next morning I did have cause to celebrate when I found a large bundle of mail for me at company headquarters.

The army post office had lost track of me when I went with the British group to Vietri. There were sixty-three letters and two telegrams in the package. It took me one whole day to read them. I learned that my new little daughter, then six months old, had been named Carol. I read and reread every letter, studying the snapshots, crying over them, thinking about my family. Did they have enough to eat? Would I ever be able to care for them?

That night I sat down and wrote the first letter home in months, telling Eva how much I loved them all and how I thought Carol looked like her.

Being a father of two and having just celebrated my twenty-second birthday, I felt I was getting on in years, especially when the new replacements began streaming into camp. They were 18 and 19-year-olds in fresh new uniforms. As I passed them in the company street, I'd catch them staring at me. I remembered how awed I had been by the first combat veterans I'd seen in Oran. That was only nine months before.

As soon as our group reached full strength, we moved up to the front at Monte Cassino, the "Gateway to Rome," and joined the British Black Cat Division to give our new replacements some firing experience. As our troops struggled slowly up the boot of Italy, they met fierce resistance.

We reached the Black Cat Division after they had made dozens of assaults on the impregnable Monte Cassino. We existed in a no-man's land. German artillery methodically worked over our area and except for patrols we huddled in our burrows munching D-ration chocolate bars and figuring out ways to meet personal needs such as urinating in one's helmet and pitching it up over the side.

Cold winter rains lashed the area and a deep depression settled on me. I worried about Eva and the girls. What would happen to them if I died? I was now convinced that I would never leave Italy alive. The loss of my comrades on the exploding ship in Anzio Harbor haunted me. Had I been spared by a supernatural act of God?

When they announced that a chaplain would be holding Palm Sunday services, I felt impelled to go. It would be the first worship service I had attended since going overseas. After so many narrow escapes, I felt that I had better make peace with God.

Under a rainy gray sky, I knelt before a Catholic priest to take communion. As he worked at the little altar set up on the hillside, I thought about the Catholic Father back home. This priest worked hard, too. Only twenty-five of us were allowed to attend at a time, to cut down casualties from shellfire. The priest had to work steadily through the day.

I didn't understand all the words as he stood there in his soaked uniform and squishing GI boots serving us communion, but I did sense his selfless spirit. I asked forgiveness for my many sins, committed Eva and the girls to God and told Him I was ready to go at any time. Afterwards, I slogged back to the front and crawled into my foxhole, feeling strangely at peace even though I seemed to be destined to remain in that wasteland of shell bursts and slimy mud forever.

It seemed that all of the Allied troops were destined to remain bogged down before Monte Cassino.

But just before Easter our company was transferred back to Naples where we boarded an LST and headed for the Anzio beachhead earlier established by that leapfrog operation which placed our troops on the coast sixty miles west of the Allied troops halted by fierce enemy resistance at the inland city of Cassino. We found our troops boxed in on the Anzio beach. Encircling it were four German divisions with tanks and artillery, including heavy railroad guns that lobbed in huge shells every night.

As our ship moved into the Anzio harbor, I thought about the ship that had blown up landing troops there. But our LST was able to nose to shore, drop its ramps and we double-timed into a town which had become a battlefront.

After returning from patrol one night, I found myself shaking with chills and fever. My malaria had returned. Half delirious, I was sent to the 34th evacuation hospital. The flimsy tent seemed to shake continuously from bombing raids, and those of us who could do so crawled out of bed to lie on the floor as the planes passed over. We were in an area called "Hell's Half Acre," where almost 500 medical personnel alone were killed or wounded during the beachhead operation.

However, as I began to recover I had a most pleasant surprise. Through one of the nurses I learned that the National Guard ambulance company from Ida Grove was located just across the road!

We had a great reunion. The men came roaring over to the hospital and surrounded my bed. They brought bottles of something they had distilled from fermented raisins called "P-38." We had several great evenings, talking about old times and toasting Ida

Grove. We also had occasion to toast some Allied victories. Monte Cassino finally fell on May 18th and our troops began closing in on Rome.

Despite the celebrating, I began to get my strength back and though still shaky, was sent to a replacement center. Each day I would check in at the center's headquarters expecting orders to return to the front. One morning the sergeant said: "Get ready, Hughes. You'll be leaving for the States tomorrow morning at five o'clock."

I was dumbfounded. Going home? It turned out that a medical review board had gone over my case and felt I had had enough combat. I was being returned to the States for other duties.

I left Naples, Italy, on June 1st, 1944. When our ship was five days at sea, word came over the loudspeakers that the Allies had invaded France at Normandy. The long-awaited Western Front had begun.

As the hospital ship neared Newport News, my sense of impending death began to lift. As I stood at the rail of the ship studying the curling bow wave, I began to wonder. Why me? Out of all the men who had died over there, why was I spared? And for what?

However, my questions were soon lost in the excitement of docking at Newport News. I learned that I was to report to Camp Butner, North Carolina, where I would join a military police unit. But the good news was that I was given a delay en route of three weeks. Three weeks to spend at home! The furlough for which I had waited one and a half years.

I ran for the telephone to call Eva. But the lines of men waiting to call home stretched around the building. I didn't have the strength to stand that long. Instead, I rushed to the railroad station and took the first train in the direction of home. In two days I reached Des Moines and then hitchhiked the rest of the way.

It was a hot sunny afternoon in Odebolt, twelve miles from Ida Grove, when the last driver picked me up. He was a grizzled farmer driving an ancient pickup with bald tires and a C gas rationing sticker on the windshield.

"Well, soldier," he said as he shifted into third with an ear-shattering rasp, "was it rough over there?"

"Oh, uh, what did you say?" I asked. I had been watching the empty highway, bemused by the fact that we rarely met an oncoming car. The gas shortage, I thought.

"Where have you been?" he asked. "The fighting?"

"Oh, yeah," I grunted.

The driver went on talking; I could sense that he wanted to hear more about my experiences but I had no wish to talk about something I wanted to forget.

My mind was on Eva. As we neared Ida Grove, the anxiety within me mounted. What if her feelings for me had changed? After all, a year and a half had passed since we had seen each other. How did she feel about me? Emotions churned within me, an anticipation and apprehension at meeting my wife, family and the daughter I had never seen.

5

Homecoming

THE DRIVER LET me off in front of the Baxter Hotel. I stood squinting for a moment in the hot afternoon sun as he accelerated up the street. Nineteen months had passed since I had last stood here. The exhaust of the departing truck seemed to be the only sound in Ida Grove. It was two o'clock and most of the townspeople were off the street, probably escaping the heat with a soda at Skaglund's Drugstore or a beer at the tavern.

I looked up at the old hotel, its sign creaking slightly in the hot breeze from the cornfields. Was it in another century that I had huddled under that same sign with the other draftees. How many of them would return? I wondered.

I heaved the duffel bag onto my shoulder and started walking down the sidewalk and across the tracks toward Old Town and home. As I approached the highway I passed Baxter's Garage where Jesse used to work; a grizzled mechanic with gray hair looked up from under the raised hood of a 1939 Chevrolet; I didn't recognize him.

Forrest Avenue looked the same, yet something seemed different about it. Or had I changed? The air was quiet except for the humming of locusts. Gardens flourished in backyards. In one a woman in an old-fashioned sunbonnet wielded a hoe. She didn't look up, so concentrated was she on her work; I thought I recognized her.

And then I saw my folks' house, the low yellow frame cottage with the green-roll roofing. It looked shabbier than I had remembered it; paint peeled from its weathered siding and screens rusted red. A large vegetable garden had been planted behind it. I cut

66

across the lawn toward the house, my heart beginning to pound. My feet sensed a flint-hardness to the earth under the dusty grass; evidently it had not rained for some time.

The house dozed quietly. There was no car in the tire ruts beside it. Was anyone home?

Then I heard it: a whoop from inside a window where a curtain fluttered. I had not heard that whoop since before Jesse died. The screen door flew open and Mother bounded out of the house.

Laughing, I ran toward her, dropping my duffel bag. We met on the dry grass where we stood hugging each other, her tears on my cheek as she cried over and over: "Harold . . . Harold . . . Harold . . . we thought you were never coming back."

I was surprised at how much she had aged in the nineteen months since I had seen her. Her auburn hair was streaked with white, lines etched her pale face and as I hugged her I was shocked to find how thin she was. We walked into the coolness of the kitchen, mother more animated than I had remembered seeing her.

"Your father's at work," she said. "Eva and the children are at her mother's. You going there now?"

Something gripped my heart. "No," I said, glancing at the window. "I thought I'd phone her first." I looked back at Mother who was busy getting food out of the ice box. "I want to give her a chance before barging in on her." Again that turmoil within me, the fear of facing the girl who seemed to be from another lifetime.

What was she like now? Had she changed in the time we'd been apart? Had I changed? And the two little girls? What would they think of me? A puzzling mixture of anticipation and shyness filled me.

Walking over to the phone, I called her mother's number, my hand trembling. Eva answered. For an instant I couldn't speak, and then said: "It's me, Pack. I'm home."

I could sense her shock over the wire. "Where?"

"At my folks' house."

"When will I see you?"

I hesitated for a moment. She'd want a few hours to get ready for me, I thought. "I'll be over around four."

Walking to her house that afternoon was like walking to a girl's house on that first date, a mixture of trepidation and anticipation.

Eva met me at the door, her dark brown eyes frightened for a moment as she looked into mine, as if she had expected me to be terribly changed. Then evidently recognizing the same husband who had left her, they softened and we clung together for a long moment, her raven-tressed head pressed against my chest. "Oh, Harold Everett Jones," she murmured. All my fears vanished. I was home again.

A little girl in blond braids peeked around the door at me. I knew she had to be Connie but I didn't recognize her; she was almost two years old. "Come kiss your daddy, honey," said Eva.

The little girl hesitated, her head down. I picked her up. "Honey," I said, "you'll never know how much I missed you." Slowly she put her arms around me, her brown eyes inquiring into mine.

Eva took me into the bedroom where Carol was awaking from her nap.

She looked just like the tyke in the snapshots. Eva picked her up. Big luminescent brown eyes looked at me, then she shyly buried her head in Eva's shoulder.

"It will take them both a little time to get to know me," I laughed. I felt at peace and relieved. I was home with my family; Eva had not changed; neither had I.

We lived in my mother-in-law's house the two and a half weeks of my furlough. A good-natured soul, she did everything possible to make us feel at home. But it was an unreal time; I felt I was partly at home and still partly at the front. Nervous, jumping at every loud noise, I still suffered from battle fatigue. I tried to avoid drinking— but it was difficult not to relax this way.

One morning I awoke to find Eva sitting by the window. "What's the matter, Honey?"

She looked at me, rushed over and threw her arms around me, burying her head in my shoulder, "Oh, Pack," she sobbed, "you must have suffered so."

It developed that I had been having terrible nightmares, leaping up in my sleep, screaming out warnings, as Eva cowered in fear beside me.

"Don't worry, Honey," I soothed her, "give me a little time and I'll be back to normal."

As days went by, the tensions within me seemed to subside. Dad and I went fishing at Lake View. His thinning hair was now silver, but his gray-green eyes sparkled as he baited his line. Sitting in the sun with the wavelets lapping the bottom of the boat, I felt really at peace.

I left Ida Grove the second time for camp, but this time in an optimistic mood. I was eventually assigned to a military police company at Fort Benjamin Harrison in Indiana.

When I was off duty I probably provided more work for my own M.P. unit than any other drunk. However, I was rarely punished with much more than a stern chewing out. After all, I had been in combat. And to my mind, I had earned my right to get high whenever and wherever I pleased.

After all, we were winning the war in Europe; so why not wink at a man's night out?

One night, two soldiers and I were in a riverfront bar in Evansville, Indiana, bragging about how we each had won the war. The more we drank the louder our boasting and finally the bartender ordered us out. We told him where to go and he called the police.

I had a hazy view of two blue-coated policemen coming in through the door. But there were no M.P.'s with them.

"Listen, you guys," I said, "I'm going nowhere without an M.P."

"Well, you're leaving this bar," barked the policeman.

"The hell we are!" we chorused. The next thing I knew the cops had grabbed us and that started it.

I woke up in the morning with a large knot on my head. Painfully hoisting myself on one elbow, I saw my two buddies slumped on the bunk next to me. One had blackened eyes and the other's face was bandaged.

They said it had been a whale of a fight. It had taken two more police squads and some M.P.'s to get us out of the bar and into jail.

"Well," I groaned, "what's going to happen now?"

"The lieutenant is coming after us," one said.

The lieutenant. I tried to smile but my jaw hurt. He was a "90-day-wonder," a product of the Army's Officer Candidate School still wet behind the ears who had never been overseas. Since our entire military police company was composed of combat veterans, all of us looked on this young man with disdain and pity.

As he had done several other times, he patiently came to the jail that morning and listened to the charges against us: drunk and disorderly and resisting arrest. Again, he secured our release to the military for punishment. The turnkey unlocked our cell and the three of us limped outside to the lieutenant's waiting jeep.

He was still inside signing papers for our custody. Finally he came out grim-faced, sat down in the front seat for a moment, then turned around with tears behind his glasses: "I really don't know why you guys do this to me," he said, his voice breaking. "You're making me look like a fool. I ought to let you all rot in jail."

He should have. Perhaps I might have been saved the hell to come.

Why did I keep drinking? I ended up sleeping off drunks in jails in Columbus, Ohio; Morganfield, Kentucky; and other places I can't remember. Two forces seemed at war inside me: one decent, one destructive. The deadly pattern was long set and I didn't realize what a prisoner I was to it. Fall and winter of 1944 waned into 1945 and by spring Germany had surrendered. With the easing of the war, some of the combat veterans began getting their discharges and in July 1945 I found myself once again coming home to Ida Grove, this time, I thought, for good. I had gone into the army as a private and had come out as one.

Eva and I and the babies moved into the little frame house on Forrest Avenue with my folks. We had no other place to go. We squeezed Carol's crib into our little bedroom, and put Connie's baby bed in the living room.

Finally I got a job pumping gas at Chuck's Standard Station on the highway. Dad and Mother did everything possible to make it easy for Eva and me in the house. But four adults and two toddlers couldn't live together in a two-bedroom crackerbox without grating on each other.

It was a blistering summer that year. Often Eva and I would spread a blanket out in the yard and lie there most of the night, at least until Carol awoke and began crying. She had a bad case of heat rash.

"Have you ever thought about going back and finishing college?" asked Eva one of these nights.

"How can I do that with two children to support?" I retorted, feeling anger grow within me. Deep inside I shrank from the future, as if I sensed something was waiting for me out there which I didn't want to face.

"Well, I can go to work."

I sat up and slammed the blanket with my fist. "No you won't. No wife of mine is going to go out to work while I take it easy in school."

Feeling another argument coming on, I jumped up and strode

down Forrest Avenue into town. At least there I could find bar company who'd understand how I felt. Early in the morning, I reeled home, half conscious, and fell into bed.

At work as I pumped gas, I could see the high school on the hill where I had graduated. "Most likely to succeed" the yearbook said about me. What really hurt was when an old classmate would drive in to fill up his car. "How ya doing, Pack? Gee, it's good to see you back."

"Yeah," I'd mutter, and keep my head down until his tank was filled.

If he were a drinking buddy, I might look up. But something was twisting my insides. Maybe it was a combination of all the things that happened to me overseas and the terrible difficulty I was having adjusting to becoming a husband and father. I deeply sensed my responsibilities to my family, but the few dollars I was bringing home from the gas station wasn't doing it.

Something had happened to me over there. I couldn't explain it; no one could. And I realized that no one in my family really knew me.

When well-meaning people praised me for what I had done for my country, I exploded. "If I'd had a white flag in my hand, I would have waved it."

I was sick of the adulation of war. Its hideous evil had permanently seared my spirit. How could anyone, I wondered, raise a boy, teaching him to love his neighbor because God is love, and then watch him be trained to become an efficient killer?

I was sick of killing. A vision of Scott with his entrails in the sand, and the blond Illinois boy's dead eyes staring at the Italian sky, came before me. Both of them had gone to Sunday school, their mothers and fathers had given their lives for their education. And now . . . ?

I felt no great honor about being in the army and helping defeat the enemy. But I did feel a deep compassion for those who went through the same hell.

There was old Spike, forty years old, one of the older men to leave Ida Grove for World War II service. He'd served all his time in the front-line infantry. Now he could be found most any night or morning dead drunk up against a building on the sidewalk.

When people would talk about him, I irately defended his right to lie in that gutter. "You do what he's done," I'd say angrily, "and then come back and talk to me about it!"

God? I wasn't thinking about God. All the Sunday school talk about a God of love didn't jibe with what I had seen. And the goodie-two-shoes who streamed in and out of the three white churches at the corner of Main and Fourth just didn't know the score. That's what I told Eva when she would leave for church with the girls and Mother and Dad Sunday morning.

Why didn't she stay home? I brooded about it. Outside of those few months in that Des Moines apartment, Eva and I never had a chance to really live together as man and wife.

Mother just couldn't understand my dark moods. "Harold," she said softly one day, "you've changed so much since you were a boy. I . . . I had thought the Lord had something for you, but . . ." She began to weep. "I just want you to know that I'm still praying for you. With Jesse gone . . . and now you." As she buried her head in her apron, I turned and walked out of the house.

Dad also tried to talk to me. Once while we were fishing together, he was rummaging in the tackle box for another plug, and then said: "Harold, is there anything you need, anything I can help you with?"

I looked at him sitting in the other end of the rowboat, his gnarled hand tremoring as he held the plug, and lines of worry deepening his eyes. My heart went out to him. Dad had a hard life. But there was no way I could tell him what was gnawing at me.

"No, Dad, nothing . . . ," I said, shaking my head, "but thanks anyway." Then I pointed to a bobber. "Hey, you got something working on that."

I just couldn't stand anyone trying to help me. Eva brought up the college thing again.

"You know, Pack, you could go on the G.I. bill; we'd be able to get by."

"No!" I shouted, "didn't I tell you? I'm not going to let you work!" I stormed out of the house. After what I had been through, college seemed so non-essential, so useless.

No one seemed to understand me until I had stood for some time at a bar and then a good discussion seemed to get going. There I found myself able to express my innermost thoughts in a deep and philosophical way. But I always seemed to forget what I had been saying. However, one day after a particularly busy night, one of my companions stopped me on the street. "Pack," he laughed, "that was some sermon you gave at the bar last night. Why, if I hadn't known better, I would have thought I was at one of those old Hardshell Baptist meetings with the preacher giving 'em hell."

"Sermon?" I laughed. "I must have drunk more than I thought!" I turned to see Mother coming out of the drugstore. She looked the other way as she passed. I knew she blamed my companions for my drinking. She couldn't believe that her son who had grown up in a home where liquor was not allowed would do such a thing on his own.

One afternoon after a particularly rough day at the gas station I had a few shots and walked home. As I stepped into the kitchen, Mother was rolling out noodles.

As I passed her, she evidently caught the odor of whiskey, set the roller down, and turned to me, pain in her eyes. "Harold, please," she choked, "please don't come home like that . . ."

Rage filled me. I rushed into our bedroom, rummaged behind the shoes in the closet, pulled out a fifth of whisky, stamped back into the kitchen and slammed the bottle down on the table so hard it foamed. "By God," I yelled, "I'll drink wherever I want to: I'm a man now, fought through a war for my country, and am sick of being treated like a kid!"

Mother's face blanched as white as the flour on her trembling hands. As she stood there silently, the fear in her glistening eyes knifed my heart.

Turning, I rushed out of the house and roamed through the darkening streets of Old Town, cursing myself for hurting Mother, who never smiled anymore in her grief for Jesse, and who now had a good reason to grieve for me as well.

Not too long after that Dad met me as I was finishing work at the gas station and walked home with me. As we scuffed through the dry leaves on the sidewalk, he said: "I've been thinking, Harold, I've got the offer of a good job as a groundskeeper on the Maytag estate in Newton. If I go, would you be interested in taking over my job at the hardware store?"

I didn't answer for a while; only our feet scraping through the rusty leaves broke the silence. A great feeling of love for my father overcame me and I wanted to put my arms around him. But all I could do was say: "Yeah, sure, Dad, if they'll take me."

Two weeks later Eva, the girls and I stood next to the old Ford piled high with my folks' things. They were ready to drive the 150 miles to Newton. Mother was crying and I had a hard time keeping my eyes dry. I leaned in and said goodby again, kissing her wet wrinkled cheek, promising her that I would stop drinking. Dad stuck out his hand and I felt the callouses that had been building for sixty years. Carol gurgled "Goo-by Gwama, Goo-by Gwampa." Connie sobbed, asking them not to go.

The ancient Ford rolled out into Forrest Avenue. I watched it until its tail lights winked at the highway and disappeared.

The gloom of the darkening street seeped deeper into my soul.

6

Downhill with No Brakes

IT WAS NEARLY eleven o'clock on Saturday night, closing time for Wilkins Hardware. It was a typical old-fashioned store, walls and ceilings festooned with shovels, pitchforks, chick feeders and tricycles. Some hundred thousand other items from sink stoppers to eye bolts nestled in a myriad of wooden drawers, the right item to be miraculously plucked by Tiny Wilkins or one of his clerks almost before the customer finished trying to describe it.

I kept busy there six days a week doing everything from installing light fixtures in customers' homes to repairing washing machines in the store's basement.

On Saturday night when a clerk finally pulled the cracked green oilcloth shade down over the glass front door, Tiny ambled his tall frame over to me and handed me the twenty-five dollars I had earned for the week.

"You going straight home, Pack?" His pale blue eyes questioned me hopefully. I knew why he asked. It was normal for me to stop at a local bar.

"Yeah," I answered, "in a little bit."

The "little bit" usually ended in the early morning hours when I'd stagger up Forrest Avenue singing "Red Wing" at the top of my lungs.

The first time I did this after Saturday night closing was when I discovered that Dad had left his job in the store to make room for me. Good jobs in Ida Grove were scarce in 1946, since so many retired folks had gone back to work during the war. Once used to the extra money they didn't want to give it up.

75

It really got me that Dad had to sacrifice on my account. I knew his caretaking job in Newton would end in April. Then what would he do? I was brooding about this one morning as I worked in the store's basement on an old Maytag washer. I heard a heavy step on the stairs. It was Tiny. He sat down on the bench next to me. "Pack," he ventured, "I've been meaning to talk with you . . . Have you ever wondered . . ."

"Wondered what?" I grunted. I knew he wanted to talk to me about my drinking but I was in no mood for lectures. I kept working on the machine.

Tiny gazed at me sorrowfully for a moment, then got up: "Nothing, Pack." As he slowly climbed up the stairs, I sat there looking at the broken washing machine's gear in my hand, angry at Tiny for getting into my personal life and angry at myself for not being able to discuss it with him.

I was still morose that evening at the dinner table. Eva had prepared chicken in her special way, simmered with onions and other vegetables. But I just picked at it. Why did Tiny have to stick his nose in my business? I never tippled on the job and hadn't lost a day's work because of it. I was getting sick of being regarded as one of the town's drunks.

"Pack?"

It was Eva across the table; her eyes were puzzled. "Is there something wrong with the chicken?"

"No, Honey," I sighed, "it's fine." I shoved my fork into the food on my plate and forced it down. Little four-year-old Connie had just about finished her plate and Eva began helping three-year-old Carol with her milk. As I looked at my two daughters, I thought: What kind of a father do they have? And yet, why was I berating myself? None of us ever had to go hungry; we always had a place in which to live. No, I vowed, I wasn't going to let any raised eyebrows about my Saturday night relaxation bother me.

"Pack?"

"Yeah?"

"I heard that the old Idso place was for sale."

I grinned. "That big barn?" For several months Eva had been talking about buying a house, but I had shrugged off her idea. We couldn't even afford a car, much less a house.

But she persisted in bringing it up. "You know your folks will be back in a few months and I don't think we should impose on them any more," she reasoned. "Besides," she added, "the girls do need a room of their own."

She was daydreaming, I argued. In no way could we ever come up with a down payment. Then one evening Eva pointed out an article in the *Record* about a new veterans' program called the "G.I. Bill." "Look, Pack," she said, "it offers vets an opportunity to buy homes with little or no down payment at a low rate of interest."

Encouraged by this, we had started looking at houses. However, the post-war building boom hadn't started yet and in several weeks of looking we found little in our price range.

But the price Eva said they were asking for the Idso place—$3,000—seemed like something we might be able to swing. I had known the big old house most of my life; it was only a block from my folks' house. Old man Idso wanted to move to Marshalltown to live with relatives. I smiled, recalling how he had called the place "Mount Olive." It had seven little olive trees growing on the property.

"Well, all right," I told Eva as she cleaned up the table, "let's take a look at it." She put the girls in their snowsuits and we walked down Main Street toward the big house. An early April breeze brought the rich scent of spring-freshened loam down off the fields. Soon we were on the corner looking at the Idso place. Looming against a gray sky, it looked foreboding. Rusted gutters hung loose from the eaves and old paint flaked from bare wood. I knew it meant a lot of work. A tour of its interior verified my fears. But I could also see Eva's vision; it did offer room for a growing family.

Back out on the sidewalk, I looked up at it once again, then turned to Eva. "Well, OK, let's make a try for it." She gave me a big hug.

I applied for a G.I. loan. Weeks went by and we didn't hear a thing. All Eva did was eat, sleep and dream the house. She didn't care that with our buying a house we had no hope of owning a car. She'd gladly walk the two miles to shop.

Then one afternoon at the hardware store Tiny called me to the phone. It was Eva. Our loan had gone through. It turned out that ours was the first G.I. loan ever granted in Ida County. The *Record* asked Eva and me to pose for a picture in front of our new house as we held the loan papers in front of us.

With our $100 down payment, we were able to arrange this government-guaranteed loan with a local lending institution.

Dad and Mom helped us move into our new home. That first night a light spring rain fell. And as I lay in bed I could hear the steady dripping of water in the hall. I wondered how many other leaks there were. It also wasn't insulated and the window frames rattled when the spring winds buffeted the old house. Thus, practically every Sunday found me working on repairs. Still, it was our own home and I got a real sense of satisfaction out of it.

However, the $24.77 monthly payments left us strapped. I had to earn more money. Someone told me about a job opening at the creamery which paid more than the hardware store and I headed right over to it. I got the job and was thrilled, even though it meant getting up at 3:00 A.M.

Each morning Dad would be waiting outside the house in his Model A to take me to the creamery. There I'd pick up my cream truck, come home to where Eva had a hot breakfast waiting and take off on my route. At each farm I'd pick up the dairyman's full cans of cream and leave empties for him to refill. He would be paid for each can we took to the creamery. I'd cover some fifty farms a day, picking up around 90 five-gallon cans of cream. I enjoyed driving over the rolling hills and watching pheasant flutter up from the fence rows and deer bounding across the fields. If I saw milk cows heading for their barn and the place wasn't on my route list, I'd stop in and solicit the dairy farmer's business.

Finally, in the afternoon I'd head back to the creamery where I'd wait in line with the other trucks, unload the cans and wait for the cream to be tested, weighed and emptied into the big holding tank. Then we'd wash our cans on the steam rack, reload the truck with empties, refuel and service it for the next day. The drivers would help each other out in this. Most were war veterans, too; after work we'd stop somewhere for a few beers, and tell lies to each other about how we won the war.

However, even though I earned a little more money, the battle with poverty continued. My finances became even more threatened the winter I slipped on the ice, fell and wrenched my back carrying a cream can in each hand. For days I could hardly walk but forced myself to go back to work each morning. There was little employee protection in those days and if I took any time off I felt sure I'd lose my job. My boss recommended I go to an orthopedic surgeon in Omaha for treatment.

"But I can't take that much time from work, much less pay a doctor," I said.

"All right," he answered, "then all we need is for you to sign a release form before you go back to work." I did not realize that the release absolved the company from any responsibility for insurance purposes. I signed and continued working, stiff with pain. Gradually it got better, though I always had to be careful when lifting. Not until years later did I realize how serious and long-lasting my injury would be.

But it was money that continued to be the real problem. We owed to the hilt for furniture and had borrowed from a finance company. The interest was high but when I had tried a bank they'd asked me for collateral. "Collateral?" I remembered asking. "If I had anything worth something I wouldn't be asking to borrow money." Finally, an old schoolmate, Jim Lipton, who was with a bank in a nearby town, helped us out with a loan. Even so, when payday came it was exchange day for us, most of my salary going into payments.

It hit me especially hard one evening in October when Eva was going over our finances. She looked up at me and shook her head. "Pack, we're not going to have any money for Christmas."

I looked at Connie and Carol playing on the floor, then thought back to my boyhood days and remembered how Jesse and I had made extra money. Trapping. The game was there and pelts still brought good money. I bought a dozen traps, got permission from the property owners, and set out early one morning along the Maple River west of town. I set my traps, steam rising from my breath in the icy dawn.

The season lasted about three weeks. But I did get some mink, raccoon, muskrat and possum. Eva relented about allowing me to skin them in the kitchen if I promised to keep everything scrupulously clean and do it when she and the girls weren't around. I stretched the pelts and set them up in the attic to dry. Eva and I made an agreement. Half of the money would go to pay bills and the rest would be for Christmas. We had a wonderful Christmas that year. And I kept my trap lines going every year after that, getting up each morning before dawn just as I did back in my school days.

But the old house continued to soak up money like a thirsty sponge. If the ancient furnace didn't need fixing, the water pipes would freeze and burst every time the temperature dropped.

One night after again coaxing the furnace into action, I collapsed into a chair in the living room and picked up the paper. As my eye traveled over the "help wanted" ads, I read where a man was looking for a truck driver. The salary was more than I was making.

After having driven a cream truck for a year, I figured I qualified. I phoned the number printed in the ad to find that it was a local gas station. The man who placed the ad took his calls there. "Yeah," a voice said, "that's Gordon Hinrichs. Come on down in the morning tomorrow and you'll find him here."

The next morning I walked to the filling station. A youngster leaned against a gas pump, swigging a bottle of Nehi. "Gordon Hinrichs around?" I asked. The boy leaned forward and called around the corner. "Hey Gordon, someone here to see you."

There was a rustling under an old Dodge truck parked in back and a man worked himself out from under it. As he stood up I saw a big raw-boned man about ten years older than I. He brushed back his sandy hair with a grimy hand and walked over to me.

"I'm Pack Hughes," I said, "I'd like to apply for that job." Hinrichs studied me for a moment; then as we leaned against the service station wall, he described his equipment as an old Dodge straight truck with an 18-foot box, plus a tractor truck with semitrailer. I had never driven a semi before but knew I could handle the Dodge.

"OK, Pack, you're on," he said, shaking my hand. I felt that I was going to like this big hearty guy with the steel blue eyes and sun-freckled face. Gordon Hinrichs was one of the many thousands of small trucking operators that serve communities all over our nation. He would haul everything from a farmer's soybeans for storage in the local grain elevator, to cattle and hogs for the Chicago stockyards. To succeed, the small truckers needed to keep the trucks operating as many hours each day as possible.

I started right out that day hauling shelled corn in the Dodge straight truck. Soon I was learning to load hogs and cattle and take them to local packing plants.

In a week, Gordon came up to me and pointed to the tractor truck which coupled onto a semitrailer. "Get in behind the wheel," he said. I crawled up into the driver's seat and he got in beside me.

With the 34-foot trailer extending behind me and sitting so high up, I felt like I was driving a house. The tractor had 5 speeds forward and one had to double clutch with a 2-speed axle giving it the capacity of ten speeds total. Gordon went over some pointers with me and then said, "Let's get started." With the engine trembling beneath me, I guided the big rig out onto the highway. As we rumbled along, I sweated each time a car came toward me, feeling sure I was taking up the entire highway. We had reached Battle Creek, a town about seven miles from Ida Grove, when Gordon said: "OK, Pack m'boy, turn her around."

Back in Ida Grove, he clapped me on the shoulder and said: "You're on your own." Then he told me to go to Kewanee, Illinois, a city about 300 miles distant, pick up a load of grain elevators and deliver them to various customers. He named a half dozen towns in Iowa and added, "You ought to be back in four days."

I said goodby to Eva and with heart in mouth, took off down the highway. By the time I returned I could handle a semi-rig. But I still had some things to learn.

Near disaster came when I hauled steel girders to a plant in Sioux City. Gordon cautioned me about a low viaduct under which I'd pass just before my destination. "You may even have to let some of the air out of your tires to make it," he said.

When I reached the viaduct I could see why Gordon was concerned. Carefully easing the semi up to it, I stopped just before my trailer reached it. Climbing up to the top of the trailer, I sighted down its top and saw that I had about one inch of clearance. Holding my breath, I slowly drove through and then breathing easier rolled over to the loading dock.

Delivery papers signed, steel unloaded, I swung back up into the cab, put my truck in gear and pulled away from the loading dock. Then I headed back toward the viaduct and confidently accelerated. There was a terrible shriek of ripping steel and a giant hand seemed to stop the truck. The accident hurtled me against the wheel and I then fell back gasping.

Dazed, I climbed out of the cab and looked back. The trailer top was crumpled into jagged wreckage. I had not reckoned that minus its load my rig had risen several inches on its springs. I drove back to Ida Grove in a state of panic, worrying about Gordon Hinrichs' reaction to what happened to his only trailer.

However, the big sandy-haired man was forgiving. He clapped me on the back with his ham-like hand and said: "Aw, don't worry about it, Pack." Then he grinned: "Next time, look *both* ways."

It took a week for the damage to be repaired. In the meantime he bought a new International livestock-hauling truck.

Two months later he purchased a few acres of land a mile west of town. On it we built a small frame building for an office and some livestock pens. "We're on our way, Pack," said Gordon. We began buying hogs on order for firms like Swift and Armour; then we'd transport them to packing plants in Omaha, Sioux City, Dubuque and Davenport. We'd also buy yearling calves and haul them to local feeders where they would be fattened for market on golden Iowa corn.

Once a week we'd take a load of cattle to the Chicago stockyards. I'd usually leave Ida Grove early Saturday morning with our stock truck and drive fifty miles to a livestock raiser. We'd get the cattle up into the trailer and by noon I'd be ready to take off for Chicago.

I had to be at the stockyards by Sunday morning. This would give the cattle a quiet Sunday to rest, fill up on corn and drink water to help replace the weight they lost on the trip, putting them in prime shape for market Monday morning. On the way, I'd pull in at a truck stop every hundred miles, check the cattle to make sure none were down, grab a mug of steaming black coffee and go on. Sunday morning I'd turn off Chicago's Halsted Street into the teeming, odorous stockyards where I'd unload my cattle, then drive over to a load-out office. Here commission men would locate a Chicago area firm with material to haul back to Iowa. Without this return load, we'd make little profit. The load back might be roofing nails, sheet metal, barbed wire.

Sometimes my return load would be heavy steel building girders which I had to pick up in East Chicago, Indiana. First I'd remove the tarp top and side ribs from the trailer so the girders could be hoisted into the truck. Then I replaced the ribs and tarp, weighed the truck so as not to be fined for an overload, and headed back. There was something good about being behind the wheel of a load and by now I figured I could handle anything on wheels.

Months went by and our trucking and livestock hauling business thrived. As it grew, I found myself dealing more and more with customers. So often it turned into a social time where a drink would seal a deal. One night after a lengthy time in a local bar, the customer drove me back to the trucking office. I knew I couldn't make it home in the pickup Gordon let me use so I parked it next to the office and fell asleep behind the wheel.

I drove home the next morning to find Eva almost hysterical. When I confessed to sleeping down at the stockyard, she looked up through tear-filled eyes and said: "Yes, in the hog pen; right where you belong!"

I glared at her and stormed out of the house. I stopped at my parents' and found my father building a greenhouse. He had long talked about getting into the flower-raising business. "How about some fishing?" I said. He was glad to go and a half hour later we were sitting on the bank along the Maple River.

"Trouble with Eva?" he ventured.

I grunted.

"Well, Son," he said slowly, measuring his words, "Your mother and I have been worried about you. You're a father now with a wife and two little children to support." He rebaited his hook and threw it back into the stream. "What I mean is, Harold," he said, looking at me sorrowfully, "when are you going to stop drinking?"

I stood up, took in my pole and started back to the car, swearing. "When is everybody going to lay off me?" I barked.

Dad was quiet as he drove me home. Just before I got out, he laid a gnarled hand on my arm. I stared stonily ahead. "Remember, Harold, your mother and I are praying for you."

I got out of the car and stamped into the house. Eva was listening to Billy Graham preaching on the radio and I was galled even more. Why do preachers have to tell others how to live?

"Praying for me," I muttered to myself. A lot of good *that* was going to do. Eva had been taking the two girls to the white frame Methodist church at the corner of Main and Fourth Streets and occasionally I'd go with her. But it was only for social reasons. I felt I had as much likelihood of communicating with God as with a fence post along the road.

But inside me forces were at work. One winter's afternoon found me returning from Council Bluffs hauling a tank trailer of gasoline. Sleet rattled against the windshield and it was snowing heavily by the time I started home. As evening fell I worried about making Honey Creek Hill on Highway 75; ice was beginning to build on the highway. When the hill loomed ahead, I shifted into low gear and touched a button on the dashboard which shot sand under the drive wheels. I was able to burn my way up. After mounting the peak, a long expanse of highway dipped before me into the snowy gloom. Carefully, I touched the trailer brakes of the giant tanker brimful with 6,000 gallons of gasoline. We started downhill in first gear, air brakes hissing, exhaust barking.

Suddenly, an ominous shape filled my side view mirror; it was the trailer, beginning to slide on the ice around me! I touched the trailer-brake lever but it kept advancing.

I quickly shifted into a high speed, fighting to keep ahead of the trailer. Perhaps I could straighten it out. Now we roared down the hill. I thought of the sharp curve at the end of the hill. My heart froze as I saw it ahead in the pale dusk. On its outside edge was a dance hall with scores of cars parked in front of it. On this ice I wouldn't make the curve!

I could see my rig smashing into the dance hall, exploding into a mountain of flame. My God! All those people.

My truck hurtled toward it. If I touched the brakes we'd jacknife into a wild twisting juggernaut. I could only grip the wheel and struggle to keep the rig on the road. Now I became one with the truck. As we roared into the turn, the rig shook like a bone in a terrier's teeth. In terror I clung to the wheel. Hold it . . . hold it . . . now, at the top of the turn give it gas! I shoved the pedal to the floor, praying that the acceleration would hold us on the road.

The dance hall and parked cars flashed by my side window and suddenly we were on the straightaway again. Breathing hard, I slowly let up on the accelerator, gently bleeding the trailer brakes, and watched the speedometer edge down to 40 mph, 30 . . . 20, and finally I was able to bring the rig to a stop on the side of the road.

For a moment, I sat behind the wheel too weak to move. Then I got out of the cab and stood by the roadside, shaking so badly I could hardly light a cigarette.

I stood there in the lightly falling snow, sucking deeply on the cigarette. In the distance I could hear the strains of a saxaphone and the thud of a danceband drum. The people laughing and chattering inside that building would never know.

I looked back at the curve and the hill. How did I make it? I shrugged, flipped the cigarette into the ditch and swung back into the cab. Just one of those things, I figured.

However, as I related my experience to some friends in a bar that night, it became even more clear to me. I was one topnotch driver.

Later that night I lurched into the house. "No doubt about it, Eva, I'm one helluva good driver." Then I sank onto the sofa.

Eva, her face white and strained, tried to shush me. "Please, Harold, the children." I tried to rise from the couch and caught a glimpse of Connie and Carol peeking at me from behind their bedroom door. I tried to say something to them but couldn't get the words out.

In the morning I awoke to a patter of sleet on the window. My back ached and my throat burned. I had spent the night on the sofa. When I made my way into the kitchen, Eva was sitting at the table, an untouched cup of coffee in front of her. The dark circles under her eyes seared me. She was staring out the window at the ice which was building on the black tree branches.

"Honey," I said, putting a hand on her shoulder. "I'm sorry about last night." She stiffened.

"All right!" I barked, going over to the stove. I poured the coffee so fast it sloshed onto the floor. I ripped off a paper towel to clean it up. "All right," I said, "so I had a few last night. Is this any way to treat me after the kind of day I had?"

She didn't answer. I looked around the kitchen with its green walls I had painted only a few days before and slammed my cup down.

"The hell with it," I snapped, turned, went out of the house, jumped into the pickup and headed for my office. But all the way my conscience bothered me. I couldn't blame Eva. It seemed I was coming home senseless every Friday and Saturday night and some nights in between. By the time I reached the office I had calmed down. I picked up the phone and dialed home.

"Eva? Look, Honey, I want to say I'm sorry. And I want to tell you that you have every right to feel the way you do. And look . . . I have something to say to you." The phone was very still. "As true as I'm sitting here, I promise you, Eva, that I'll never take another drink again. I mean it."

The next few months were idyllic. By now the pickup truck had become our family car. Eva couldn't drive and I figured it was time to teach her. So after supper, Eva, the girls and I would go out on the back roads for driving lessons.

In a few weeks Eva was doing well at the wheel. One warm

summer's evening as we were crunching along a gravel road on the brow of a hill, Eva pulled over to the side. The girls had been laughing and talking, the setting sun had filled the sky with flaming colors. Eva shut off the engine and in the evening quiet a melody of sounds filled the air, a meadowlark trilled, and the leaves of a cottonwood rustled above us. Even the girls hushed. Eva stared poignantly across the valley.

"What's wrong, Honey?" I asked, putting my arm around her. She turned to me and sighed: "Why can't it always be like this?"

"What do you mean?" I shifted uneasily on the seat.

"Your not drinking."

My hands tightened on the edge of the cushion. Why did she have to bring *that* up? "You're expecting me to fall off the wagon any minute," I snapped. I found myself becoming angrier. "Besides, even when I did drink, did the kids go hungry? Weren't the house payments made?"

I didn't say anything more but got out of the pickup, walked around to the driver's side. Eva slid over and I climbed in behind the wheel. I spun the tires on the gravel and drove home silently.

When I walked into the office the next morning, Gordon Hinrichs had his feet up on the scarred old desk and was talking into the telephone. "Okay," he said into the receiver, "you got a deal." He hung up the phone and grinned at me. "Well, Pack," he said, "we've just leased a grain elevator in Battle Creek."

Our business was really growing. We already had two semitruck trailers, five livestock trailers, five straight trucks. Besides livestock, we were also selling and hauling fertilizer and feed. I had already started taking over some of the buying and selling of livestock, not to mention managing the trucking operations. Of course, this meant spending quite a bit of time with customers and drivers.

It seemed every time a deal was made it called for a drink. I kept waving the liquor aside and taking a Coke and then one night in the tavern, after completing a particularly good transaction, I said to myself, "What the hell. One drink won't hurt."

I didn't stop until I was almost senseless. Evenings like this increased, and often I would avoid going home but would bed down on the old sway-backed davenport in the little cubicle that served as my office. One of the reasons I avoided going home was that I discovered Eva was afraid of me. I couldn't understand it until one night I saw the two little girls cowering behind a closet door. It was then I realized how angry and belligerent I became.

The next Sunday one of the men from church stopped at the house. "Is there some place we can talk, Pack?"

"Sure," I said, leading him out into the yard. We sat down on a bench making small talk. It was fall and I wished I could have used this time to rake leaves.

With some effort he said what was on his mind. "Pack, have you ever thought about joining Alcoholics Anonymous?"

I stared at him. "Alcoholics Anonymous?" Sure I had heard of it. I reached down, picked up a stick, crumbled it, and looked back at him. "No, Bob. I don't need *that*."

My would-be benefactor gulped and said. "Well, just thought I should mention it. I hope I didn't get you angry."

"No, you didn't get me angry," I laughed, standing up and clapping him on the back. I watched him walk away and shook my head. Alcoholics Anonymous; that was for the bums and down-and-outers, the guys who had hit the skids.

It was far from my life. Things had been picking up more and more in my job. I was earning $100 a week, plus five percent of the net profits. That year it looked as though I'd be making a bonus of $300.

I was working on the accounts one morning when a young fellow drove in looking for a load. I knew him; he had seven kids and lived on a run-down place seven miles out on Schleswig Road. He had an old Ford half-ton truck which filled our driveway with blue clouds of burning oil. He left the motor running and I could hear the rattle of a worn clutch. One end of the truck sagged on a bad spring.

His pale blue eyes were desperate and he said that if we gave him a load he'd do it for ten cents a hundred less than the going rate. Trucking rates in Iowa, as in every other state, are regulated by the State Commerce Commission, so that everybody is supposed to charge the same; otherwise it would become cutthroat competition.

When I presented this offer to Gordon, he gazed reflectively at the livestock cane he always carried with him, then looked back at me. "Give the guy the full rate," he said.

The man left happy, his truck leaving a fresh puddle of black crankcase oil on the driveway. Gordon sat down at my desk, put his feet on a wastebasket which he usually did when he philosophized. "You know, Pack, I can sympathize with that guy. I remember being in the same spot myself. You have three payments due on your rig at the bank. So to get a load you find yourself offering less than the going rate. But it's no good. You just run yourself into the ground doing that."

He leaned back, balancing his cane on his knee. "If it weren't for the Association, guys would be going out of business all over the state."

He was referring to the Iowa Motor Truck Association and he was on its board of directors. Composed of truck owners, their objective was to present a united front to help each other maintain standard rates. The commerce commission was supposed to do this, but the state inspectors who came to our office hardly glanced at our books. They took my word for what we were paying, gabbed for a while, then climbed into their state car and drove away.

"If it was left up to them," said Gordon one day as he watched an inspector leave, "the truck business in this state would go to pot in six weeks."

He got up from his chair and started to leave, then hesitated. "Is it tonight when you close that deal with the livestock shipper in Ames?"

"Yeah."

He hesitated. "Well, take care."

I squirmed because I knew what he meant. The Ames man enjoyed his bourbon as much as I. We closed the deal and when the celebration was over, I was reeling. Fighting to stay awake, I drove back to the office, staggered in, fell down on the couch and passed out.

In the morning I awoke with a raging headache, drove out to a restaurant for coffee and aspirin, then returned to my desk to fill out some rate books. About ten o'clock that morning a big form filled the doorway of my office. I looked up to see Charley Yousling. I had worked for his son at the gas station. Charley had been County Sheriff since I could remember.

"Hey, Charley," I greeted him, "How you doing, ol' buddy?"

He looked down at the floor, then back to me. "Well, this ain't exactly a social call, Pack," he said. He stepped forward and put a paper document in my hand. I looked down to see the big words SUBPOENA printed on it.

"I'm sorry, Pack," said Charley, "delivering this is the hardest thing I've ever had to do."

I opened the document. It was an order that I appear before the Ida County Sanity Commission that afternoon to show cause why I should not be committed to the state asylum as an inebriate.

The name of the person filing the subpoena was in a handwriting that I knew well: Eva Hughes.

7

Broken Promises

I SAT IN MY chair stunned, the paper trembling in my hands. Charley Yousling's anguished face swam before me. "I'll see you, Pack," he muttered and quietly walked out the door.

A shocked stillness filled the office; the lowing of cattle in the pens outside seemed strangely distant. I picked up the subpoena, brushed away a blue-bottle fly, and reread the document. An *inebriate*. I knew what the word meant but leaned down into a lower desk drawer and pulled out a battered Webster's. *One who is drunk; an habitual drunkard.*

I didn't consider myself an inebriate. Sure, I drank too much. But an inebriate? Again a view of a man I saw lying in the gutter one night in Des Moines flashed before me, his rumpled clothes stained with vomit and his purple face showed no connection with this world. No, I wasn't like that.

What was Eva trying to do . . . get rid of me? Perspiration soaked my shirt. The hearing was only a few hours away. I picked up the phone and called Gordon who was out at the elevator in Battle Creek and told him what had happened. "You'd better get a lawyer fast," he advised.

There were five lawyers in town. I knew four of them fairly well. I frantically phoned each one. None could take my case on such short notice. The fifth lawyer, whom I hardly knew, said he would represent me. I only had twelve dollars in my wallet. He agreed to take my case for ten. I put the phone back on the hook, slumped at my desk and wiped sweat from my forehead.

We met that afternoon on the steps of the county courthouse. I was shaking inside as we walked into the hearing room, our steps sounding loudly on the wooden floor. The first person I saw was Eva. She looked like a frightened bird, huddled with her mother on one of the long pine benches. Her face was chalk white and she wouldn't look at me. Her mother glanced nervously at me once and quickly turned her head away.

Four men, all of whom I recognized, sat around a long wooden table in front of the room. One of them was Arthur Johnson, our Republican county chairman, the man who had helped me get into the University of Iowa. He got up and introduced the other three men as members of the Sanity Commission. As the commission's attorney, he would be the prosecutor in this case.

Art took my attorney to one side, talked with him for a moment, and then asked me to come into an office just off the hearing room. Inside, he waved me to a chair, sat down behind a desk, leaned back and asked me. "Now what's this all about, Pack?"

I stared at him for a moment. "I've been drinking too much," I said.

He looked down at the desk for a moment, then back up. "Have you lost your job?" I shook my head. What was Art getting at?

"Well," he said, picking up a pencil and holding it between his forefingers. "Are you supporting your family?"

I nodded.

"Are you beating your wife?"

I straightened in my chair. "Of course not, Art! Sure, we've had arguments, but I've never touched Eva."

I leaned forward in my chair, hands on my knees. "Art, I can assure you that I have never missed a day of work or not paid my bills. Check it out with Gordon Hinrichs if you want."

Art looked at me, his face serious. "I'll do that." For a moment only the ticking of a wall clock broke the silence. I watched a long ray of afternoon sun slant across Arthur's desk. Suddenly, I lowered my head into my hands. "For the life of me," I said huskily, "I can't understand why Eva is doing this thing."

Art put down the pencil he had been holding and his light blue eyes bored into me. "Pack, would you make me a promise?"

"Yeah?"

"That if you can get out of this hearing you'll not drink for a year?"

I sat back in my chair, drew a deep breath. "Art," I said, my throat catching, "if we can get this thing dropped, I promise; I won't take a drink for at least a year."

He got up from the desk and headed toward the door. "OK," he said, "let's see what we can do."

In the hearing room he spoke to Eva, the commission members and my lawyer. Everyone agreed not to proceed with the hearing. Then Art made a statement for the records that I had provided adequately for my family, had not harmed anyone and had promised not to drink for a year.

My mind reeling in a mixture of relief and wounded feelings, I hurried out of the courthouse, jumped into the pickup and drove home. The house was empty; I felt sure Eva was still with her mother. I packed a suitcase with some clothes and then went back to the office.

I sat at my desk wondering what I was going to do. The sun set behind the stock barn and the office melted into darkness. I did not feel like turning on the light.

At six o'clock the phone rang. It was Eva. I held the receiver, emotions whirling within me. "Are you coming home?" she asked in a tiny, strained voice.

"No," I said swallowing hard, "I didn't think you wanted me home; I thought you were finished with me."

"Well, I was only trying to help you." She started to cry. "Your own father thought it would be the best thing for you."

I wiped my eyes and swallowed hard. "Well," I said huskily, "I can't understand how having me committed would help. I know what I have done was wrong but . . ." I leaped to the question I most wanted to ask: "Do you really want me to come home?"

Within a minute I was in the pickup heading home. That night Eva and I sat at the kitchen table talking into the early morning hours about our life together. I repeated my pledge that I wouldn't touch liquor for at least a year.

It was a promise I found most difficult to keep. Drinking had become a ceremony in doing business. And I found the physical craving almost overwhelming. However, I would remember my promise to Eva and Arthur Johnson, and keeping it had become a special point of honor to me. It was like back in my high school days when I had promised myself a certain number of tackles a football season. I had pledged not to drink and my ego would suffer if I failed.

Others would also try to help me, like Father Harry Dailey, the priest who now lived in the white frame parsonage near our house. From our garden I'd look up to see his car, always tan with dust, bob into his driveway. The little red-haired priest would leap out, wave and in his Irish lilt call: "How ye doing, Pack, me boy?"

"OK, Father," I'd answer. I loved this man who seemed to be always on the go. His was the only Catholic parish in Ida Grove and his flock extended far into the country. Late at night we'd often hear his old car grind out of the driveway on the way to some sick or needy parishioner.

Often while I worked our garden, we'd get into conversation, I resting on my hoe and Father Dailey leaning on the fence, as we talked about the best fishing holes on the Maple River.

Every once in a while he'd say something about the need for prayer and for a man to discipline himself. There would be deep concern in his blue Irish eyes, but I'd quickly change the subject.

In trying to quench my desire for alcohol I immersed myself deeper into the trucking business. Gordon reciprocated by increasing my responsibilities. In addition, I found myself doing more work for the local Republican Party, to which everyone in Iowa seemed to belong.

One morning Gordon walked into the office and set a large bundle of cardboard signs on my desk. "How'd you like to do some work for the party?" he asked, holding up one of the signs. It was an election poster for our local Republican state representative.

I spent that afternoon and the next morning traveling all over the county, nailing up the posters on telephone poles, vacant buildings and fences. By the end of the second day, I was so tired of facing that man's grin that I had difficulty voting for him in the election.

I also walked door to door soliciting financial contributions for the party, and ended up attending some county and state Republican conventions as a delegate from our area.

My interest in politics was stirred by its involvement in the trucking industry. It still hurt to see a gaunt-faced man in worn overalls step down from a wheezing truck and offer to haul for less than his published rate. And from what I saw, little was being done by the State Commerce Commission. It seemed that as long as a trucker paid his five-dollar permit fee, had insurance, his name on the truck, and filed his rate with the commission, that was all that mattered.

The trucker who insisted on charging the established rate lost business, while the trucker who cut his rate too low would eventually lose his truck to the bank. Everyone seemed concerned, even the other directors of the Iowa Motor Truck Association, made up of fleet owners and individual truckers.

One day while I was spouting off about rate cutting, Gordon said: "You're talking to the wall, Harold. Why don't you speak to the truckers themselves?"

"What do you mean?"

"Go to one of the Truck Association meetings and talk to the men about the need for uniform trucking rates."

"I'm no speaker."

"What do you mean?" Gordon laughed. "I've heard you do some mighty fine speaking when you ran for delegate to the state convention. And I heard you were a crackerjack orator in high school and," he laughed, "in almost every bar in the state. Besides, Pack, with that deep resonant voice of yours, you could charm tires right off their rims."

I figured Gordon was laying it on thick to get me off his back. But the rate situation had become an obsession with me. If talking to the men would help, I'd do it.

By that time I had become manager of the Hinrichs trucking and livestock operations and thus came in close personal contact with the State Commerce Commission men. I had also begun to learn the ins and outs of the political structure that governed these commissions and so was able to translate some of this to the truckers in the speeches I began giving at Association meetings.

It was easy to relate to these men because we all shared the same problem—lack of money. All of us were mortgaged to the hilt on homes and furniture. We talked the same language. It was more like gutter language.

I figured that if I were going to reach these men, I'd have to swear more than they did. The only problem was that Eva complained it was slipping over into my talk at home.

"OK, Eva," I said one evening, walking up and putting my arms around her as she stood at the stove, "I promise you, not one bad word here in the house, OK? Just like drinking. I've proven I can handle that. And I'll be able to handle the language."

As we started supper, I told the girls that if they cleaned their plates I had a surprise for them. Eva looked at me questioningly. "It's a surprise for you, too, Honey," I smiled. Right after supper I took them into the driveway to see our "new" car, the first one we ever owned. It was a 1942 Buick Century which I had bought for $150 from a friend who ran a tavern. Despite the fact that it was nine years old and rust had eaten out much of the body and fenders, Eva and the girls were as excited as if it were a brand new 1952 model.

Of course we had to take a ride in it then and there. We stopped for ice cream and sat in the parking lot eating our cones.

A few days later as I worked in the garden staking tomato plants, I thought about how good life had become for us in the fourteen months since I'd stopped drinking. Eva had lost the dark hollows around her eyes and I was feeling a lot better.

"Pack." A voice greeted me from the corner of the house and I looked up to see a friend walking toward me. I hadn't seen him for some time and we exchanged pleasantries. He put his arm on my shoulder and spoke confidingly. "Pack, I understand you've been off the sauce for over a year now and I want to congratulate you. You know, I haven't touched a drop myself for two years and I give the credit for it to Alcoholics Anonymous. Before joining, I was powerless, just couldn't stop drinking." He talked some more about his group and then invited me to come to a meeting with him that night.

"Friend," I said smiling, "thanks but no thanks. Now I know you had a big problem, but mine isn't that bad. I'm able to handle it and I don't need any club to help me do it."

As I watched him walk back to his car, I thought that there were some fellows who didn't have the moral strength or will power to help themselves. They must need a supportive group like the AA's. I thought back on my fourteen months of sobriety and felt a sense of satisfaction on how well I had been able to handle it.

I seemed to have been asleep for a long time and it was difficult to awake. Yet I really didn't want to awake. My head was swimming. The room seemed to explode into light and then become dark, light, dark, light, dark.

"Eva?" I called out weakly. There was no answer. Where was I? I sensed I was lying on a bed but still dressed. I struggled to sit up, swung my legs over the side of the bed and sat there staring at a strange rug intermittently revealed in the flashing of a light. Nausea welled within me and my head pounded. Now I could see that the light flashing was the hotel sign outside the window. I leaned on the sill and looked down into the street. Des Moines; that's where I was. But how did I get there? The last I remembered was being at a truckers' meeting in Ames.

I couldn't remember taking a drink. But there was that familiar dryness in my mouth, that stale taste. The room whirled as I stood up, went to the bathroom and washed my face with cold water. I noticed vomit covering the toilet bowl. I slumped back on the bed. It must be morning. There was a gray light in the sky. A Diesel locomotive moaned in the distance. How did I get there? What had I done? Where was the car?

I reached inside my sweat-dampened coat for my wallet and looked in it. Some sixty dollars was gone. Where had I spent the money? I fell back on the bed flooded with despair. Eva? I had better call her. I flicked on the bed light and with a feeling of dread picked up the phone.

There was relief in Eva's thin voice when she heard me speak. "Where are you?"

"Eva, I'm here in a hotel in Des Moines and I've been drunk. I have to tell you that." I almost sobbed. "Eva, I can't remember a thing."

A horn sounded from the street and I had a sudden vision of a man in a rumpled, soiled suit lying in the gutter.

"Eva," I said, "I'll start for home right away."

Her voice was cool and measured. "Don't you think you should wait until morning?"

"Why, is it night?"

"Yes, it is."

I sank deeper into the bed. "What day is it?"

"Thursday, the 16th."

Good God. I had been gone two days.

"Eva," I said, gripping the phone, "I'm sorry."

There was silence on the other end. "Look," I said, struggling to maintain communication, "I'd better not start for home now. I'll get something to eat. I'll see you in the morning."

"All right." The phone clicked.

I got up and snapped on the ceiling light. Standing on the dresser was a fifth of bourbon, almost empty. All I could figure was that I had come into the hotel room with it two days before and started drinking.

I carried the bottle into the bathroom and poured the rest into the sink. The whiskey fumes nauseated me. I dropped the bottle into the wastebasket vowing never to drink again.

On the long dreary drive home that morning I again found myself wondering what was wrong with me. Why couldn't I handle alcohol like other people seemed to do? Somehow my male virility was mixed up in it; a man should be able to hold his liquor.

I thought of the hard-drinking men I had known since youth. Some of them didn't make it home after drinking bouts. Did they have the same problems as I? Or was I an unusual case?

Yet the truth burned deeply within me as the asphalt highway rose into the Iowa hills: I was crucifying my family, my parents and myself.

Eva was quiet and cold when I walked into the house. I put my hand on her shoulder. It seemed so frail. I could feel her shudder. "It won't happen again, Honey." She turned and went upstairs to check on the girls who were getting ready for school.

I stood watching her climb the stairs. I knew she had absolutely no faith in what I said. She didn't believe me any more than if I had said I was preparing to study for the ministry.

Later that week my father pulled up in front of the house in his old car and asked me if I'd take a ride with him. He drove out to the park and we sat there and talked. "I understand how you feel, Harold," he said, "what with the war and all."

I grimaced. All he and Mother could attribute my problem to was the war. But I knew that wasn't it; I had begun drinking long before the army. Dad tried that day, but I didn't hear him.

Back at the livestock depot, Gordon Hinrichs gave me a quizzical look as I came to work the next morning. "Got kinda worried about you, Pack," he said. I shrugged and dove into the stack of papers that had mounted on my desk.

Immersion in my work was one way of forgetting my problem. And it was easy to do. For my meetings with the truckers were giving me an education. And I was beginning to focus on the problems of the smaller truckers who simply weren't making it. The banks got full interest on the money they loaned the men to buy their trucks, the insurance company made profits, but those who had just one truck and operated out of their back door and shirt pocket were hurting.

About every three weeks Keith Olson, a State Commerce Commission inspector, would come to our office to check out our trucks.

The earnest, young, blue-eyed inspector and I had become good friends by that time and during one visit I opened up to him about my concerns. He nodded and said he was also worried about the many small truckers who had their insurance canceled for non-payment of premiums. "It kills me to put them out of business," he said, filling his pipe and lighting it, "but I have to do it."

Gordon Hinrichs felt as I did. We talked it over with Keith Olson and it was arranged for me to call a meeting of local truckers in one county. We chose the town of Mapleton. The idea would be to convince them all to file a uniform rate and stick to it.

Some fifty truckers showed up, all fiercely independent men. With every sentence punctuated with oaths, I explained the purpose of the meeting; Keith Olson then spoke about the law, pointing out that each driver had a right to expect a uniform tariff and the legal right to file a complaint against any one of their number who undercut it.

"Nobody can be forced to join this group," he said. "But if you join, you'll be assured of actually getting the kind of rates that will keep you in business."

There were sharp questions from the men and some suspicion. But I knew them; I had spent much of my life as they did, trying to make a buck. Their interest encouraged us to hold similar get-togethers in other counties. Finally we got enough truckers together to set up a rate structure.

As I was setting up some files for this operation in the office, Gordon came in, sat down on a chair and leaned its back on the wall.

"Pack," he said, a big hand pushing back his sandy hair, "can I give you a little tip for your talks with truckers?"

"Yeah," I said, emptying a drawer into a wastebasket, "I can use all the help I can get."

"Well," he said, shifting his chair, "this is the last thing you would have thought I'd be saying, but . . . it's your language."

"My language?" I glanced at him puzzled.

"Yeah," he grinned sheepishly, "believe it or not but some of the truckers have complained that you swear too much at the meetings."

I threw my head back and laughed. "Why, those no-good s . . . o . b . . . . . s."

When I enthusiastically told Eva about my work helping the truckers, she didn't act as thrilled as I thought she'd be. I sensed her thoughts. This activity would involve more traveling and more opportunities to drink.

Her brown eyes had dulled and new worry lines had etched her face; guiltily I realized that I had put them there.

After falling "off the wagon" in Des Moines, I had been coming home drunk more often. At times I'd be belligerent and foulmouthed. Though I never struck Eva, my verbal abuse made her cringe like a beaten kitten. One night both Connie and Carol were awakened by my shouting and I almost stumbled over them at the top of the stairs where they were huddled crying.

By then, I had decided that drinking was an inevitable part of my life and I no longer made claims about trying to stop. Anyone who tried to talk to me about it was curtly rejected, for I would always tell them I could control it. But deep down I had begun to hate myself. I wasn't at all sure I could control my drinking. I was still haunted by the fear in Mother's eyes when I slammed the whiskey bottle down on her kitchen table. I had trouble sleeping; when I did I'd have nightmares of men dying around me in shellbursts and I would awaken screaming and crying. And I had lost count of the jails I had been in for drinking or brawling.

A drum beat of doom seemed to fill my days and nights. I cringed at people's comments, at knowing winks, at seeing the flush in my face in the mirror, at the deepening fatigue which racked my body. Yet I was powerless to stop doing the one thing that caused it all. It was as if a malignant force was whirling me toward a frightening precipice.

The year 1952 dawned cold and bitter. The hills above Ida Grove were heavily blanketed in snow and the Maple River was frozen deep. My spirits had lifted; I had not had a drink for two weeks after months of heavy drinking.

As I kissed Eva goodby that January morning she reminded me we had a dinner date that evening with friends. We had a very limited social life, mostly because of my problem, and I knew this dinner was very important to Eva. I promised her I'd be home early, turned and headed for the car. As I drove away, I looked back to see Eva still standing at the door. She looked so small, so sad; I reminded myself to bring her some flowers.

It was a busy day, starting with a meeting with drivers who had a rate structure grievance. It went through an extended lunch. That afternoon I met with some shippers involving a knotty problem and the meeting lasted far longer than I expected. I kept glancing at my watch. Finally, everything was settled and one of the men suggested that we all retire to a bar and confirm our decision.

I hesitated. Eva wanted me home early. Just one drink, I decided. It tasted so good. Later through a murky maroon fog I heard someone say something about it being eleven o'clock. Eleven o'clock!

I hurried to my car and raced home. The house was dark. I pushed open the front door calling out "Eva?" But my words echoed hollowly in the hall. I stumbled and fell into the couch, breathing heavily. Cold sweat beaded my forehead. I knew Eva was not home. It had happened before. When Eva sensed I'd be coming home drunk, she would take the girls and go to her mother's.

I slumped on the couch, hopelessness overwhelming me. I remembered how long Eva had sewn material to make a new dress for the dinner that night, how we had arranged with my mother to sit with the girls.

Again I had hurt loved ones. My head pounded in guilt and nausea. Slowly the alcoholic fog seemed to lift. As it did the sense of shame sank deeper into me. I felt helpless. I was a father just in his 30s who was worthless, a sot. What was the point in going on any longer? I couldn't face Eva, the girls, our parents. I couldn't even walk downtown any more and meet the many good friends whom I had insulted during drinking bouts.

Trying to escape the horrible self-loathing, I found myself wandering about the house, a sense of blackness closing in on me. In the bedroom, I slumped onto our bed. I sat there, realizing the awful hopelessness of my condition. I couldn't control my drinking; for ten years alcohol had controlled me.

What was the point of living? I'd failed everyone who had meant anything to me; I was a disgrace to my town. I didn't go to church —that would be phony. I was a hypocrite in everything I did; I couldn't even tell the truth anymore.

I couldn't do anything right. Why not just end it?

The thought hung there, like the echo of a tolling bell.

A cold feeling of logic overcame me. Why not? I had thought about this before but had brushed it away. Yet the more I considered the alternative, the more sense it made. Why go on doing the things I hated? The more I thought about the disorder in my life and the inability to control it, the more I wanted to end it. I was just an evil rotten drunk, a liar. And what should happen to evil men? They deserved to die.

I remembered enough Scripture to know that suicide was not God's way. But as I weighed the balance, I felt it better to be eternally lost than to bring eternal hell to those I loved.

No, my mind was clear now. I hated what I did, but I still did it. When I promised loved ones I wouldn't drink and even prayed to God that I wouldn't drink, and did it again and again, I realized in my heart that there was no way on earth I could ever control it.

I got up from the bed and went to the closet where I kept my rifle and shotgun. I opened the door and considered both, then reached for the shotgun. It would be the most certain. It was a single barrel Remington pump gun, 12-guage.

As I lifted the gun into the room its walnut stock glowed in the bedroom light. The gun had belonged to Jesse; he had been so proud of it. I thought about Jesse, then considered what I was going to do to Mother, Dad, Eva and the children. Eva was still young and beautiful. She would easily find someone else to marry and have a decent life. The thought hurt me. The girls would eventually forget me. As I was then, they would never forget, suffering only disgrace and sorrow.

I thought about insurance. I had let my G.I. insurance lapse, but I did have a benevolence society policy which would pay my burial expenses.

I slid three shells in the magazine and pumped one into the chamber. Tears streaming down my face, I lay down on the bed, rested the shotgun on my chest and put the muzzle into my mouth. The cold steel rasped my teeth and tasted of oil. Reaching down, I found I could push the trigger with my thumb. This way everything was certain: I did not want to botch it and spend the rest of my life as a vegetable.

Then I thought of the awful mess and stains this would leave in the bedroom. I remembered the men I had seen shot overseas. I was leaving Eva and the girls with enough bad memories. Getting up, I walked into the hall and into the bathroom. It could be cleaned easier. Carefully holding the Remington, I climbed into the tub.

8

A Time to Die

IT WAS AN old-fashioned claw-footed tub. The porcelain was cold to my hand as I stepped into it, my shoe soles squeaking on the tub bottom. In it, I lay down, feeling strange to be in a tub with my clothes on. With the shot gun resting on my stomach, I positioned it with the muzzle in my mouth toward my brain. Reaching down, my thumb found the trigger and I was about to push it.

A terrible sadness filled me. I knew what I was doing was wrong in God's eyes. Yet, my whole life had been wrong. And God had always been very remote. In a few years my family would get over it, I reasoned. They would have an opportunity to rebuild their lives. But if I remained here, I would never change and only hurt them more. The thought came that I should explain all this to God before pushing the trigger. Then if He could not forgive this sin, at least He would know exactly why I was committing it.

Climbing out of the tub, I knelt on the tile floor and laid my head on my arms, resting on the cool tub rim.

"Oh, God," I groaned, "I'm a failure, a drunk, a liar and a cheat. I'm lost and hopeless and want to die. Forgive me for doing this . . ." I broke into sobs, "Oh, Father, please take care of Eva and the girls. Please help them forget me . . ." I slid to the floor, convulsing in heavy sobbing. As I lay face down on the tiles, crying and trying to talk to God, my throat swelled until I couldn't utter a sound. Totally exhausted, I lay silent, drained and still.

I do not know how long I lay there. But in that quiet bathroom, a strange peace gently settled over me. Something that I had never experienced before was happening, something far beyond my senseless struggles. A warm peace seemed to settle deep within me, filling the terrible emptiness, driving out the self-hate and condemnation. My sins seemed to evaporate like moisture spots under a hot, bright sun.

God was reaching down and touching me. A God Who cared, a God Who loved me, Who was concerned for me despite my sins. Like a stricken child lost in a storm, I had suddenly stumbled into the warm arms of my Father. Joy filled me, so intense it seemed to burst my breast. Slowly I rose to my knees and looked up to Him in the awe of gratitude.

Kneeling on that bathroom floor, I gave Him myself totally. "Whatever You ask me to do, Father," I cried through hot tears, "I will do it."

For a long time I knelt there. Then I stood up, breathing heavily as if I had just climbed a long hill. Reaching into the tub, I picked up the shotgun. I shuddered as I thought how close I had come to using it. Taking it to our bedroom, I unloaded the shells and placed the gun back in the closet. As I closed the closet door, a faint accusatory echo sounded: "Coward . . . afraid to pull the trigger."

Doubt chilled me. Had my experience in the bathroom been another of the many illusions I had gone through before? I was so deceptive to myself and others. But something far stronger kept saying: "Stay with God, follow Him, *believe.*"

I knelt at the bed: "Father," I prayed, "I don't understand this or know why I deserve it. For You know how weak I am. But I put myself in Your hands. Please give my family back to me . . . and give me the strength never to run again. Father, I put myself in Your hands."

For a long while I knelt there. Then I climbed into bed, rested my head on the pillow and for the first time in months slipped into a deep, peaceful sleep.

Bright sunshine streaming through the window awakened me. An exuberance filled me, and then I remembered the night before. I got up and made coffee, thinking how close I had come to killing myself. I knew that if I drank again I would put myself under the control of dark forces that would lead me to the same horrible pit.

But I also knew I had Someone with me, a personal Being Who had reached down in my desperation and comforted me. As I thought of Him, again that strange joy filled me.

Eva! I wanted to call her but I could not summon the courage to pick up the phone. Finally, as it neared nine o'clock, I dialed the number hoping that Eva's mother wouldn't answer. Eva answered and I sighed inwardly in relief.

But what could I say to her? Again I thought of my Helper.

"Eva, I'm sorry. I don't blame you for never wanting to see me again. But Eva, I want you home more than anything else." The words came, not tearful, pleading, phony promises, but honest communication. "Eva, I'm going to try . . . really try not to fail you again. Please bring the kids and come home."

For a moment the phone was silent. It seemed both our lives hung in the balance and I found myself praying silently. Then Eva answered. "You had better go on to work, Harold. Then the girls and I will come home."

That evening as I drove into our driveway and saw the house lights glowing, I suffered mixed emotions, as I did when I came home from the war, both a joy and an embarrassment about seeing my loved ones. It seemed as if I had been gone a long time.

Though I wasn't able to tell Eva what had happened in the bathroom, I felt she saw something different in me. After the girls had gone to bed, we sat up late in the living room talking in the light of a glowing fire, something we had not done for a long time.

"I wonder if we shouldn't move out of here," I ventured.

I could sense Eva stiffen. "Why?" she asked.

"Oh, go some place where we can start over. Maybe California . . ." I picked up a poker and stirred the fire, "Someplace where we won't have to face people who know me."

I looked at her across the dim room, firelight flickering across her pale heart-shaped face. "Eva," I said huskily, "I believe I have changed. But I don't think people will accept me as changed."

My wife was silent for a moment, then said: "You mean run away from the problems?"

I looked down at the floor. She was right; that's exactly what I wanted to do. But I knew that wherever I'd go I would take my problems with me.

As I leaned back and watched an ember flare into a bright flame, I thought—wouldn't God be with me right here in Ida Grove where I could work my problems out?

The next evening after dinner I found our Bible in the bookcase, took it into the living room and sat down with it under a lamp. I wanted to know God. I had made a commitment to Him for the first time in my life and I meant to keep it. To keep it I had to know what He wanted me to do. And the best way to find that out, I felt, was to study His Word.

As I looked at the black leather-bound book in my hands, I remembered the last time I had read the Bible. It was while I was in the army; in fact, I had that little metal-covered pocket volume in a drawer somewhere. In the army I had tried to read it as an obligation, forcing myself through the gray type without getting any meaning out of it.

This time I sensed an expectancy as I picked it up. My heart was open. As I opened the pages, there was a movement at my elbow.

I looked up. It was Connie and Carol standing in their nightgowns. Connie was approaching her tenth birthday. And Carol—where did she get those large brown eyes?

"Daddy," said Carol, "we've come to kiss you goodnight."

My eyes blurred. It had been so long since the girls had done this. Either I had not been home or had been in such a dark mood that they had shyed away from me.

Their kisses felt like angel wings brushing my cheeks and I remembered words I had heard as a youngster: "I will restore to you the years the swarming locusts have eaten."

I thought back to when I was a child standing out on the hillside at night, before the locusts came, looking up and feeling the nearness of God, feeling He had something important for me to do.

What of the wasted years in between? What had happened to the boy who had memorized the twenty-third Psalm in Sunday school? I leaned my head back and found I could still say some of the words . . . "Yea, though I walk through the valley of the shadow of death, I will fear no evil; for thou art with me . . ."

Excitement surged through me. I *had* walked through the valley that night in the bathroom and He *had* been with me! Eagerly I opened the Bible and turned to the Psalms, found the twenty-third and read. This time instead of dry printed words it was as if that same Being Who had comforted me in the bathroom was speaking to me. I *would* be restored. He would be beside me, guarding and guiding me all the way.

Surely His goodness and mercy would follow me the rest of my life. I found myself being lifted as I read His powerful promises, and when I finished the Psalm I rested the book on my lap and shut my eyes, flooded with that wonderful assurance.

The following Sunday morning Eva did not seem too surprised when I told her I would be taking her and the girls to church. Before, I had accompanied her only intermittently and then with grumbling.

A new minister had come to our Methodist church and I found myself listening to what he had to say with interest. Wayne Shoemaker was a tall, dark-haired man about my age. I wasn't sure whether my attention was caught by his direct and interesting way of speaking or whether it was because my whole being seemed to be directed by God.

One Sunday morning he talked about how men plan for their retirement. My ears pricked up because I had no retirement program and I often wondered about this. Social Security would help but it wasn't the answer.

Wayne Shoemaker spoke about how men put their money into the bank for things of this world. "But the only thing that really matters," he emphasized, "is what we put into the spiritual bank."

He stressed that our investment in the spiritual kingdom—what we do for God through helping others—is far more important.

It was a stunning revelation. Since boyhood I had scratched to pay bills; my life had centered on making money. I had not considered eternal life. I had heard about the physical resurrection of the body but dismissed the thought as something that might happen a million years away. Suddenly, a new world had opened.

Early one morning as I followed my trap lines along the Maple River, I stopped for a moment on the bank. Mist rose from waters which mirrored a deep orange sun rising above the maples. I stood there remembering a Bible verse Pastor Shoemaker had quoted. "For what shall it profit a man if he shall gain the whole world and lose his own soul? . . . And do not lay up for yourselves treasures on earth, where moth and rust consume and thieves break in and steal, but lay up for yourselves treasures in heaven."

Somewhere upstream a waterbird called and I thought of my father lying in agony on his bloodied bed and Neil Nelson driving up in his old Pontiac and like a gentle giant picking Dad up and taking him to the hospital. I thought of the many times Gordon Hinrichs had every reason to fire me and had overlooked my transgressions. And I thought about Father Dailey, always helping others, who would leave this earth without a cent in the pockets of those faded black trousers. But what treasures he had laid up in heaven!

Still, I figured, if I hadn't arisen early in pre-dawn blackness to run this trapline, we wouldn't have enough money to meet our financial obligations. Well, I thought, as I headed back to my car, if the Lord would allow me to make enough money to feed my family and pay our bills, that's all I would ask.

That's about all anyone should ask, I reasoned. But there were so many people who had a hard time even doing that, like the small truckers I was trying to help. That was where I could really forget myself, I felt, and be about doing His work.

When Gordon Hinrichs told his fellow directors on the Iowa Motor Truck Association about my work with the small truckers, they invited me to acquaint them with the problems of these men. Then they offered me a part-time position in their organization which would allow me to continue my work with Gordon. Within a year my work so expanded with the Iowa Motor Truck Association that they asked me to come on full-time to help straighten out the tariff and rate structures for small truckers in eighteen counties of northwest Iowa.

It wasn't easy to leave my old friend Gordon Hinrichs, even though I'd still be working with him in a way since he was part of the organization. At the end of my final day in the office, we both found it difficult to say goodby.

We stood there by my car, not saying much while cattle lowed in the pens and the sun sank behind the little office building where I had spent so much of my time.

Finally, Gordon slapped me on the back with his big hand and laughed: "Don't forget, Pack, to tell those truckers to check the viaduct *after* they unload their steel!"

In the meantime our family life had improved dramatically. In fact, it was difficult to get my arms around Eva at that time. She was carrying our third child. Ten-year-old Connie and nine-year-old Carol were hoping to have a baby sister. I sat at the kitchen table and enjoyed watching the two little brown-haired girls busily helping their mother put supper on.

On June 4, 1952 our third daughter was born. We named her Phyllis and I celebrated her birth with 7-Up. Phyllis' arrival was very special to me. I had left for the army shortly after Connie's birth and was overseas when Carol came. Finally, I was immersed in the delights of a brand new baby firsthand.

With the arrival of this laughing child a new brightness seemed to fill the house. Mother, Dad, and Eva's mother came over often and the house resounded with laughter as we played games and sang the old songs in the living room. There were picnics with Eva and the girls, taking Connie to her Brownie scout meetings, and regular family drives after supper through the countryside.

Yet, underneath the new joy, like a minor key constantly sounding, was the realization that as far as drinking was concerned, I would be walking a tight rope from then on. One drop and it would all be over.

For strength to start each day, mornings found me reading my Bible. So often verses that I had read became particularly helpful to me that same day as they related to a problem I faced. By then I felt that if one studied the basic word of God, he would hold the key to solving all problems, worldly and personal.

Everything about God began to interest me. I found myself looking forward to listening to Billy Graham on the radio. I was impressed by his straight-on-for-Jesus stance. Already, I was beginning to notice a wishy-washyness in some Christians and at that stage in my development it was helpful to see someone stand firmly on what he believed.

Sundays found me increasingly eager to go to church. I began singing in the choir and enjoying it, even appreciating the compliments on my voice. However, when I was asked to substitute as a teacher in Sunday school, I tried to beg off. I had never taught before, I maintained. But they persisted.

Finally, I agreed and they started me off with high school students. However, when I was given the course material I had second thoughts. The teaching didn't seem to meet the basic needs of these youths. Though my own daughters weren't teen-agers yet, I could tell that young people of all ages needed help in meeting everyday problems.

I agreed to teach if I could use only the Bible as curriculum. Some adults were a little dubious at first. But when my class started to seriously read the Gospels, there was an eager interest among the students. Each week they had an assignment to read and the next Sunday they returned with questions. Bible verses sparked comments which led into deep discussions on various personal problems. As we began sharing more openly, I found myself admitting that I had nearly ruined my life with heavy drinking.

This seemed to unlock doors and they began bringing me their innermost worries and confessions; often we'd end up in one-to-one counseling sessions. Some wanted to know what they could do for a father or mother who had a problem with alcohol.

Soon I was serving on the official board of the church.

But if I had any ideas that I was a candidate for sainthood, they were shattered in Kissimmee, Florida.

9

The Kissimmee Caper

IT STARTED WITH an errand of mercy. Jack, a close family friend, had a drinking problem and left his wife and children. For three or four months his wife had no word from him. Since he and I had been friends, one day I received a smudged postcard from him in my mail at the office. He was in Kissimmee, Florida.

Eva and I decided that I should drive down to Florida to persuade him to return to his family. Three days later I arrived in Kissimmee, found the address given on the postcard and rang the bell.

The door opened and there stood Jack.

"Well, Pack," he grunted, sticking out his hand, "c'mon in."

I told him his family missed him and it was time to come home. He amiably agreed that I might have a point. "Let's go get something to eat and we'll talk about it," he said.

We walked a block to a local cafe, sat in a booth and reminisced about old times. Jack ordered drinks and I was about to push my glass away when I stopped. Would this be right? My refusal might turn him off. And this was a mission of mercy. Surely, for old time's sake I should sip just one drink. Something deep inside said no. But looking at my friend sitting across the table, I strongly felt the need to relate to him. Just one drink.

Hours later, I found myself behind the wheel of my car being jolted unmercifully. I stopped the car to find out what was wrong. Jack was sound asleep, his head against the door. I was driving down a railroad track and the jolting was the car wheels bouncing on the

110

ties. I got out and was bending over a bent wheel when a bright light blinded me.

It was the police. They helped me get the car off the tracks and Jack and I were thrown in jail as drunks.

The next morning I awoke in a cell. Jack was still snoring peacefully on the other cot. In agony of spirit, I called to the sheriff's aide sitting at a scarred desk in the corridor. A heavy, short man, he got up and waddled down to our cell.

"What do we have to do to get out?" I asked.

"Wahl," he drawled, "you'all have to wait for trial for drunken drivin'."

"When's the trial?"

"Next Friday, when the judge gets here."

It was then Tuesday. My heart began to pound.

"But I've got to get back home," I said. "Isn't there something I can do?"

"Sure," he drawled, "you can post bond."

"How much?"

"A hundred dollars for you, and twenty-five for your partner."

"What happens if we leave and forfeit the bond?"

"Nothing, you'll just lose your $125, that's all."

I had $150 hidden in my luggage at the motel. I asked the sheriff's aide to drive me there. I checked out and returned to the jail where I wrote out the bond for $125 and gave the sheriff the money. Jack and I took off for Iowa with $25 left, buying a bag of oranges to eat on the way.

Back home I said nothing to Eva about our trouble in Kissimmee and explained away the bent car wheel as a minor accident.

Once again the fact was rammed home—I could never, ever touch alcohol. I prayed and received God's forgiveness. But that night in jail would come back to haunt me in an embarrassing way years later.

Four months later I got a notice in the mail from the Florida Public Safety Commission that my driver's license had been revoked for a fourteen-month period for driving while intoxicated. I broke out in a cold sweat. Lies came back to trip me every time. Drawing a deep breath, I went to the county sheriff, showed him the notice and explained what had happened.

"What should I do?" I asked.

"Well," he said, "far as I'm concerned, Pack, I'll not pick up your license until I get notification from the Iowa Department of Safety. They're the ones from whom I take orders."

That night after supper, I told Eva the whole story.

She came over and put her arms around me. "I love you and forgive you, Pack," she said. "And I know you really are changed."

Aware that deception always tripped me up, I decided to tell the truth to the executive director of the trucking association. Together we went to the Iowa Safety Commission. Since I needed my driver's license to make a living, I was given a license suspension for sixty days from the date of the accident. Since the sixty days had passed, I could apply for a new one.

It was a painful, costly experience which drove home the truth that my life was just one drink away from disaster. Nor did it help to bring Jack home. He couldn't reconcile with his wife and left within a few weeks.

Some months later the father of an old high school friend called me one Monday morning.

"Pack," he said, "Dave is bad off. His drinking is fouling up his whole life. He's gonna lose his job and his wife is about to divorce him. Can you help?"

"I don't know," I said. "I've never been able to help anyone with that problem before."

"Well, would you just try to talk with him? He admires and respects you."

I said I'd try, wondering how I could handle someone with whom I used to do a lot of drinking.

Late that afternoon Dave and I sat in the car in front of his house. He admitted he was in a lot of trouble. "But there's nothing I can do about it, Pack," he said, sadly shaking his head. "I know I'm going to lose my job and my wife, but I'm powerless.

Powerless. I had heard that word before, used by the friend who had first approached me about joining AA.

I had a sudden revelation. "Dave," I said, "there's this group called Alcoholics Anonymous and I don't know much about them. But I hear they're meeting over in Storm Lake on Monday nights. Let's go over there tonight and see what it is. If it's no good, we'll just not go back."

He shook his head and tightly clasped his hands together.

"Dave, do you think you're better than I am?"

"No . . ."

"Well, we both have the same problem. If I'm willing to go, why not you?"

Finally, he relented and I told him I'd pick him up at six-thirty so we could make the eight o'clock meeting.

That night as I was leaving the house, the phone rang. It was Dave's wife. She sounded depressed. "He says to tell you he's not going, Pack."

I gripped the phone. "Well, you tell him I'm going to be there at six-thirty and if he isn't going he'll have to whip me."

I drove up and Dave came out of his house, his face black with anger. "I'm not going, Pack," he growled at me through the car window. "Who in the hell do you think you are?"

"Dave," I said, praying inwardly, "get into this car and shut up!"

We reached Storm Lake with Dave still muttering, but something inside him wanted to see what this AA group had to offer. I felt the same way.

We found the address in downtown Storm Lake and climbed up a narrow stairway between two stores into a big room in which a bunch of men were standing around. I recognized two or three. Some of the fellows spoke to us, telling how glad they were to see us; they said they had been wondering when we'd show up.

Dave glanced at me in irritation, and I felt the same way. They were taking a lot for granted. We certainly weren't going to stay.

The meeting started and the man who spoke of his own alcoholic experiences must have been following me for the past ten years. For he seemed to be telling my very same story.

Then they had a chip ceremony. I was called up first and handed a chip. "You keep this chip in your pocket change," I was advised. "If you are ever tempted to drink, take a dime and call one of your AA brothers first. If you do take that drink, then throw the chip away."

I wouldn't take the chip. "You know, I'm not really sure I'm an alcoholic," I said. "I've been on the wagon for so long. Besides, I added, "I don't like that term 'alcoholic.' "

Dave wouldn't take a chip either.

However, we were both impressed by these men who had stayed sober so long. They all looked hale and healthy, so I knew they weren't faking it. I knew their backgrounds because I had been drunk with several of them.

The next week Dave and I found ourselves driving the forty miles back to Storm Lake. After the meeting we stayed on for over an hour, talking with the men.

"You know, fellows," said one man we'd known since boyhood, "I'm still an alcoholic, even though I've been dry for years. It's just my physical makeup, I guess. But do you know how I handle it?"

We shook our heads.

"If someone told me that I couldn't touch a drop for a year, I'd go out of my noodle for that would be impossible. But I know that with God's help I can stay away from the stuff today. So I don't worry about tomorrow. That's how I've been able to handle it, one day at a time."

Dave and I didn't talk much as we drove back to Ida Grove. We were both deep in our own thoughts. The most important thing I had learned during that year was that despite my pride in not having taken a drink for some time, I was still susceptible to alcohol. I *was* an alcoholic and would be for the rest of my life. I had also seen something special in that little band of men. They were comrades, yes. But that was not what sustained them. Beyond any person or group was a far greater Power. And it was this Power on Whom I could depend.

It was brought home to me later one night in a hotel in Des Moines.

As it takes a flame and wick to set off a powder charge, so do alcoholics suffer syndromes which start them drinking. They find themselves in a situation where a combination of elements sets up a deadly desire.

With me it was usually a lonely hotel room after a hard day's work. No one would see me, and my family wouldn't know.

Such a chain of elements was created when I checked in at the Savery Hotel in downtown Des Moines one night after a series of hectic business meetings. Before leaving my room to go to a restaurant for dinner, I thought I'd relax for a moment.

I had picked up a copy of the evening newspaper and was scanning the pages when I suddenly felt the urge. By that time, I had not touched alcohol for over a year, and though there had been many urges I had been able to overcome them. However, my long-time habit of an evening drink coupled with being alone in a hotel room generated a powerful force deep within me. I wanted a drink. I needed it. I had to have it.

Desperately I battled. I turned back to the paper and tried to read. Drumming incessantly within me, however, was the demand for a drink.

I stood up, the paper falling to the floor. Suddenly, I felt like two different people, the new and the old Harold Hughes. The urge became overpowering. I knew that in a very few moments I would be going to dinner at a downtown restaurant. To reach it I would pass an old drinking spot. And I knew as well as I stood in that hotel room that I would go into my old haunt for a drink. I could already savor its delicious burning strength.

I felt lost, defeated. And then I remembered one of the teachings of the AA's. "If you're in trouble and need help, call a local AA group wherever you are. Someone is always manning the phone and you'll get help."

There was still enough of the new person within me to pick up the directory and, like a man searching for a life preserver on a sinking ship, look for "Alcoholics Anonymous."

I dialed the number. It rang twice and someone picked it up.

"Look," I said, my voice trembling, "I'm down here at the Savery Hotel and am just on the verge of getting drunk. I need help."

"Well, come on over," the voice said.

"Look, man," I retorted, "if I could come over there without drinking, I wouldn't have bothered calling you!"

"Why can't you make it here?" he asked.

The phone was shaking in my hand. "Because if I go out of this hotel room I'm afraid I won't get past the bar."

"You can make it," he wheedled, "come on over."

"The hell with you!" I shot back and slammed down the receiver. I stood there for a moment, anger rising in me. If a guy had no more concern for me than that, he could drop dead.

I grabbed my coat from the back of the chair. This is it, I figured. Nobody's going to know about my getting drunk. I'll just get it out of my system.

In the exhilaration of decision, I pushed out the door and into the corridor of the hotel, heading for the elevators. But as I stood waiting for the elevator, something came over me. What was I doing?

I leaned against the wall and prayed. "Oh, God, please don't let me do this." The chime of the "down" elevator broke the spell and

I headed for the open door. The lust for a drink was in charge again.

I strode through the hotel lobby out into a warm Iowa evening. The traffic hubbub did not distract me from the neon lights of the bar down the street.

One last spark of resistance flickered within and like a drowning man clawing at a reed, I clutched a parking meter.

"Pack!" Above the rumble of traffic I heard my name being called.

I looked up and coming toward me down the sidewalk was an old friend I hadn't seen in years.

"Imagine that!" he exclaimed, pumping my hand. "I step out of a cab and there you are. What are you doing for dinner?" he asked.

"I was on my way," I managed to say.

"Well, come join me."

As we walked together into a restaurant, I sensed a malevolent power leaving me.

We had a good dinner, chatting over old times, and as we paid our bills, I realized the desire was completely gone.

"Say," said my friend, looking up at me, a toothpick in his mouth. "Wasn't that a coincidence, our meeting like this?"

I thought of my feeble prayer at the elevator, and clapped him on the shoulder. "No, Sam, no . . . I don't believe it was a coincidence at all!"

It really struck me. I had prayed and He had answered. It was a prayer of desperation, but then it was a prayer of desperation that had turned my life around months before.

Wayne Shoemaker and I had some long talks about prayer and one's relationship with God. I found him easy to relate to; he seemed to be a man who met others where they were at that moment.

As I became more deeply interested in the Bible, Wayne encouraged me to take some correspondence courses from our denominational headquarters. I took several on the Bible, plus creative writing. The lessons illuminated the reality of God speaking to His people and how He communicates with us . . . individually through the Holy Spirit. They caused me to examine myself even more carefully.

At the time I did not know that I was being prepared for a far greater ministry than I could have even dreamed of. But as I immersed myself deeper in these studies, I found a revelation building within me. One night as I sat at the kitchen table studying my lessons, I knew what it was. I didn't continue reading but sat staring out the window far into the night. Finally I went to bed but couldn't sleep.

Early next morning at breakfast I mentioned my thought to Eva. She stood at the stove for a moment, the coffee pot poised in her hand. "A minister?" she said. "You mean you think you should become a minister?"

It was as much of a shock to her as to me when I thought of it. And yet, when I examined myself, it wasn't too far out. It may well have been a germ planted by my mother long before when she spoke of my uncles and cousins who were ministers and how she hoped that one of her sons would so serve God.

"You know what that would mean if I went to seminary?" I asked.

Eva nodded and poured us both a cup of coffee.

"We'd have to completely change our life style." By now I was making $125 a week plus traveling expenses, and living had become easier.

She smiled, "I know."

"Then you'd go along with it?"

She took a deep breath and sat down at the table.

"Harold, if this is what you feel God wants you to do, then I'll be happy to do anything."

"Even if it means living in poverty and serving some little country church?"

She smiled and took my hand. "Even that, Harold Everett Jones."

Somewhat hesitantly I asked Wayne if there were any way a man like me could enter the ministry. By now he knew all my faults, and I was afraid he might put me down. But Wayne was gentle and encouraged me to start.

"Why don't you begin by becoming a licensed lay speaker?" he suggested. This spoke to me and I took the correspondence courses needed to go before the Methodist board and become licensed for this position.

I'll never forget that first time I spoke as a lay speaker in our own church. I was scared to death up there in the pulpit. When I looked into the faces of the congregation, I realized most of them knew what a rotter I had been. The sermon that I had written in long hand on a little tablet was on the reality of Jesus Christ.

At first I felt like a hypocrite standing up there talking about God, but then came the assurance that He was with me. Other churches in the area asked me to speak and no one was any prouder than my mother. In a way, she felt her dream was coming true.

Then the Lord began to gently move me in a different direction. As I talked with small truckers in my work with the motor truck association, I could see that they still were not getting a fair shake. My concern poured out in pleas to the association executives for a uniform rate structure for the small drivers.

They said that it was difficult enough to work this out for the major lines without worrying about the independents. And to be patient. But the more I looked at it, the more I saw that the little fellows just weren't able to fight their own battles. Not only was the red tape too complicated, but most were under such financial pressure that if they lost any business at all by getting personally involved, they would fold.

Then one day as I brooded about this at my desk, a thought struck me. Why not start a separate trucking bureau keyed to the little man's needs?

I felt that the best way to find out if this idea had any merit was to check with the truckers themselves. But how? I went to a stationery shop in Ida Grove and bought a little postcard mimeograph machine.

That night I set it up on our kitchen table and ran off hundreds of postcards announcing a meeting to be held Saturday, November 5, 1955, in the Ida Grove Armory to discuss the formation of a new association. It would be called the Iowa Better Trucking Bureau and the card described something about its goals.

Thirteen-year-old Connie and twelve-year-old Carol helped me with the cards. Even three-year-old Phyllis tried to join in. Together we carried the big box of cards down to the postoffice where we sent them to small truckers in eighteen northern Iowa counties. On Saturday morning I went over to the Armory, wondering if anyone would show up.

The place was jammed with nearly 600 men, some of whom had driven 150 miles.

Standing before them I said that I felt I had led them astray in the past—that I had talked most of them into becoming members of the big trucking association to get better representation and that it had not happened.

What we should do, I suggested, was to start a new organization to represent them, that we would have their concern at heart and they would not have to fight the big guys.

Two directors of the Iowa Motor Truck Association had showed up and they argued that the truckers would be wrong to leave the big group. The meeting got rough, with much shouting and arguing late into the day. Finally, we agreed to take a hand vote. I got a lump in my throat when most of the hands were raised in favor of the new association.

So it started—the Iowa Better Trucking Bureau. We set up an office in a building on Main Street in Ida Grove. A friend joined me as a partner; I did the work and he furnished the capital.

We started out on the same arrangement I had with the other association, $125 a week and my traveling expenses. As we expanded, we reached a top membership of about 1,500 small truckers. They ranged from a guy with one truck hauling corn to men operating up to ten trucks in the grain and livestock business. The typical member owned a combination truck, hauling grain by day. Come sundown, he would knock out the slats used for ventilation in the side of the sixteen-foot combination livestock and grain box, then haul steers into Sioux City, returning home to clean up, wash down the truck, and replace the slats. Soon after sunup, he'd be on the job again hauling corn, oats and beans. This man would usually work out of his house.

To keep everyone informed we published a small monthly sheet called the *Iowa Better Trucking Bureau News*. Advertising helped pay printing costs. Soon I was in the insurance business, too, because every trucker had to be heavily protected.

By now the spectre of alcohol had left our home. Permanently, I prayed. For I was really learning to live one day at a time. Furthermore, Dave, the man who went up with me to that first AA meeting in Storm Lake, had joined me in starting our own group of Alcoholics Anonymous in Ida Grove, and both of us carried chips. Regular meetings were held in the basement under my office which our wives helped decorate. We started inviting ministers, priests and doctors to the gatherings, so they could find out firsthand how to treat their patients and parishioners who had this problem.

Times were better, but with Christmas approaching I was glad that I still had kept my trap lines running. I was dressing out a muskrat skin one evening when Eva came to me with fear in her eyes. "The doctor called," she said in a strained voice. It was about Carol, who had gone for a checkup after having some persistent abdominal pain. "Carol has a growth on her lower intestine. The doctor feels it's serious, Pack," said Eva, her lip tremoring. "He says she must have an operation as soon as possible."

10

Crossroads

THE DATE FOR Carol's operation was set for shortly after New Year's Day.

The United Methodist Church in Ida Grove had a special New Year's Eve service. Candles glowed as many of us went forward and knelt at the polished walnut altar rail for communion. Tears ran down my cheeks. How great to be able to start the New Year with Christ. Again, I asked forgiveness for my sins, and resubmitted myself to Him, offering Him my body, soul, spirit and life to use as He willed.

As our family left the church, Phyllis was asleep in my arms, her curly brown head nestled on my chest. I looked up into the winter night where stars sparkled like crystals and really sensed the awesome magnificence of being part of His great plan.

A week later Carol went into surgery at the Methodist Hospital in Des Moines. Eva's mother and mine offered to stay at our house to care for Connie and Phyllis. Phyllis was too young to understand, but Connie was in tears over missing Carol.

However, I knew they would soon be listening to stories their grandmothers liked to tell. Eva's mother would describe when their grandfather was a newspaper linotype operator and the many different cities in which they lived. Mine would tell of the long ago day when Dad and Jesse thought I was too sick to accompany them hunting. Undaunted, I went out alone and brought home a big red fox which made a prize pelt. When the girls tired of stories there would be hot apple and lemon meringue pies, and always Buddy, the black

121

cocker, and Taffy, the golden lab, plus thirteen cats to keep them company.

Wayne Shoemaker accompanied us to the hospital. It was a gray blustery morning, snow whipped around building corners and dark clouds scudded across a dirty sky. We waited in the family room while Carol underwent surgery.

Suddenly, I had an impulse to go to the hospital chapel. Wayne said he would stay with Eva and I headed to the little room. Six seats were on each side and a window was inset high in the wall. I knelt at the altar rail, asking the Lord to take care of Carol.

As I prayed I felt a warmth on my arm. I looked up to see a ray of sun beaming through the window. Evidently there had been a break in the clouds; but could it not be God answering? I felt His peace. I thanked Him and returned to Eva and Wayne. In a few moments the surgeon stepped in. He reported that he had made a resection of Carol's lower intestine and she was doing all right.

Again I was impressed with the Lord's words: "All things are possible to him that believeth." It had happened with Carol.

But there were some things that didn't seem to succumb to prayer. Or, perhaps the Lord had plans of which I, as yet, did not have the faintest comprehension.

Troubles had developed among the truckers I represented. There were now some 1,500 members of the Iowa Better Trucking Bureau from all over the state.

We still battled for rates that would make it possible, for example, for a man to haul a ton of gravel fifteen miles, make installments on his GMC 10-ton tandem truck, keep up house payments and support a wife and three kids. Often the cards were stacked against him. A stone quarry might team with a bank financing a rockhauler's truck and force the owner to take a lower rate. Trying to right such things found me in close touch with our State Commerce Commission's three-man board which regulated all public carriers' rates. The commission had a number of inspectors who were supposed to enforce the board's rulings. But not a lot was being done.

Time and again I would drive into Des Moines to meet a number of truckers outside the state house. Together we would troop in to attend a formal hearing by the commission. We'd spend hours telling our problems, pleading for support. Little happened and too many inspectors continued to slough their jobs.

One evening in our living room as I sat brooding about it, a thought struck me. I turned to Eva who was sewing on one of the girl's dresses.

"Eva," I said, "I'm going to see the governor."

"The governor?" she echoed, dropping her work in her lap. "You really believe in going to the top!"

Herschell Loveless was one of Iowa's few Democratic governors. He had wrought a small miracle by defeating an incumbent Republican governor. And though I had supported his opponent, I admired the way he fought an uphill battle. I respected his honesty and felt he would be concerned about our problems.

A friend was able to get me an early appointment. I felt a sense of awe as I walked from the parking lot up the long sidewalk to the Statehouse. A bright winter sun glinted on its giant gold dome soaring into the cold blue sky, and I remembered those warm summer nights when Eva and I laid on a blanket in the grass near this very sidewalk. I smiled. What would we have said if someone had told us that I would actually be coming here to visit the governor?

The governor's secretary ushered me into the waiting room. As I sat watching impressive-looking people go and come, I asked myself what a country fellow like me was doing wanting to talk to the governor when I wasn't sure I could sell my case? Why would the governor even be interested?

I glanced at my watch. My appointment time had passed and still people were entering and leaving his office. Nervous, I wondered if I hadn't just better get up and quietly walk out.

Then the secretary came over to me: "The governor will see you now."

With pounding heart I was ushered to one of the high-backed ornate wooden chairs lined before the governor's desk. Governor Loveless, sitting behind the massive desk smiled, shook hands, invited me to sit down.

Suddenly, in that spacious wood-paneled office, my problems didn't seem very big any more. Lord, I wondered, this man must have so many things on his mind, why should he worry about some little truckers?

Encouraged by his friendly warmth, I started talking and to my surprise found him listening. Not only did he seem to understand, but he was interested. He called in a sandy-complexioned man, a little older than I, and introduced him as his administrative assistant, Park Rinard. Mr. Rinard took me into his own office. As I poured out my concerns to this warm, friendly man, he leaned back in his chair listening, thoughtfully drawing on a pipe, and every once in a while asking a perceptive question.

When I was gathering up my papers to leave, Park Rinard leaned across his desk, put down his pipe, and said, already using my nickname naturally, "You know, Pack, I can't figure out what you're doing in the Republican Party. You talk like a Democrat."

I glanced at him sharply. Was he joking?

"I grew up a Republican," I laughed. "I don't know any Democrats in Ida Grove."

A month later I encountered Herschell Loveless again at a festival at Spirit Lake. It was late afternoon and we were seated by the water talking about the commerce commission. The sun was a low fire ball over the trees. A deep sense of peace had settled with the hush of evening and the lake was a scarlet mirror, dotted by rowboats with silent fisherman hunched over cane poles.

"Pack," said the governor, who seemed to be in an expansive mood, "if you're really concerned about the truckers, why don't you consider running for one of the seats on the commission?" He chuckled: "You might want to consider changing parties, too."

I sat in quiet shock for a moment, my hand gripping the rattan arm of my chair. "I've never even considered the possibility of running for office," I finally said, not wanting to tell him that with my background I could hardly hope to win a race for bulb changer on street lights.

But Loveless pressed on, pointing out that two seats were open on the commission in 1959. "That's a year and a half from now," he said, "plenty of time to prepare."

"Well, Governor," I said, "I'll think about it." We shook hands and I walked toward my car, my mind whirling.

It was a hot summer night and a three-hour drive home. A lot of time for thinking. What about a new career in politics? I shook my head at the idea. Two of the commission members were former district judges, all were college graduates and skilled in the transportation field. My credentials? I was a college dropout, a drunk with a jail record. They'd laugh me right off the ballot.

There was little traffic on U.S. 71 and white corn-borer moths fluttered into my headlights like snowflakes.

Still . . . I had been close to politics the past five years. I had been a delegate to the county convention and two state conventions, had been credentials chairman for Ida County and had done legwork for various candidates. In fact, just a few years before, I had campaigned for John Ropes who in 1955 ran for a seat on the commerce commission and won.

My concern was to meet the truckers' needs by helping elect the right people. What could I give if elected? A lot of inner convictions began to bubble up. Years of self-deception had made me prize blunt honesty when I saw it. Many people considered politics the art of deception. If I had to play that game I wanted no part of it. Could I be myself? Could I tell the people the truth as I saw it? Deep in my gut I knew that people wanted officials they could trust. I would love to be the kind of man in office who would fight for the little guy.

Something happened to me there on U.S. 71. The truth was shown to me as clear as a vision: God who had given me life had a special purpose for me. To turn away from it would be denying Him.

Sweat broke out on my forehead and I gripped the steering wheel. Changing parties would anger my friends. I'd have to give up at least a year of my life to campaign. My trucking association and insurance business would be neglected, perhaps lost. I had no money, didn't know where it would come from, or even what running for election would cost. If I lost, everything I had worked for all these years might go down the drain.

A voice out of the blackness seemed to whisper: "What sort of fool are you? One false step and you'll be back in jail sleeping off a drunk. No one will take you seriously."

My mind was seething by the time I arrived in Ida Grove and turned onto my street. As I drove into the driveway, nothing ever looked so warm and familiar as my home. I could see the light in our bedroom and knew Eva was waiting up. Picking my way past Phyllis' tricycle and doll buggy on the sidewalk, I opened our front door to find Eva waiting for me.

I took her in my arms. "Honey," I said, "we've got a lot to talk about."

11

The First Hurrah

EVA AND I SAT up late that night at the kitchen table over coffee talking about my running for the commerce commission. Even after we got into bed and turned out the lights, we continued our discussion. Finally, Eva sleepily murmured: "Pack, let's talk about it in the morning?"

But I couldn't sleep. I lay there, my mind racing. And then a completely different thought struck me: how great it was to come home clearheaded and be able to talk to Eva. Along with this came the strong affirmation that I was not to worry about this new path but to trust Him.

Eva confirmed it in the morning. She was getting ready to do the laundry and as she headed for the washer with a big armload of clothes, she stopped, and turned: "Pack," she said, looking over shirts and underwear, "if you feel running for the commission is what you have to do, do it." Her brown eyes were shining: "You know I'm with you."

I was sure then what I wanted to do. But would the Democrats want me? I went to Edith Hansmann Julius, chairwoman of Ida County's Democratic party. An educator and music and fine arts teacher in the area for many years, I also knew she would level with me.

We sat on her front porch. "Pack," she said, handing me a cold glass of lemonade, "don't worry about the past. You have something we Democrats need, and that's the gift of leadership." She eyed me perceptively: "I haven't spent twenty years teaching not to be able to see it in someone. Besides," she laughed, "there aren't that many of us Democrats around. Maybe you can help bring us together."

It was all I needed. I headed up the hill to the red brick county courthouse to change my party registration. As I was signing the documents, the county clerk, well acquainted with my Republican activities, looked at me in astonishment.

Leaving the cool interior of the courthouse, I stepped out into the bright July sunshine and was walking down Moorehead Street when I saw Arthur Johnson approaching. I was always glad to see him; he had done so much, from helping me get into college to mediating at my inebriety trial. Today his face was strained.

"Pack," he asked, "why? Why did you do it?"

I winced, realizing that someone in the courthouse had phoned Art with the news. He stood there, his blue eyes questioning me.

My heart went out to my old friend. "Art," I said, "from where I stand right now, I just cannot agree with Republican ideology. Please don't take it personally," I urged. "You know how much you mean to me; I want us always to be friends."

He stood quietly for a moment, shaking his head. "Pack," he said sadly, "let's talk about it some other time."

As I watched him walk away, a sadness filled my heart. Was this the way of politics? Hurting good friends? Practically all of my family and friends were Republicans. In no way did I want the love between us impaired by how we looked at earthly problems.

Even though the 1958 election was over a year away, I drove to Des Moines, parked at the state house and walked into the Secretary of State's office to take out nomination papers. I would also need petitions. These would have to be signed by enough people in each county to get my name on the primary ticket.

The secretary, who knew me, was surprised at my request. "We don't have any petitions yet," he said. "Usually, folks don't start campaigning until election year." He thought for a moment. "But I can give you some petitions from the last election." As he assembled them, he said: "All you have to do is change the date."

He looked up at me over his glasses. "You're running as a Republican?"

"No, a Democrat."

His eyes widened. "Well, I wish you luck," he said doubtfully, handing me the bundle of petitions.

But if I was worried about hurting Republican friends, it seemed I had ruffled Democratic feathers much more. To many I was an upstart and the state party rushed to get an old-line Democrat on the ticket. It ended up with three of us competing in the primary.

I sent out notices of my candidacy to all trucking association members and everyone else I knew. The petitions were circulated through friends in the trucking industry. Contributions began dribbling in, a dollar or two at a time.

In the meantime, Edith Julius and I got together with my old friend, Arthur Johnson who had since forgiven me, along with Republican county chairwoman Hulda Besore. Together we thought we'd try something new—a joint fund-raising drive in which we would split the proceeds proportionately between both parties to help underwrite our expenses.

Aware that I was an underdog, I knew I had to take the offensive and speak to the man in the street. Soon it was clear that I had made more friends than I realized among workingmen throughout the state. On top of that, having three names on the primary ticket may have been in my favor. The votes for my opponents were divided.

And yet, I was probably as surprised as anyone the day after the March primaries to find that I would be one of the two Democrats vying with Republicans for the two seats open on the three-member commission.

But where would my little group of supporters get the money for the long haul to the November election? Our campaign fund started out at $300, and we eventually spent $6,000, which is almost nothing in a statewide contest. We scraped, we improvised, we stretched. I spoke wherever and whenever I could. Truckers were very helpful in seeing that posters were put up in different parts of the state.

Eva and I would get tickled when driving down the highway to hear six-year-old Phyllis standing in the back seat point to a telephone pole and squeal: "There's Daddy!"

In addition to posters and bumper stickers, television was already a factor in 1958 campaigning. After careful study, we felt we could afford two 15-minute live programs. I just sat down in front of a TV camera and spoke off the cuff. Somehow I managed to pull through with no grievous errors.

One night after coming home from a Farm Bureau meeting where I addressed thirty people, I stretched out on the sofa, rubbed my eyes and yawned. "Eva," I sighed, "if I get any votes at all, it's going to be a miracle."

"Don't worry, Pack," she said in her matter-of-fact way, "I have a feeling you're going to win."

A phone call came one day from the office of Governor Loveless who was running for his second term. He was supposed to be at a county fair up in Rock Rapids where he and his opponent, Dr. Bill Murray, were scheduled to speak. However, because of a date conflict, the governor couldn't make it. Would I go up there and speak for him?

I drove up to Rock Rapids in trepidation. Dr. Murray was a Ph.D. and highly respected throughout the state as a brilliant professor of history and economics at Iowa State University. Few had even heard of me; the commerce commission race didn't excite people.

Under a hot August sun, Dr. Murray and I climbed makeshift steps to the hay rack on which we would speak. There was a festive spirit among the assembled farmers, townsfolk and children. Bill spoke first; the people standing on the hot dusty grounds listened attentively and applauded enthusiastically.

When I stood up to speak my heart sank. People started to drift away. After a quick, silent prayer for help, I started talking. We needed to hold the line against an increase in sales taxes, I started. The folks yawned and chatted with each other, some began letting children tug them to the cotton candy and ice-cream stands.

Then I brought up the problems of people in our state institutions. "Those poor folks hurt from neglect and indifference," I said. "Nobody cares what happens to them. Our institutions are becoming warehouses for those unable to help themselves."

This was where my heart was: people like me—defeated, sometimes despised, full of fear. Needy people. Something happened at that moment. The crowd quieted down. Mothers shushed their children. Others began drifting back from the refreshment stands. A thrill surged through me. I had caught their attention. People were always interested in what was happening to people. During that hot afternoon, they seemed to forget the heat, their whimpering children, the biting flies.

After the event, the Democratic county chairman accompanied me to my car. "Pack, I was frankly a little worried when the governor couldn't make it," he said. He clapped me on the back. "But they sent a good substitute." He laughed: "One of these years you'll be back here campaigning for the governorship."

I laughed uproariously as I put the car in gear and headed home, hoping I had enough money for gas.

But that speech seemed to confirm something. I felt the Lord's support as if I was properly using the gift He had given me.

Not long after I filled in for Governor Loveless, he invited me to accompany him in his plane to several television appearances. He also contributed $500 from his own campaign fund to mine. It was a real lift, both emotionally and financially.

Even so, I still felt at a disadvantage in campaigning for a seat on the three-member commission. Four men fought for the two open seats—two Democrats, Bernard Martin and I, and the two incumbent Republicans, Dave Long and John Ropes. The ironic twist was that only a few years before I had helped work for John Ropes' election to this very post.

When election night arrived, Eva, the girls and I settled in front of the television set to watch the returns. Governor Loveless had invited all of us to an election-night party in Des Moines. But it would have meant our getting two hotel rooms which we couldn't afford. In any event, the girls were quite excited as we all settled down with popcorn Phyllis had made. I could feel my heart begin to pound as the first returns were flashed on the screen.

After about an hour of returns, Phyllis turned to me and asked: "Where are you, Daddy?"

As it turned out, the commerce commission was the last state office on the ballot. Ahead of us was the whole state ticket—including supreme court judges, circuit judges and all the congressional offices.

We waited, yawning between munching popcorn. The girls went to bed. In a few hours, Eva and I followed them, still in the dark about the outcome.

However, I was up at five o'clock to catch the local radio station news. At 5:30 I learned that I had won a seat on the commission by twenty thousand votes. Bernard Martin was the other winner.

I sat at the breakfast table stunned, the coffee in front of me forgotten. I hadn't expected to win, much less by such a margin. Eva came into the kitchen in her robe and kissed me. "I heard it," she smiled. "Congratulations, Mr. Commerce Commissioner."

On January 1, 1959, Bernard Martin and I went to Des Moines to be sworn into our posts. Later, Eva and I went house hunting. Even with selling our Ida Grove home and my business interests, we were still deeply in debt because I had borrowed so much to get the trucking bureau going. However, we salvaged 1,500 dollars and put it down on a house in the west part of Des Moines on 58th street. It was a two-story older frame home. But I liked the giant. oaks surrounding it, for I knew I'd miss a rural atmosphere.

I wasn't the only one. Though six-year-old Phyllis acclimated to city life fairly well, Connie, a sixteen-year-old high school junior, and Carol, a sophomore, sorely missed their Ida Grove friends and had difficulty adjusting to a metropolitan school.

I tried to be with them as much as possible. But almost immediately after taking office, I found my time being swallowed up by my job.

Hearings were held constantly as we three commissioners—representing both the public and transportation utility industry—listened to applications for rate increases, territorial authorities and rights to deliver. Through it all, we did get transportation rates under control and hired honest and qualified inspectors to enforce regulations.

It was a growing and learning experience. Eventually I was appointed chairman of the commission, and became familiar with all departments of state government.

The position brought me in touch with every segment of the Iowa economy. I met the farmer worried about transporting produce to market, sat down with the utility-company executive seeking to store natural gas underground, and talked with small-town businessmen fighting to keep their local railroad freight depot open.

For some purpose, of which I had no inkling as yet, I was being steeped in an understanding of my state's needs and its development opportunities.

Through it all I endeavored to live in the present, savoring each day at a time as I had learned to do through my fellowship in the Alcoholics Anonymous. How this helped was driven home to me one evening as Eva, the girls and I prepared to go to one of the AA fellowship's family get-togethers.

Little Phyllis, now seven, and I were waiting inside the front door for the others to come downstairs. As I stood, impatiently jingling car keys, Phyllis looked up through innocent brown eyes and asked: "Daddy, why do we go to these meetings? You never drank." Tears filled my eyes and my heart swelled in gratitude for the gift just given me. I sat down on the steps and pulled her to me. "Honey," I said, looking into her cherubic face, "I did drink once. Much of it happened before you were born and I stopped drinking before you were old enough to remember.

"Yes, Honey," I added, "your daddy did have a very sad drinking problem."

She threw her arms around my neck. "But you don't now," she said, "and that's all that matters."

I hugged her tight and savored the wisdom of an innocent. Yes, I thought, what we are today is all that matters to a child . . . and to God.

I was free of my past. But because of that very past I found myself facing a special responsibility which I knew I would keep meeting for the rest of my life.

In Des Moines, it first came with an unexpected phone call which awakened me long after midnight.

12

Turning Points

THE INSISTENT ringing of the phone finally roused me from a deep slumber. It had been a rough day and I had gone to bed exhausted. Sleepily, I picked up the phone to hear the blurred voice of an old friend.

"Pack?"

"Yeah?"

"Pack . . . I'm drunk . . . sick . . . and broke. Can you help me?"

I rubbed my eyes and looked at the clock. It was two in the morning. Even the thought of getting out of bed was agonizing.

"Howard," I groaned, "how about our meeting in the morning?"

"But Pack, I need help now," he pleaded, explaining that he was in a bar downtown.

Supported on an elbow, I thought: He's drunk, he wants money for more booze, and he doesn't even know what he's saying.

"Howard," I said, "I'm not sure I can come."

"But I need help . . ."

"I just can't do it, Howard," I said. "Let's get together in the morning." I hung up. Surely by then he'd be sober and we could talk sensibly.

I snapped off the light and fell back on the pillow. For some minutes I stared into the darkness. Suddenly, I sat bolt upright.

"What are you going to do?" murmured Eva.

"I'm going downtown and get him. What else can I do?"

"I figured that's what you'd do," she said. "Please be careful."

It was cold in the car as I started the engine and eased it back down the steep incline of our driveway. In twenty minutes I was downtown. The streets were empty. Lights swayed eerily in the cold wind and shadows darted. Old newspapers rustled along the curbs. I reached the bar but it was dark and shuttered. My heart wrenched. Why hadn't I said something to Howard on the phone? Then I saw a slumped heap on the curb. I rushed over. It was Howard in grimy bib overalls, almost unconscious. I helped lift him up. It was easy to see that he'd been on the bum for some time. I took him to an all-night restaurant, then to a cheap hotel. I left him sitting on his bed blinking at me in the glare of the naked bulb.

"Hey, ol' buddy," he said, "how about a buck for breakfast?"

I shook my head. He'd be right back on the street trying to buy liquor. "No," I said, "I'll see you in the morning."

Next day I found him a job on a loading dock and also brought him to the local AA chapter. He worked for a month, borrowed money from everybody on the dock and took off.

When I heard about it, I wondered: Does God save some people and not others? Why me?

Should I have taken more time with Howard? That was impossible. My schedule was such that I was spending less and less time with my family as it was. I didn't even have time to read the Bible in the morning anymore.

A few days later I had to go to Washington, D.C., to attend a joint board hearing of the Interstate Commerce Commission. I had never been there and as Eva packed my bags, I found myself getting excited. I took the Chicago & Northwestern to Chicago where I transferred to the B & O and got a Pullman compartment. It was intriguing, except that to use the toilet in the middle of the night one had to fold up the bed. In Washington I walked out of Union Station gawking like a tourist.

There it was, the United States Capitol, its massive snowy dome rising to the sun. After my commerce commission work, I joined a group touring the capitol and was thrilled to get into the visitor's gallery overlooking the Senate floor. I recognized some of the senators from newspaper photos, and thought of the great men of history who had served there—Clay, Webster, Calhoun.

But Washington was not for me. Instead, my ambition was to become director of the Interstate Commerce Commission in Alaska. The territory was battling for statehood at the time, and to me Alaska was the last frontier. There I could go hunting and fishing to my heart's content in the unspoiled wilderness.

Meanwhile I was primarily concerned about the politics of my own state. After almost two years of involvement with nearly every branch of its government and contact with its people, I saw a growing need for stronger leadership.

At the same time, I sensed a powerful national surge. We had gone through an economic recession and now America seemed to be entering a new era of strong growth.

It impressed me even more as the train carried me home across the rolling Iowa hills. Our state possessed greatness in the wealth of its soil, in the cleanliness of its cities, in the honesty and willingness of its people. No state was more American than Iowa, I felt. Yet America seemed to be going forward—but not Iowa.

"Almost everything I look at in the state is wrong," I told Eva one night as we ate supper, "and I don't think anything is going to be changed unless someone really gets out there and does something about it."

"And you're the one who feels he can do it," she said, giving me that knowing look.

"Well, I could do a better job than the guys who want to take over from Loveless," I said.

After two terms as Iowa's governor, Loveless had his sights set on the United States Senate. His lieutenant governor, Nick McManus, announced his candidacy for the governorship.

Some of us in another faction of the party felt our slate needed a more positive leadership.

One afternoon, six of us were discussing the situation in a club in Des Moines. We all agreed that somebody had to represent our viewpoint. But no one had any idea of who would do it. Finally, I turned to John Hanson, a local businessman, and said: "John, one of us ought to run for governor and the other for lieutenant governor; I don't care which. But since you're older and more experienced, you ought to try for the governorship and I'll run as your lieutenant governor. Anyway," I laughed, "it's pretty clear we'd both get beat, but this'll be an opportunity to get all the issues aired."

John sat silently for a while, studying his folded hands, then looked up and said he agreed, but because of the press of business, he'd rather run for lieutenant governor.

I felt like the man who had been asked to hold the bull while the veterinarian gave it a shot with a needle. After much meditation, prayer and long talks with Eva and the girls, I agreed to enter the race. By then I was beginning to think I had a chance. But if I knew what was coming, I would have gone back to the trucking business.

In the first place, Iowa was always considered a conservative Republican bastion. Out of the thirty-four elected governors that had headed the state since 1846, only six had been Democrats. Governor Loveless had been the only Democrat to be elected in the previous twenty years.

In the second place, old-line Democratic regulars strongly resisted my decision. I was a Johnny-come-lately. Sure, I had been elected a commissioner on the party ticket in 1958, but that didn't make me a real Democrat.

"Wait until you get more years under your belt," said one of my primary opponents. Many in the State Central Committee felt the same way.

I felt like someone who stood looking in on a birthday party to which he was not invited. I tried to attend every county dinner I could. Instead of being welcomed as a candidate, I was often told: "If you want in, buy a ticket like everyone else."

Then, my major opponent would stand up at the head table to tell how he went to his first Democratic convention as a four-year-old holding onto the hand of his grandfather who was then the state senate majority leader. "Yes, my friends," he continued. "I have been born a Democrat, lived a Democrat and have a life-long heritage of Democratic service."

There were times when I wasn't allowed to speak at dinners. And if I did, I could find no one to introduce me. Often I would just find a seat somewhere and end up introducing myself to individuals. Once I was even stopped from passing out my brochures.

When I was able to speak along with my opponent, there was a patter of hands for me and great shouts, stamping and whistles for the other candidate.

Even so, my supporters, concentrating on the issues, worked hard. In avoiding comments on personalities, we not only gained some basic areas of support, notably among the universities, but made many loyal friends throughout the state.

But when the primary election was held, I was soundly defeated by a three-to-two majority. Nick McManus would run for governor.

The girls claimed they didn't want their daddy to be a governor anyway. And Eva said she felt it was for the best. But I found myself becoming bitter, not because I lost the election but at the way I felt my own party had treated me.

For some time, I brooded about this. However, I couldn't let my feelings get in the way of the upcoming November election.

To prepare for the National Democratic Convention, our party had its state convention that summer of 1960 in the Des Moines Armory. As chairman of the Commerce Commission, I was one of the speakers. My vision for Iowa still burned within me. And as I stood before the vast assemblage representing every town, city and county in the state, I expressed my dream for Iowa, the programs for cities, for agriculture, the young, the old, the sick and the poor. Where I had previously felt frustrated in reaching people during my primary campaign, I now felt an exhilaration in expressing my vision for Iowa's vast potential.

There was a thundering ovation when I finished. "A lot of people who hadn't supported you before," said an aide, "are looking at you with new eyes now. One thing's for sure, Pack," he added, "you're established in Iowa politics."

If my ego needed any deflating, it was well taken care of later that summer. The national campaign hit a local high point when presidential candidate John F. Kennedy came to Des Moines. We planned a big parade downtown and one of the party heads asked me to drive my convertible in it.

We had recently traded in our ancient Ford station wagon on a brand new white Ford convertible, something I had dreamed of since boyhood.

It had a unique metal top and Phyllis squealed in fascination as I showed her how it slid back into the trunk. Now, I proudly told Eva that John F. Kennedy would be riding in it. On parade morning, we washed and waxed the convertible, shampooed the leather upholstery and polished chrome until it sparkled.

Then I proudly drove downtown. When I reached the parade staging area, a crowd of men with television cameras leaped into the car. Then I learned someone else was driving the candidate. My white convertible was for the TV newsmen.

"Hey!" I yelled, as a heavy boot crunched down the back of the seat, "watch out for the upholstery!"

As the parade headed down Locust Street, I found myself under a barrage of orders from the cameramen.

"Hey buddy, pull closer to Kennedy!"

"Take it back; I need a long shot!"

As we wove in and out down the street, one man endeavoring to get a better camera angle clambered onto the hood; in anguish I watched deep scratches grow under his shoes. I heard metal buckling and glanced in the mirror to see another man crouched on the trunk deck.

"Lay off," I yelled, "you're wrecking my car!"

"The hell with it," he grunted, aiming his camera at the important car. Then the upholstery ripped as another man braced himself in the back seat, one foot on the chrome window moulding.

Finally the parade was over, the newsmen tumbled out, and I went up to the hotel where I finally got to meet the youthful-looking presidential candidate.

We accompanied him to the airport where he thanked us all and disappeared inside the airliner. I turned to one of his aides and asked about the damage to my car. He gave me an address. The repairs amounted to $340. I sent the bill but never heard a thing. I guess I was supposed to consider it as a campaign contribution for a worthy cause. For the young man whose visit I helped cover photographically went on to win the election.

Iowa Democrats did not fare so well. Nick McManus was defeated by Republican Norman Erbe. Herschell Loveless lost his race for the senate. Fellow commissioner Bernie Martin and I seemed to be the only Democrats left in the statehouse.

"You know Pack," he laughed, standing at my desk the day after election, "we could hold a caucus of the entire Party in a telephone booth!"

It looked as if our state would have a Republican administration for some time to come.

Where was my future? Ever since that life-changing night on the bathroom floor, I had submitted every important decision to the Lord. At age 38 I needed to know if I was to stay in public life or perhaps reconsider the ministry. Or could politics be considered my ministry? What about the desperate needs in our educational system, mental institutions and prisons?

I would often pray while walking outside at night. Still an outdoorsman, I liked to feel the grass under my feet, hear the insect sounds, smell the honeysuckle, breathe deeply of the cool night air. As I looked up into the firmament one night, I remembered how I had stood on a snow-drifted hillside as a boy gazing up into the same heavenly lights. "If I'm to stay in politics, please give me some sign, Lord," I asked.

A few weeks later several Democrats in northwest Iowa asked me to consider running for Congress. That didn't appeal to me, but their interest encouraged me to seriously consider the 1962 gubernatorial election.

One night in April after returning from a walk, I mentioned this to Eva as we prepared for bed. She had been sitting at her dressing table, brushing her long raven hair. She put down her brush and turned to me. "I'm not surprised."

"It will be rough," I warned. "Worse than last time. You'll have to accompany me to a lot of places you won't like and," I added, "you and the girls will be home alone a lot too."

She looked pensively at her brush. "I know," she said. She stood and put her arms around me. "But if you believe in your heart that this is God's will, I'm with you all the way." She smiled, "So Harold Everett Jones, you start off with one vote already."

The girls were for it too. "I'm not sure I'd like to live in the governor's mansion, though," said Carol. "It's too big."

"And spooky looking too," said Phyllis. She reached down and tousled the hair of the red Irish Setter who had joined our family. "But now that we've got Mike I'm not afraid."

I contacted Park Rinard, the man I had met in Governor Loveless's office six years before who had told me that I talked more like a Democrat than a Republican. Through the years we had become good friends. Park had a fine grasp of Iowa politics. Earlier he had been secretary to Grant Wood, the famous Iowa artist. I often felt that some of Grant Wood's inspiration came from this astute man whose unassuming exterior covered great perception and ability. Park's head just about reached my shoulders but I found myself looking up to him in matters of political judgment.

We spent several evenings in my living room discussing the pros and cons of my entering the gubernatorial race. One night, Park, who had been sitting across from me in an old easy chair, took a long draw on his pipe and exhaled. "Of course, you understand, Pack," he said, "that much of your opposition is again going to come from your own party."

I nodded. I was still the brash newcomer.

"You went through a lot of heartache in the last primary," said Park, relighting his pipe. "Do you want that all over again?"

I leaned my head back on the sofa and looked at the ceiling, feeling resentment as I thought of what had happened two years before. I looked at him. "No Park, but I feel there's a reason for me to run, even though I know how hard it is to beat an incumbent. If I get clobbered, I get clobbered."

Park got up, knocked out his pipe, "OK, Pack, I admire your guts and I'll help you in any way I can."

The next morning I went to the Statehouse to get nomination papers and start seeking signatures to run in the June primary election, four months away. In the spring of 1962 my name was presented as the first major Democratic candidate for the governorship. Soon three other Democrats joined the primary race.

We were all just names. Reaction was unanimous. The incumbent Republican governor had nothing to worry about.

Meanwhile the Des Moines *Register* was quietly conducting a survey which would plunge me into the middle of a red-hot campaign issue—liquor-by-the-drink.

Harold's parents, Lewis and Etta Hughes
Insets: Top—Harold; Bottom—Jesse

Above:
Jesse Hughes, 15
Harold Hughes, 12

Right:
Harold Hughes practicing shot put for high school track meet, in back yard of home in Ida Grove.

Below: **Harold Hughes and his father after fishing trip in 1940.**

Right:
Eva and Harold Hughes, 1944

Below:
Eva and Harold holding Carol and Connie with representatives of local bank and loan agency. This was first GI loan given in Ida Grove.

VICTORY DINNER

Famous cartoon which ran in Des Moines *Register* Nov. 8, 1962 following Hughes' election. (By Frank Miller.) Used by permission of the Des Moines *Register*, Des Moines, Iowa.

Meeting John F. Kennedy   **Meeting Lyndon B. Johnson**

Below: **Harold with Mother and Dad at meeting when Governor of Iowa.**

GOVERNOR HUGHES SPENDS A NIGHT IN THE WHITE HOUSE

Cartoon comment on Hughes' visit to White House with President Johnson. (By Frank Miller.) Used by permission of the Des Moines *Register*, Des Moines, Iowa.

Right:
With Robert F. Kennedy at fund-raising dinner for Hughes' Senate campaign, 1968. (Photo by Chris Hansen.)

Below:
Harold Hughes on "Meet The Press" television program with Senator Edmund Muskie.

Above:
Political comment found on brick wall in Cedar Rapids, Iowa, during Harold Hughes' campaign for Senate.

Below:
With Senate office staff.

With Senator Edward M. Kennedy, 1969. (Photo by Okie Okamoto.)

With Mercedes McCambridge during Senate Hearings on Alcohol and Drug Abuse. (Photo by Gus Pasquarella.)

KICKING THE TIRES

3-10-71

Cartoon comment on Hughes considering presidential nomination.
(By Frank Miller.) Used by permission of the Des Moines *Register*,
Des Moines, Iowa.

Hughes related well to college people.

Typical campaign stop during presidential race. (Photo by Dierdre Pirie.)

Aspirants in 1972 Democratic presidential nomination race. From left: Hubert H. Humphrey, Edmund S. Muskie, Birch Bayh, George McGovern, Harold Hughes.

Hughes with Senators Humphrey and Gaylord Nelson (far right).

Hughes visits *U.S. Frigate John F. Kennedy*. Beard was short-lived experiment.

**With Julian Bond, Georgia state representative, at opening
session, Democratic National Convention, Miami Beach, July 10, 1972.**

Above:
With Senator Sam Ervin. Fund for New Priorities in America Congressional Conference: The Constitutional Question— Congress and the Executive (March 5, 1973). (Photo by Wm. M. Horton.)

Below:
With Demos Shakarian, President of Full Gospel Business Men's Fellowship National Convention, 1974. (Photo by G. Horton.)

The Hughes family in Senate dining room. From left: Connie and her son, Jon; Harold; Eva; Carol (standing); Connie's daughter, Tracy; Phyllis.

Eva and Harold Hughes (left) with President and Mrs. Jimmy Carter who visited the Hugheses' Cedar Point farm Sunday, November 12, 1978, for a special, private religious retreat. (Photo by Bill Fitz-Patrick, the White House.)

Cartoon comment when Hughes announces he will not run for Senate reelection. (By Frank Miller.) Used by permission of the Des Moines *Register*, Des Moines, Iowa.

13

A Fiery Issue

FIFTEEN CAMPAIGN advisors faced me through a blue haze of smoke. The issue before us glowed as hot as the ends of the cigarettes. What stand would I take on the liquor-by-the-drink issue?

I was facing my old enemy in a new way. In Iowa only beer could be sold over the bar. Selling liquor by the glass was against the law. Those who drank had to buy a bottle at a state-owned liquor store and take it home. However, if one belonged to a private club, he could bring his unopened bottle there and mix drinks from it. Usually the club would charge for mixes, ice and glasses.

Naturally, I was very familiar with the many ways in which this law could be side-stepped. The definition of "club" became very broad. Anyone could step in off the street into a wide variety of bars and restaurants, pay a dollar or more for instant "membership," and drink from his bottle. If he didn't have a bottle, the club would illegally sell him one at an inflated price.

Because private clubs were legally immune from search and seizure, all kinds of corruptions—gambling, prostitution—flourished. Age meant little. As a teenager I had done some of my heaviest drinking in these clubs.

Many places, depending on the attitude of local law enforcement officials, didn't even bother with "key club" dressings. I had patronized bars where liquor was sold openly. The sheriff in one county had no complaints. "If that's what people want, that's what they get," he said. Investigative reporters from the Des Moines *Register* found they could easily buy liquor by the drink in 75 out of our state's 99

157

counties. And of course, the state didn't get any revenue tax from
these sales.

One day a news reporter asked my opinion and I said I'd either
shut down these places or legalize serving liquor by the drink. "We
could then at least control it," I added.

My comment steamed like a redhot horseshoe thrown into a water-
ing trough. This was why my campaign advisors had called for an
emergency meeting.

The consensus was that the liquor-by-the-drink issue in Iowa was
political death if not handled correctly.

"I wouldn't touch it with a hundred-foot pole," said one man,
stabbing his cigarette into an ashtray.

"He's right, Chief," spoke up the man across from me. (By now
my aides were calling me this in reference to my distant Indian relative.) "Just glide over the issue . . . say the law will be enforced and
you'll do the best you can."

"Yeah," agreed another, "candidates have been winning with that
approach for the past several elections."

I drove home from the meeting troubled. I had to agree it would
be much safer politically to duck the issue. Yet the law then in effect
was pure hypocrisy. It promoted disrespect for the law, it spawned
the very evils it was trying to prevent.

"I know it sounds crazy," I said to Eva over dinner. "A guy like
me who's had so much trouble with alcohol should not be pushing
for liquor by the drink."

Eva looked at me over her coffee, "I don't think you could live
with yourself if you were to be phony about this, Pack."

That night in prayer I got an answer. If I went into this campaign
smothering my true feelings for the sake of avoiding controversy,
then I had better get out of the race.

The next evening I talked it over with my chief advisor, Park
Rinard, and he agreed. We prepared a statement stressing that liquor
sales by the drink should be legalized, thus diverting the revenue
from illegal operators and suppliers to the state treasury.

In speech after speech I addressed the subject bluntly. As a youngster, I had found that if, when pulling a thistle from the ground, I
held it timidly, I got stuck. But if I grasped it firmly, it would not
hurt me.

My campaign advisors were right. I had stuck my head into a
hornets' nest. Angry criticism came from well-meaning citizens who

felt I was an agent of Satan and from political adversaries pouncing on a vulnerable spot. Even some in my own party sniped at me.

One gray rainy spring day while driving back into Des Moines, I saw one of my roadside campaign posters with the words "Lose with Hughes" spray-painted across it.

It was like a slap across the face. I almost skidded to a stop on the wet pavement, wanting to tear it down. Instead I accelerated into town, burning to punch someone in the jaw. I knew who was behind it. One of the opposing groups had been bandying the phrase "Lose with Hughes." But hearing about it didn't hurt as much as seeing it in bold black letters.

That slur wasn't the only wound. Some of the opposition were making personal attacks on my character, easy to do if they wanted to dig back far enough. A sickness filled me as I continued driving into the city. Politicians were supposed to develop casehardened hides, but the insults and now the "Lose with Hughes" campaign rubbed me raw.

By the time I got into downtown Des Moines traffic, I had calmed down. Resentment could hurt only me. I had no wish to tear the party apart. Swallowing hard, I headed toward my office.

The spring rains so welcomed by the farmers in 1962 ended, and on a warm June day Eva and I traveled back to Ida Grove to vote in the primary election. When the late returns came in that night, I had won.

"People *believe* you when you speak, Harold," concluded Park.

We had five months in which to convince Iowa voters that I—a Democrat—should be their next governor. It was considered an almost impossible task. I was relatively unknown. Norman Erbe was a successful Republican governor for one term and he hadn't made any real mistakes. The Des Moines *Register* statewide poll, usually accurate, put me 22 percent behind Erbe.

I could well appreciate his popularity. Though I disagreed with Governor Erbe philosophically, I liked him as a person. He was honest, a fine family man. To me he had not been aggressive enough in facing human issues or showing effective concern for the poor and handicapped. His party also seemed more concerned in keeping a low tax base than in assessing business and corporate interests their fair tax share.

It was going to be an uphill battle all the way, especially in view of our limited funds. Our war chest had only $66,000, most of it from small givers. It was a pittance for a governor's campaign. My hopes centered on county Democratic organizations, truckers and womens' groups who had supported me in my commerce commission days, plus individual men like Chuck Iles, Des Moines mayor and a trucking executive, and Bill Knapp, a real-estate developer from Beaverdale, who shared my vision for the state.

With the sixty-six thousand dollars, we were able to get some radio and TV spots plus a light covering of billboards and bumper stickers. My big problem was the recognition factor. Many people were saying "Harold who?"

"We need better newspaper coverage," mused an advisor after studying the latest polls that showed me still far behind. Then he brightened. "I have an idea."

He suggested that I challenge Norman Erbe to a debate. I hand delivered it in a letter to his office. He wasn't there at the time. But the newspapers picked it up and the challenge received statewide coverage. Though we never had the debate, the publicity began to let people know that there really *was* someone representing the other party in the upcoming election.

Another problem was myself. "You've got to get out into the shopping centers and press the flesh," urged one of my advisors. I had always rebelled against this as phony.

"If a person votes for me just because we shook hands, he's an idiot," I argued.

Truth was that I was shy. I shrank from walking up to people with the old catch words: "Hello, I'm Harold Hughes and am campaigning for governor. I can do more for this state than any other man. And I need your support."

It wasn't true. I couldn't do more for this state than any other man. All I could do was try. Meanwhile, another piece of advice shook me up.

"I hate to have to tell you this, Chief," said one, "but you look like you slept in your suit. You wear those mismatched pens and pencils in your front pocket along with eye glasses and notebooks. There must be about ten pounds of stuff you carry around. When you stand to speak you look like a bulging bag of potatoes."

The words hurt but he was right. I had never thought much about clothes. I tried to change, watching what I stuffed into pockets, being careful what I put on before going out. Even so, Eva would often stop me at the door to do some gentle rearranging.

Then there was the language. As we sat over breakfast one morning, Eva laid down the morning paper. "Pack," she said, "they keep referring to your speaking like a truck driver, using words like 'hell' and 'damn.' "

I winced. The report was right. Moreover, I spoke haltingly, and my grammar was poor; I certainly didn't sound like a man running for governor.

"I don't know, Park," I said one day as my friend and I sat in my office. "I'm painfully aware of not having finished college. And, after all, what does four years on the commerce commission mean to anyone?"

"One thing the people *do* know," said Park; "they know you talk straight. They can tell that you'll try to do what you *say* you'll do."

Despite my earlier reservations, I did get out and shake hands with more people. Though the opinion polls showed me slowly edging up, six weeks before election day I was still behind by 15 percent; it didn't look as if I'd ever catch up.

I intensified my efforts. Most mornings found me driving our Ford down our driveway at 5:30 while a moon still hung in the west. I'd pick up an aide and we'd head for a breakfast gathering, go on to several coffees, a luncheon, drive 150 miles to a town, walk down the street introducing myself to people, stop in at the local newspaper and try to get the editor to run something on me, knowing that it would probably be derogatory since few editors at the time had much confidence in me. But, I felt like the politician who said: "I don't care what they print as long as they spell my name right." Often at a dinner meeting, the chairman would introduce me as "Howard Hughes."

As I spoke, I'd bring up the usual issues of a new reapportionment plan to give urban voters a fair voice, introducing a withholding system for state income taxes, increasing aid to state education, and consolidating state government for greater efficiency. Yet despite these important points, the emotion-charged issue of liquor-by-the-drink captured the limelight.

My opponent, of course, took the opposite stance. Then the letters started coming, hundreds of scathing denunciations; and since I was Methodist, many came from ministers of my denomination, some calling me a force of evil trying to lead people astray. "You can't be a man of God and propose selling liquor this way," was the common charge.

By this time Wayne Shoemaker had a church in north central Iowa and it was fairly easy to slip up there to discuss my problems.

I found Wayne, who had been more helpful to me in my spiritual life than anyone else I could remember, also was a competent advisor on some secular problems.

"Wayne," I groaned, "you know how I, of all people, hate liquor. If I could pull a switch that would eliminate liquor from the face of this earth forever, I'd do it. But the thing is here and we've got to face it."

After some discussion, I decided to write a letter to each of the fifteen hundred Methodist ministers in Iowa. In part it read:

> Thousands of good people who oppose any change in liquor laws because of temperance convictions may not realize how disgraceful and dangerous the present breakdown of the liquor law in Iowa has become.
>
> It is difficult for people whose basic moral convictions are for prohibition to make a realistic judgment concerning handling of the liquor traffic of which they disapprove under any circumstances.
>
> But the biggest mistake of all would be to assume that the advocacy of legalized liquor-by-the-drink—in preference to illegal liquor by the drink—is simply another chapter in the wet-dry issue. It isn't. It is an issue of law and order over crime and confusion. It is an issue of honesty over hypocrisy.
>
> If temperance is our goal, as it should be, then we are at the furthest point from our goal under the present system. The utter breakdown of liquor law enforcement has created the most permissive atmosphere in our history for law enforcement in general. Disrespect for one law creates disrespect for others and the whole structure of public morality is damaged.
>
> Under the plan I advocate, establishments selling liquor by the drink would be under strict licensure requirements and the laws would be enforced. This is the obvious reason that illegal key club and tavern operators are deadly opponents of legalized liquor by the drink. It would simply put them out of business.

Whatever the letter's effect, I was beginning to feel that my stance was going to put *me* out of business. Four weeks before election the *Register* poll still put me behind my opponent—by 12 percent. Even so, I found myself addressing the liquor question whenever possible. "We cannot shove it under the rug any longer," I told audiences. "We either face it squarely or let ourselves in for more years of corruption!"

"If I'm defeated," I told Eva one morning, "it means I have eight weeks to find a job." For in effect, I had given up my commerce post to run for governor. Unemployment was a grim prospect at age 40. As always, we were financially strapped. Even though the size of our family had dwindled, the cost of living kept rising and a commerce commissioner's salary was small.

For by this time Connie, 20, had married Dennis Otto. She and her husband were living across town. Carol, 19, was attending business college and living in her own apartment in Des Moines. There was just 10-year-old Phyllis with us at home.

But even at her young age, she was far more involved in my campaigning than I realized. Eva told me about it one night after Phyllis had come home crying from school.

"She said the other children were saying nasty things about you," said Eva. "I suppose they were just passing on what they had heard at home."

I went upstairs to Phyllis who had just gone to bed. She was clutching her Raggedy Ann doll and her face was tear-stained. "Honey, don't worry about it," I said smoothing her long brown tresses. "No matter what anyone says about me, pay no attention to it. Words can't hurt anyone, you know."

Even so, I was letting them hurt me, for the published polls showed me still running far behind. Thus I resented being called to Washington, for I didn't want to step off the campaign trail for a minute. But the invitation was practically a command performance by the Democratic National Committee. It had arranged a meeting with President Kennedy and Vice President Johnson for all the gubernatorial and congressional candidates.

So four of us Iowans, running for representative, senator, secretary of agriculture, and governor, took time out to drive to Washington. We stayed on the road all day and night, taking turns at the wheel of an old station wagon to avoid a hotel bill. Finally, we arrived in front of the Mayflower Hotel early the next morning, tired and dirty. Just as we were climbing out of the car, Abraham Ribicoff, Secretary of Health, Education and Welfare, stepped out of the hotel door.

I was stunned. There I was, staring at that famous face I'd seen in newspapers and on television, even though he didn't know me from a bale of hay. Our secretary of agriculture candidate did know him, stepped up and introduced us. Ribicoff was warm and cordial and it was a great moment for us, even though I wondered from our appearance what he thought of the grimy characters running for office in Iowa.

After cleaning up in the hotel, we went over to the White House where, along with hundreds of other visitors, we lined up in the Rose Garden for photos. President Kennedy and Vice President Johnson stood at the head of the receiving line. One by one we stepped up and shook hands as photos were taken to be sent out to the press in our home state. Even though I had met the president in Iowa, I still felt excited.

But all I could say to him was: "I'm Hughes from Iowa." I felt foolish at not thinking of something pertinent or witty.

The President grinned at me. "I'm really expecting you to perform out there." His hand was already out to the man behind me and I walked on. The ritual was the same with Lyndon Johnson. I realized that every president has to do this and it must be a drag for him. But as I walked back to the others, I felt let down. Here we had given up valuable time, piled in that old car to save money, driven twice around the clock, and for what?

We headed right back to Iowa. "We should have stayed here and spent the time and money campaigning," I told Eva. And judging by the continuing Des Moines *Register* poll, I could have put the time to better use. For surprisingly a late October poll showed me edging up. I was only eight points behind Governor Erbe. What gave me more hope was the high percentage of "undecided." These voters could be swayed.

We redoubled our efforts. I sought radio and television coverage. Only one broadcaster really welcomed me. That was Russ Lavine who hosted a radio talk show; he was a colorful maverick who would put on speakers many felt were controversial.

"You'll come back when you win, won't you?" he asked.

"Don't hold your breath," I laughed. The fact was that as November 6th neared, I didn't feel that I was going to make it. On the evening of election day we had dinner at home. I waited until Phyllis left the table and as Eva started to pick up the dishes, said "I'm going to lose, Eva. I just know it."

She stopped in the middle of the kitchen and turned to me. "Please don't say that, Pack," she exclaimed.

"Well, the polls show me still behind Erbe," I said. "I don't think I reached as many people as I should have. And I'll have to tell you, Eva," I continued, staring at my plate, "when I'm out in those towns speaking at meetings and dinners, I don't hear much yelling and yipping for me."

"Well, I think you're wrong," she said, coming back to the table and sitting down.

"No," I stated, rising from my chair. "I'm going to call Park Rinard right now and ask him to write me a statement of concession. At least I'll have that ready."

Park was aghast. "Pack," he barked, "you and Eva go down to headquarters, listen to the returns and greet the people. You've already won the election!"

Was he crazy? "Park," I pressed, "I can't believe that. I know I'm running fairly close but not *that* close."

"Well, Pack," he said in that even measured tone when his inner toughness surfaced, "you go on down there and be confident because I'm convinced that when the returns are in you'll be governor. I just sense it, Pack, for I feel you're right on all the issues," he emphasized, "and I'm not going to write any stupid statement of concession!"

His attitude lifted my gloom somewhat but I still had doubts, and wondered if Park hadn't gone ahead and written a concession statement anyway. Shortly, Phyllis, Eva and I drove downtown to the Savery Hotel and took the elevator up to our campaign headquarters. Connie, her husband, Denny, and Carol met us along with a crowd of people. I had no idea we had so many workers. The hotel was jammed with people and there was a festive spirit in the air. Folks started slapping me on the back, calling me "Governor."

The family and I settled down in front of a TV set and began watching the returns. A chill went through me as I noticed that practically every Democrat seemed to be losing. Between Governor Erbe and me it was a back and forth battle.

Then, almost in disbelief, I watched the figures begin to edge ahead in my column. The room quieted and Eva reached for my hand. As my votes mounted to a 25,000 lead, I could feel Carol, sitting next to me, stiffen. Everyone seemed to be holding his breath.

Then, after a flurry of news comments and rapidly shifting scenes on the television screen, Governor Erbe issued his statement of concession.

The entire hotel seemed to explode into one roaring cheer. Workers and celebrants flooded our floor, bellowing and banging on the door. People surged into the suite in a pandemonium of shouting, crying and laughing. Phyllis was jumping up and down. I could hear Connie's voice breaking. And every telephone began jangling continuously. Newspaper flashbulbs flared and television and radio crews lunged at me with outthrust microphones. A police captain yelled into my ear that he had a squad of men ready to escort me from the hotel.

As the tornado mounted, I rushed Eva and the family into the suite's bedroom, slammed the door and leaned on it.

"Whew!" I said, wiping my forehead.

Eva stretched up and kissed me: "Congratulations, Harold Everett Jones."

It was a busy night, going from one broadcaster to another, starting, of course, with Russ Lavine.

Eva, Phyllis and I got home at 3:00 A.M. and tumbled into bed. I was asleep when the phone rang. Eva answered it. Suddenly she sat straight up in bed.

"Who *is* this?" she demanded. She slammed down the receiver and turned to me, her face white. "Someone said to tell you he's going to kill you!"

"It must be a joke, or a drunk," I said.

"No, Pack," she whispered, "that voice was cold and hard."

I swung my feet over the side of the bed, worried about bootleggers and key club owners out to kill me. "Well, maybe we'd better call the police."

Eva picked up the phone to dial, then swung back to me. Covering the mouthpiece she gasped. "He hasn't broken the connection; he's still on the line!"

I lunged at the phone. "Here, let me talk to him." Eva braced herself in front of the phone as if it were a loaded gun pointed at me. "No, don't talk to him." She slammed down the phone.

I felt trapped. With a maniac holding on to the line we couldn't call out.

"Where's the nearest phone booth?" I asked.

"Down the block," she said. "But he could be in it. He could be watching the house for all we know."

The phone rang again. Eva reached for it, listened, then slammed down the receiver. "It was him again!" she gasped.

"What did he say?"

She repeated the words slowly: "By God, I mean it; I'm going to kill your husband and you tell him that."

We waited a few minutes, then Eva picked up the phone to call the police. She quickly put it down and gasped: "He's still on the line. We can't call out!" Suddenly she pulled on her robe and slipped out the back door to our neighbors where she called the police. She came back and reported disgustedly.

"The police said to go back to bed and forget it; that it was probably just some nut. They won't even send out a patrol car."

We both got up and went down to the kitchen where we had some coffee. Then we went back to bed, checked the phone, heard a dial tone, left it off the hook and fell asleep.

I had been given my baptism of fire as governor.

14

The View
From the Mansion

EARLY THE NEXT MORNING the phone rang incessantly. This time it was the press. They wanted to come out to take photos, get statements.

"Hughes Wins, Upset Stuns Republicans" was a headline in the Des Moines *Register*. I had won by a majority of 40,000, polling 52.45 percent of the vote. But I was a mighty lonely winner. Every other state office in Iowa was taken by a Republican.

"Look, Daddy," laughed Phyllis. She pointed to a cartoon in the *Register* entitled "Victory Dinner." It showed a large jovial donkey at a banquet table flanked on both sides by uneasy-looking little elephants labeled "U.S. Senator," "Lieutenant Governor," "Secretary of State" and others.

Later at the breakfast table, Eva read me part of the editorial: "His election can be attributed to a more forthright stand on problems and his vote-getting strength in cities and the more populous counties."

The doorbell rang again and she sighed. "Another reporter." They were now crowding our front door, wanting stories from a family angle.

"That's what you get for winning an election," Eva said.

I shook my head. "Right now I'd rather be out duck hunting." I looked out at the gray skies and knew it would be a long time before I could call Dad and head out for the old blind we used on the Missouri River. Even then, I had little idea of how my family and I would be hurtled into an entirely new kind of life.

Though the inauguration was two months away, the whirlwind had started. Every lobbying group in the state suddenly wanted to meet with the governor-elect to get in their points on upcoming legislation.

I had to think of appointments to various commissions and state agencies. Job seekers filled our campaign office. Everyone who had been after the governor for a favor the past ten years now felt as if I was their new hope. I was deluged.

But there was one invitation I particularly appreciated. Governor Erbe invited me over to his office. At first I felt embarrassed as I walked into the echoing statehouse hall, passing the battle flags from Iowa regiments, I turned the corner and stepped into the governor's reception room.

Here was a man who had lost an election he had been predicted to win, a man whose administration and policies I had harshly criticized. And yet when his secretary ushered me into the high-ceiling office, it was Governor Erbe who made me feel at home.

A tall man with fair hair, he strode over to greet me, hand outstretched. "Congratulations, young man!" he smiled, shaking my hand. At 43 he was only three years older than I.

He invited me to sit down in one of the high-backed antique chairs. My heart was warmed by this man as he explained important details about the office and its employees. Later he invited the press in to take photos of his transferring the office key to me. He did not have to do any of this; he could have allowed the clock to run out and let me come in cold and unknowing.

"The pressures are very great, Harold," he said, "and you'll need all the strength any man can muster." He stuck out his hand. "I wish you well."

I wondered if I could have been as magnanimous as he if I were the one defeated.

A few days later I met with state comptroller, Marvin Selden. He had been appointed by Erbe and many Democrats felt I should replace him with someone from our own party. But Selden was not only exceptionally knowledgeable, he had done much good for the state. Republican or not, I felt that his benefit to Iowa far outweighed party affiliation and I appointed him comptroller. I was never to regret it.

In the meantime I was besieged with invitations to attend Democratic victory celebrations. The most touching and poignant one was held by my hometown. A lump filled my throat as I sat in the open convertible moving slowly down Second Street in Ida Grove's own version of a "ticker tape" parade. The tape, sliced rolls of wallpaper, uncurled colorfully through the air as we drove under a huge banner proclaiming: "Governor Harold Hughes is Home." I *was* home. Some 5,000 people lined the street, waving and cheering, and it seemed I knew most of them.

Eva, Phyllis and Carol sat in the convertible with me. Connie would have been with us but she was at home in Des Moines with our first grandchild, Tracy, who had been born December 28th. Also riding in the parade were Dad and Mother in a new white Cadillac loaned by the local car dealer. I think it was the first time they ever rode in one. Before us marched the Ak-Sar-Ben Shriners along with the Ida Grove High School band; twenty-three years before I would have been in the tuba section. Thoughts ranged my mind as we slowly passed Haase's Drugs, J. C. Penney's, the Smith Cash Market. Down a side street I spotted the gas station where I worked when I got out of service. Up another street was the garage where my brother, Jesse, was so proud to be a mechanic. Somehow, I felt that he, too, had joined the family in the celebration.

The parade wound in to the big new armory recently built by Ida Grove. Eva and I sat on the stage and Phyllis and Carol, too shy to join us, stayed with their former school classmates in the audience. The Cadillac carrying my parents pulled right up to the podium. With a deep poignancy I looked at the two elderly people in the back seat: Mother who couldn't attend her sons' graduations because she had no suitable dress, and Dad, balding and wizened.

It was an emotion-choked program. There was Wayne Shoemaker, my advisor, now pastoring a church in Hampton. And Harry Dailey, the Catholic priest, our friend and neighbor for so many years, stood with the light shining off his dark blue suit, his cherubic face glowing. "Harold Hughes derives his strength from God," he said in his Irish brogue.

Margaret Ferry, my fifth-grade teacher, told how her classes had given a special library book each year to the school with a picture inside of the donor class. "Yesterday my students wanted to see the book that Harold's class had presented," she said, "but none could be found." She looked around the crowd, then said. "One word explained it: Depression. No book was purchased that year."

Looking at my parents, the girls and Eva sitting next to me, my heart overflowed, not for the honors bestowed on me but for Christ's great gift in allowing me to bring honors to my family instead of the shame I had burdened them with in this town. I thought about the page in the Ida Grove *Pioneer Record* that ran that morning. "The city of Ida Grove," it read, "is intensely proud to have you as a citizen!" It was as if the Lord was saying: "I have restored the years . . ."

The weeks leading up to the inauguration were hectic. During them Eva also had her initial taste of a first lady's public life. It was a bitter one, but she learned a lesson from it.

It is customary for the incumbent governor's wife to invite her successor for a tour of the mansion. The house came furnished and included some antiques loaned by one of the state's prominent families. A woman news reporter walking along with the two of them pointed to a particularly unattractive table and said: "That one doesn't look very nice, does it?" "No," Mrs. Erbe murmured almost to herself and added that if it were her's she wouldn't keep it in her own home.

The next morning as we sat at the breakfast table reading the paper, Eva gasped. Her face was crimson and she handed me the paper. The reporter had made the comment sound haughty and crude, to the effect that the antiques in the mansion were worthless; moreover, she attributed it to Eva!

Eva called the reporter who, in defense of the name switch, said that "people are interested only in what the new first lady says."

It was just a taste of the goldfish bowl existence in which we'd be living. Before we knew it, Eva and I were getting into formal clothes for the big inauguration ball in the Des Moines armory. The next day we rode up to capitol hill in the back of a limousine. As we purred past the wide lawns surrounding the Statehouse, Eva took my hand. I knew she was remembering the two kids who used to walk up there from their apartment on hot summer evenings. Was it twenty years ago, or only yesterday?

Then we had dreamed of a house in Ida Grove. Now we would live in the governor's mansion on West Grand, only thirty blocks east of the home we had just left on 58th street, but it seemed thirty light years away. The dark red-brick house with white-frame upper story was once a private dwelling, built during the days when expansive rooms, high ceilings and extra porches were affordable. It surmounted a 1½-acre lot kept landscaped by a yard man who also daily ran the American flag and Iowa state banner up the tall flagpole on the wide manicured front lawn. Inside, a maid cared for the living room, library and dining room plus the four bedrooms upstairs. The staff also included a cook.

"I don't know if I'll ever get used to people helping me," said Eva on moving day as we drove onto the drive which wound behind the mansion.

"With the people pouring in you're going to need them," I laughed.

Among the first guests was my little AA group from Ida Grove. During the campaign they had written me that if I were elected governor it would be great to have a meeting in the mansion. After their arrival there was a lot of excited talking and good fellowship, but as the evening wore on the import of what had happened seemed to sink into all of us and the conversation quieted. As I stood by the white marble fireplace looking over my old friends, my eyes misted and I couldn't help saying, "To think that a drunk has finally become governor of Iowa." The room quieted. And then a friend added, "At least one who's admitted to being one."

Later that night, I sat alone in the library. It had been only ten years since that fateful night in the bathroom when I admitted my helplessness and asked God to take over my life. He had brought me to a position of power. Again I sought His guidance for the work ahead.

On inauguration day, after being sworn in and giving my address to the legislature, I signed into law the first bill of the 1963 legislative session, a measure to bring state income tax regulations on depreciation of equipment into line with federal laws.

Not long after that I ordered state troopers to close down every tavern or restaurant illegally selling liquor. Then I initiated legislation to sell liquor by the drink in properly licensed establishments.

Again, there was a hue and cry from many church people. After the legislation took effect, many pointed to statistics showing a greater consumption of alcohol in Iowa. The truth was that there was no more alcohol coming into Iowa than before; in fact, probably less. Under the old system, much of the alcohol coming into Iowa was bootlegged and thus never recorded. One thing no one complained about was the increase in tax revenues.

One of my post-election moves was to appoint members of the

clergy to various state commissions. I deeply trusted these men and felt that it would be good to have their influence in state government. For example, I appointed Carl Sinning, a Presbyterian pastor, to the State Liquor Control Commission, as some questions had been raised about its integrity. Russel Wilson, a Methodist minister became a member of the Board of Controls of State Institutions, and Father Phil Hamilton, a Catholic priest, served on our Civil Rights Commission.

A campaign issue which I endeavored to put into effect as soon as possible was the abolition of capital punishment. Several men had been executed within the previous two years in Iowa and everything within me cried out against it. According to studies I had read by judges, wardens, criminal psychiatrists, lawyers, governors and other public officials, capital punishment did not appear to deter crime; it seemed only to satisfy anger by taking a life for a life.

From studying the Bible I felt even more strongly against capital punishment. I could never forget the woman caught in adultery and brought before the Lord. He admitted that under the law the woman should die but added: "Let him who is without sin cast the first stone."

The words of the Lord, "Vengeance is mine" and "Thou shalt not kill," made me feel that capital punishment in its own way was premeditated murder. Each execution, I felt, demeaned human society without protecting it. I asked Iowa citizens to join me in rejecting death, in affirming life; in rejecting vengeance, in affirming redemption.

Many religious people argued for it. A number wrote me that the Bible calls for the shedding of blood for the remission of sins. And this included blood shed in executions. Others claimed that those who live by the sword must die by the sword. Though obviously sincere, I felt these people had misinterpreted what they had read.

The question came to a head early in my first year as governor. Leo Figura was slated for execution at the prison in Fort Madison. He was convicted of a murder in which he had called a doctor for help, then drove him over the river into Illinois where he robbed and killed him. This happened three years before. Since he had crossed a state line, it was a federal case and he was sentenced to death under federal law. His final plea was turned down by the Supreme Court.

My bill for repeal of capital punishment was still in the legislature.

In any event, since Figura's was a federal case, I was powerless to commute his death sentence. Nevertheless, I had contacted President Kennedy's office twice, trying for some kind of grant of mercy. I had heard nothing until 48 hours before the execution. Then a call came from the White House. It was from Ed McDermott, a close friend of John Kennedy. He wanted to discuss the Leo Figura case with me in person. "I can come to Iowa now in the presidential jet," he offered.

He came to the mansion and we sat down in my office. Knowing how I felt about capital punishment, he was concerned about my making some statement against the president.

"No," I said, "I'm not trying to harm the president. I just want to express how strongly I feel that this man's life should be spared."

"Any chance that this law can be passed through your legislature in the near future?" he asked.

"No, not now. I think we can get it through the House but not the Senate."

"Well, the president has nothing on which to base a commutation for this man. The only thing he has is his own conscience and the right to do it under the Constitution. But he doesn't feel that he can unless he can get some kind of recommendation, whether by law or reason of insanity."

"Figura had been judged sane," I said.

Ed looked at me for a moment, then said, "Would you like to talk to the president personally?"

"Sure," I said, "but I can't get through to him."

"Well," said Ed, getting up and walking over to the telephone, "you can get through to him now."

15

A Time to Laugh,
A Time to Cry

IN LESS THAN a minute Ed McDermott held out the phone. I picked it up to hear the unmistakable Boston accent: "Yes, Governor, what can I do for you?"

"I want to ask you to spare a man's life, Mr. President," I said. "I don't believe in the death penalty and I don't have anything else on which to base my request but my conscience and my faith."

I explained that there was no possibility of Iowa repealing its capital punishment law that year, adding, "But I'm pleading with you to save this man's life."

He explained that he regretted it but that he couldn't do it in view of the law and the conditions prevailing in the country.

My spirit sagged. "Well, Mr. President, I have to accept your decision, but my conscience totally rejects it." We said goodbye.

Leo Figura was hanged in an old machine shed at the Fort Madison prison. One reporter witnessing the execution said, "The guy died too easily." I pictured the man hanging there, strangling, helplessly urinating and defecating. Was it an easy way to die?

They hanged him at dawn. While the gray light filtered through the trees outside, I was on my knees in our library praying for him.

The prison chaplain had told Figura in his last hour that I had tried to stop the execution. Until that moment, this information had been withheld from him to avoid building false hope.

The chaplain told me about it later. "As we sat in his cell waiting for the call, I told him that you had been striving to save his life. He looked up at me with a strange expression, thought for a moment,

175

and then asked for pencil and paper." The chaplain handed me a folded piece of paper. "He wrote this to you."

Dear Mr. Governor:
    I don't understand why a man like you cares about me, but I thank you for what you tried to do. While in here I have come to believe in Jesus Christ and now I will soon know more about Him.
                                                    Thank you,
                                                    Leo Figura

But there were other injustices I could mend right away. Under the law, a person convicted of a felony loses his citizenship, including the right to vote. His citizenship can be restored only by the governor. My predecessor had taken the view that citizenship was a right to be earned. I learned that more than five hundred persons discharged from parole or prison in the previous two years did not have their citizenship restored.

I offered it to all of them, thinking that it would be in the public interest to make them feel useful members of society. I felt it would help remove the frustrations, resentments and hostilities in assuring a man that society was willing to give him another chance.

I also was concerned with those still in prison. Some of my advisors told me not to bother. "There are no votes for you in this sort of thing," one said. "Why do it?"

"I guess I've always had suicidal tendencies in politics," I answered, "but it's obvious to me that penal systems are failures. They are graduate schools of crime. If the purpose of prison is punishment, then we'd better go back to the stocks and whips."

As an outdoor man, I couldn't conceive of anything more cruel than being locked in a cage like an animal. Of course, for psychotics and mad-dog killers there was no other way to go. But even a hit killer for the Mafia, I felt, was not beyond redemption. Thus I became interested in the men and women my state was keeping in prison, particularly those serving life sentences. On learning that many lifers were not getting their sentences commuted, I obtained a list of them from the Department of Prisons. I decided to visit every lifer who had been in prison for over fifteen years.

The first such experience was unforgettable. I was ushered into a small room with a metal table and two chairs. While a guard stood outside the door, I sat down at the table and waited. Soon the green steel door opened and accompanied by a guard, in stumbled a wizened old man. His gray prison shirt and trousers were obviously new in honor of my visit. The guard left and I reached out to shake the prisoner's hand. Hesitantly he raised his toward me; it was slender and cold with age. We both sat down on creaking metal chairs and for a moment looked at each other; his rheumic eyes were listless, uncertain.

"When did you enter prison?" I asked.

"It was in 1922," he said.

I fell back in my chair astounded. The man in front of me had lived behind these walls for over forty years! All during the Roaring Twenties, the great Depression, World War II to the present, he had seen nothing but cold gray walls and green steel doors. Collecting myself, I asked: "Can you tell me why you feel you should now be released?"

His thin shoulders sagged and his pale blue eyes filled with tears. Through the oversize uniform I could see his body begin to tremble. Then he broke into convulsive sobs, his head sinking to his arms on the table, his back heaving.

I wanted to get up and put my arms around this old man who could have been my grandfather. I reached across the cold metal table and placed my hand on his. Finally, he quieted, raised his gray head and looked at me. "You don't know . . ." he said huskily, struggling to speak, "you don't know what this means to me. I have appealed to every governor since I came in here forty-one years ago and not one . . . no one has ever responded until you."

He looked down at the table. "I really don't know what to say. I have dreamed of this day for forty-one years and now . . ." he began sobbing again. "I don't even know what to say to you."

I wanted to open the door and let him out of that prison immediately. "What will you do if you get out?" I asked. "Do you have a family?" His eyes took on a faraway look. "None that care about me," he said. Then he brightened. "But I do have a place to go. I've saved some money over the years." There was a faint glow of pride in his eyes. "There are folks I can stay with."

This gentle old man had been convicted of murder over forty years before. A review of his case by state agencies, plus all the paperwork, took three months before I was able to request an order for the commutation of his sentence. The papers giving him his release had to be delivered to the prison hospital, however, because the old man had suffered a heart attack.

The day after the prisoner had received the news of his release my secretary came into my office with a grieved look on her face. She pointed to the phone. I picked it up; the warden told me that the prisoner had just died. I swung my chair around and sat looking out the window for a long time. The old man had completed his life sentence.

I heard later that word of my commutation order had flashed through the prison like lightning. Everyone there wanted that old man to be freed. He had become a symbol of hope to them. In the end, thirty-five prisoners after special reviews had their life sentences commuted.

There were many people who were critical of my prison visits, claiming they helped incite a full-scale riot in Fort Madison state prison. There, a large group of men, festering over grievances, burned up their laundry facility and isolated themselves in a cell block. After communication was established, the angry men said they wanted to talk to me about their problems. Both the warden and State Director of Corrections advised me not to. I don't often go against the advice of trusted associates, but when a group of prisoners have so many grievances that they will hurt themselves to get attention, I felt I should listen.

A phone hookup was arranged and when they got on the wire I promised them dialogue on the following conditions: 1) they would select two men to represent them; 2) where their grievances had merit, I would do everything I could to remedy the situation; 3) I would do nothing on grievances I felt had no merit; 4) they must understand they had broken the law and would have to take the consequences.

After some debate, the men accepted. They came up with eighteen grievances and I felt ten had merit. These involved food, work conditions, library privileges, and use of free time. These may seem inconsequential to a person outside prison walls, but when one is inside, nothing is more important than what one eats, whether he can listen to a radio, read a magazine or have access to the library.

I promised that I would do something about it, but only after they laid down their weapons, left their barricade, and suffered the consequences of breaking the law.

They agreed and surrendered. We instituted changes on the grievances and also worked out a special committee of inmates who could air their problems with the State Director of Corrections. We had no riots after that.

Communication, I was learning, was the key to understanding.

It was brought home to me again one morning about six months after becoming governor. I was in the barber shop in the Des Moines Savery Hotel and a businessman whom I had once thought was a friend of the Democratic party walked in. He gave me a cold look, and plopped down in the next chair.

I wondered what was wrong. I knew he had been contacted for a campaign contribution before the election but had not given anything.

Well, I thought, let him be. If I had heeded the Biblical admonition about going to one's brother and settling differences, I would have asked him what was wrong.

But I didn't. I buried myself in the newspaper.

Perhaps the other man read the Bible and followed it. For he got up and walked over to me.

The barber had stepped to the phone, leaving us alone.

"Hi," I said tentatively.

"Governor," he said, "I might as well be frank about it. I've been upset with you."

"What's your beef?"

"Well, we made quite a contribution to your campaign and never heard anything. It hurt."

I rose in my chair. "Contribution? My campaign committee said you folks had not given anything!"

His brow wrinkled. "That's strange. I know we contributed. The union took up a collection on the production line, and management pitched in, too. We gave the whole amount to a union man to pass on to you people."

We both checked and learned the truth. Instead of delivering the money, the man had taken it and left Iowa. If my supposed adversary had not been open with me, none of us would have known.

It was not the only lesson I would learn.

A week before my first Christmas in office, a phone call came about eleven o'clock one night. After a rough day, I was tired and ready to climb into bed. The voice had that toneless quality of one who has lost hope, but I recalled that I had given him a job when I was on the commerce commission. He was an epileptic and I didn't want to assign him to a job where he'd get killed if he had a seizure. I remembered, too, that he was married and had children.

"I'm sorry to bother you, Governor, at this late hour," he said on the phone. He told me that he was out of work, had had two seizures on his previous job and had been given a medical leave of absence. Since then he had been certified by a doctor as being capable of work. "But no one will give me a job," he added.

"Have you been drinking?" I asked, knowing that he had battled this problem for years.

"No," he said. "I don't have any money, Governor. Christmas is coming, there are no presents for the kids . . . I need a job. Can I come out to the mansion and see you?"

"Look," I said, resenting the idea of having to dress and talk to someone far into the morning, "it would take you an hour to get here, and frankly, I'm worn out. Why don't you see me in the office in the morning? I'll do whatever I can then to help you."

He pressed to see me that night.

"But there's nothing I can do for you tonight," I said feeling some aggravation building in me. With a note of finality in my voice, I added: "Come to the office in the morning; I'll be there at eight."

The phone was silent for a moment. And then in a voice that seemed to be coming from the bottom of a well, he said good-night.

The next morning was busy at the office and I was immersed in studying some papers when the phone rang. It was an associate, George McCann, secretary of the commerce commission. "Say, Governor, you remember W—— R——, the fellow who worked for the commission?"

"Oh, yes. He was the man who called me last night." I suddenly remembered he hadn't come in that morning. I wondered if he went to George's office instead.

"Well," continued George, "I just heard that he shot himself." Time suddenly stopped. "Yeah . . . sometime last night, about midnight. Despondent, I guess. Anyway, thought you'd want to know."

George hung up and I sat stunned at my desk, the murmur of the Statehouse silenced.

If I had done something for him last night when he called, it would have been different. Waves of guilt overwhelmed me. I had thought that telling him to see me in the morning was enough.

But it wasn't enough. He couldn't get through the night.

I remembered the Samaritan who had kneeled to help a man at the side of the road. He had been tired and on urgent business, too, but it waited.

The lesson was clear. Someone crying for help needs a hand held out to him immediately.

I determined to never forget that.

There were many reminders.

One afternoon as I was working at my desk in the Statehouse, I looked up to see an elderly man with a cane in each hand stomp into my office. Ruth Yauk, my secretary, and Dwight Jensen, my executive assistant, hovered behind him.

"Governor," gasped Ruth, "he walked right by me; I couldn't stop him." Dwight started to usher the old fellow out.

"No, no," I said putting up my hand. "He's in here now. Whatever his problem, I'll see him."

They retreated and I looked up at the elderly thin man in baggy worn trousers and ancient flannel shirt. Under a tattered straw hat, his bright blue eyes bored into mine with fierce determination.

"Sit down," I waved him to a chair. "What can I do for you?"

He eased himself down, placing his canes against the chair. "I'm hungry," he said. "All they give me is two eggs a day. I don't even have money for tobacco." He withdrew an ancient pipe from his shirt pocket and pointed the empty barrel at me. He was on old-age assistance and stayed at a private home for the elderly nearby. "Every month I get my eighty-dollar check; they force me to sign it and I don't get anything back."

I sympathized with him, but I was also aware of the financial squeeze faced by the private homes which cared for the elderly. Some of the boarders could only pay thirty dollars a month. And sometimes as many as ten or twelve pensioners would be living in one home. To adequately feed, clothe and care for these people on their pitiful pensions was often an impossibility.

"I'm getting two eggs and a little breakfast food, but I ain't getting any smoking tobacco," he reminded me.

I looked at the man staring at me. Since his one luxury in life was a pinch of smoking tobacco, I asked one of my aides to go out and buy him a can. It was the most important thing in his pathetic existence. Every time I found myself in political battles over providing more funds for the elderly, I was motivated by the anguished faces of this too often neglected segment of our society.

Not only did people walk into my office but they phoned me at home. In the early months of my term in office, our home number was listed in the book and often the calls were linked with legislative activities underway at the time. During the liquor-by-the-drink controversy, the phone rang at 4:00 A.M. I picked it up and the operator said it was a call from Minnesota.

"Shay, Governor Hughes . . . I'm in a bar here and I want *you* to tell thish no-good bartender to sell me another drink."

"Why?" I asked, rubbing my eyes and wondering who in the world this was. "It sounds to me as if you've had enough already."

"You believe in liquor by the drink, don't you? Well, then tell thish damn bartender to sell me another drink! I'm an Iowan and you're the governor and you can protect my rights."

I told him I thought the bartender was right and that he should go home to bed.

Not all the calls were that easy to answer. One winter's night when it was twenty degrees below zero, a woman phoned. Her voice was quavery. "We haven't had heat for three days, the children and I have been in bed under all the blankets, the pipes are frozen and we don't have any money. I'm afraid we'll freeze to death." She got out all the words in one breath.

"Have you been to your county welfare board?"

"Yes, they promised to help but can't do anything for two or three weeks while the papers go through." She said she lived about twenty miles outside of Des Moines.

"What do you burn?"

"Coal . . ." she began to sob.

I told her I'd order some coal myself and have it at her house in the morning. The next day I talked to the welfare supervisor of her district; he didn't know about the problem and got right on it, including getting her coal.

These are the calls one remembers—the poor, the lost, the abandoned who have no other place to go. It bothered me to sit down to the sumptuous banquets a governor must attend and see so much food wasted when I knew people were hungry all over the world.

This was a conflict I was never able to resolve, as the invitations began coming in from the White House, too.

I had to refuse the first two invitations because of conflicts in my schedule. But Eva enjoyed seeing the invitations. Engraved in flowing Spencerian script on heavy White House stationery, they read: "President and Mrs. Kennedy request the pleasure of. . . ."

"Look, Pack," said Eva, "they have our names done in the same style of script."

The press of my work was increasing and it was becoming more and more difficult to spend time with my family. However when the Beatles appeared in Chicago, Phyllis begged to see them and she, Eva and I slipped away for an evening. The noise was almost as bad as anything I had heard in the war and when we walked out I thought I'd gone deaf. Phyllis thought it was great. I was about to say something but then remembered what my mother thought of the Benny Goodman music Jess and I had liked so much.

The third White House invitation came in November and we planned to go. Eva was particularly keen on meeting Jacqueline Kennedy. But a few days before the dinner was held, another conflict arose and we had to cancel.

"Oh, well," I told Eva, "there will be plenty of opportunities to have dinner with the Kennedys."

A few days later I was home for lunch with Eva. It was one of our few moments for an uninterrupted time together. We had just finished eating in the little family dining room off the kitchen and I had gone upstairs for a moment. Eva called up the stairs: "The president has been shot in Dallas! They also shot the governor!"

I rushed down and waited in front of the television set. Then came the announcement: "The president is dead." Texas Governor Connally would live.

One of my first thoughts was—could it be part of a conspiracy to kill national leaders? I phoned my office and the adjutant general of the Iowa National Guard who alerted his command staff. The next morning Frank Morrison, Governor of Nebraska, picked me up at the airport in his DC-3 and we flew together to Andrews Air Force Base near Washington. As we stepped into the hushed East Room where the flag-draped casket rested in state, I couldn't help thinking of the irony of it. This was my first visit inside the White House.

The following day we had our own memorial service on the west lawn of the Iowa Statehouse simultaneously with the Washington ceremonies. Through it all—the muffled drums, the low sobbing and shattered hopes—I was reminded of Christ's words about the wheat of today being alive and thrown into the oven tomorrow.

Somehow the tragedy marked a turning point for the nation. From an optimistic spirit generated by the postwar gearing up for the good life, discords began to sound in the wings. Some Americans—particularly young people—were beginning to question the Vietnam war; the civil rights disturbances now erupted in the north as well as the south. Narcotics were becoming common in affluent suburban communities. Everywhere there seemed a growing sense of malaise and discontent.

Along with it pressure mounted in the governor's office. I felt it rather heavily one night after a hectic day during which I had an angry confrontation with Evan Hultman, my attorney general.

"Curly" Hultman was a bright young attorney who had been very successful in the Republican party. I felt that he had planned all of his life to become governor. Obviously, I was a block in his timetable. It had reached the point where I felt that, if in giving me a legal opinion he saw any latitude in it, it would not be in my favor. So for counsel I found myself turning more and more to friends at the University of Iowa Law School and other seasoned attorneys in the city.

As my limousine sped through the dark Des Moines streets toward home, I snapped off the little reading light, put down the reports I had been studying and rested my head back on the cushions. Where was my life heading? Did I belong in politics? There was so much antagonism and pressure and temptation in an elected office—could this be where God wanted me? The heavy work load had often forced me to miss church and forego my early morning Bible reading.

As the limousine with its official Iowa plate Number 1 sped on I rolled down the window. Someone had been mowing grass along the parkway and in the warm night air I drank deeply of its fresh fragrance. Not too many years before it would have been I who cut that grass with a park district lawnmower. I remembered the time they called me away from mowing the lawn in Greenwood Park to learn of Jesse's death.

The limousine slowed, swung up the driveway of the mansion and halted under the little portico by the back door. I climbed out, thanked Joe the driver, and waved him goodnight. The Lincoln purred away and I stood in the warm summer night, listening to the crickets chirp among the giant oaks towering around the mansion. Our bedroom window glowed and I knew Eva waited up for me.

But I wanted to stand there for a while, somehow to reach out and grasp something that I seemed to be missing those days. It was like a time when I followed my trap lines as a youngster. One icy morning I had overslept. Hurrying, I scrambled through brush, tripping on roots, tangling in briars, becoming panicky because I thought someone had taken my traps. And then I realized; in my hurry, I had unwittingly stepped off my regular trail.

Deep inside I knew I had stepped off His path. Yes, I would think of Him during the day and even breathe quick prayers, but it was at my convenience, not His. I had also stepped out of Christian fellowship. As a rule, my close companions and I did not talk about God; we were more concerned with political maneuvers and shoring strength for the coming election. I couldn't find time to make the AA meetings anymore.

My family was seeing me less and less. Connie complained that her little girl Tracy didn't realize she had a grandfather. Carol was engaged and I hardly knew her fiance. And too often my visit with Phyllis was a quick kiss on her cheek as she slept.

I thought about the men who had helped me so much in past years. Wayne Shoemaker up in Hampton, Father Harry Dailey, still shepherding his little flock in Ida Grove. How much I would have liked to relax in Wayne's study, or drive up to Father Dailey's white frame rectory, knock on the kitchen door to be greeted by Nell, the gray-haired housekeeper. With both men I could talk for hours about the Bible, the way God moves in our lives and how we can listen to Him.

There was a sound at the door and I looked up. It was Eva.

"I heard the car," she said, "but you didn't come in."

I walked up the steps and kissed her. "I was just studying the night."

16

The Risks One Takes

I HAD FIRST met President Johnson on his campaign visit to Des Moines and liked the man. I identified with his open casualness, was impressed with his courageous stand on civil rights and efforts to fight poverty.

So when the invitation came once again to attend a White House state dinner, we accepted. Eva and I flew to Washington and dressed in our hotel for the dinner. I felt uncomfortable in the black-tie dinner jacket but Eva looked great in the long white gown she had worn to my inaugural ball. Our invitation specified that we enter by the southeast gate and arrive at 8:00 P.M. We walked into the White House through the diplomatic reception room where Franklin Roosevelt used to broadcast his fireside chats. As we passed through this oval blue room I remembered so many years before how Mother, Dad, Jesse and I had sat around the battery-set listening to that broad eastern accent which rallied the country out of the disastrous depression.

We turned in our admittance card, checked our coats and then walked down the long wide corridor to a broad red-carpeted staircase that led us up to the white marble entrance foyer on the mansion's main floor. We received a numbered card that told us where we would sit at dinner. Eva looked at the card, gave a little gasp and whispered, "We're going to sit with the president!"

Just then Lyndon Johnson and Lady Bird walked into the room, cocktails were served, and we all proceeded into the dining room. The procession was led by Lady Bird walking with the guest of honor, and the President escorting the guest's wife.

The president and Lady Bird made us both feel very much at ease. After dinner there was music and dancing. I was surprised to see the president inviting various ladies, including Eva, to dance. Later Eva and I both commented to each other what warm and friendly people the president and his wife were.

I had no idea that in a few years I would also know what it was to incur the wrath of Lyndon Baines Johnson.

Another White House invitation of quite a different nature came in the summer of 1964. I was making a speech in Iowa City one evening. After the speech, someone said there was an urgent phone call from the White House.

It was from a Johnson aide. He was calling about the Democratic National Convention, only a few weeks away. Would I make the speech seconding Johnson's nomination?

I was startled but quickly said yes. The convention was held in Atlantic City and the president invited my family and me to Washington a few days before the event. Eva, Phyllis and I drove there with Bob Barry, our State Highway Commissioner, and his wife, Ramona. We thought we'd make a vacation trip out of it. After we checked in at the Hay Adams Hotel, I got word that my family and I were invited to spend the night at the White House.

That evening, a very excited Eva, Phyllis and I walked through the iron gates on Pennsylvania Avenue. Phyllis was given her own room and Eva and I were ushered into another. As Eva sank down on the canopied bed, she said, "I still can't believe it."

That evening we saw the musical *Oklahoma* on the White House lawn. We also enjoyed a pleasant chat with Lyndon Johnson. Afterwards, we retired to our sumptuous bedroom, almost too awed to speak. The next morning there was a polite knock on our door. I answered it to be greeted by a smiling white-jacketed steward bearing a covered silver tray.

"Breakfast for you and the madame," he smiled. He gently placed the tray on a bedside table, and uncovered it revealing steaming eggs, coffee and rolls on White House china.

For a moment, I was mesmerized. I thought of the little kid in dirty overalls following his trap lines along the Maple River and wondered how I got here.

Our visit with the President over, we returned to the Hay Adams and if I had any inflated ego over our White House stay, it was well taken care of the following morning. While eating in the hotel dining room I had noticed several diners in sport shirts. So the morning we were leaving for Atlantic City, I told Eva and Phyllis to go on to the dining room and order breakfast while I finished packing the car. I'd join them there. In view of a long hot drive, I put on my sport shirt and slacks, then hurried to the dining room where I spotted my family across the room.

As I headed toward their table, I heard a "Hey you!" I paid no attention but the exclamations continued. I turned to see the maitre d' pointing at me. "Yes you," he barked. "You can't come in here without a coat and tie!"

I walked over to him and said quietly, "But I see people in here every day without a tie. Why me?"

His voice was clipped. "Buddy, you can't eat here without a tie."

"I'm the governor of the state of Iowa heading for the National Democratic Convention and that's my family sitting over there," I said pompously.

"I don't give a hoot who you are," he said obstinately, "you are not eating here without a coat and tie."

That morning as I ate breakfast at a roadside stop on our way to Atlantic City, I mused about the incident. What was happening to me? Was it the inevitable arrogance that goes with position? If so, I had really needed that comeuppance.

If my ego needed further trimming, it was taken care of at the convention. For weeks, the party platform committee had been trying to hammer out a civil rights plank. President Johnson, although a strong proponent of such rights, felt a moderate plank would bring everyone together. But he was having difficulties with a committee member who felt it should be much stronger. She also happened to be a member of my Iowa delegation. Because of her, the Party was not even close to getting the plank laid.

One night in our suite the phone rang. Bob Barry picked it up and his face tensed. He looked at me, put his hand over the receiver, "The president!"

"What do you mean?" I asked.

He gulped. "It's President Johnson."

"Hell, you mean it's his secretary."

"No! *He* is on the phone."

I walked over and picked up the phone, my voice tight: "Hello, Mr. President."

"Governor?"

"Yes."

"We're all having trouble with that delegate of yours on the platform committee. She's not going along with our position. You all are going to have to do something about that."

This was the hard side of Lyndon B. Johnson.

"Well, Mr. President. I don't like to bring undue pressure on my people. She is a civil liberties person and will advocate a strong plank on equal rights, opportunities, the whole works."

There was a moment of silence, then: "Governor, I expect you to control these things; when we get people on these platform committees we expect them to do what we want them to do. Now I want *you* to take care of it."

I felt my hackles rise. "Mr. President, I'm not sure I can take care of it. I'm not at all sure she'll do what I want her to do, even if I agreed with your position."

There was cold steel in his voice. "Governor, I expect you to take care of it and I don't want to have any more problems with that woman."

After hanging up the phone, I sat back and wiped my brow. Although sometimes overexuberant, "that woman" was a good friend and loyal, hardworking member of our state committee. In addition, she was an iron-willed person whose mind, when made up, was impervious to being changed.

The next morning I located my delegate at a meeting and asked her to see me. As I heard her heels beating a tattoo on the hall outside my door I braced myself for what had to come. I pictured her, head held high, chin outthrust, and fiery eyes snapping.

She burst through the door in her usual flurry. "Yes, Governor, what do you want?"

"Look," I said gently, leading her to a chair, "The president called me last night about the civil rights plank." I explained they needed her vote to get a workable plank, and added how much I'd really appreciate her going along with the president's position.

As I awaited her outburst, I was surprised to see her looking at me calm and poised. "Well, Governor," she said quietly, "I really wasn't going to go along with him, but . . ." She explained that she would agree with the proposed plank. It seemed that on her way to my floor, she had met some of the well-known civil rights leaders in the hotel lobby. A great admirer of them, she had rushed up and started to talk. Hurrying to an appointment they had cut her short. Offended by this she had changed her mind on the plank in the elevator. It intrigued me how a cause could suffer through failure to use a bit of courtesy.

Making the speech seconding Lyndon Johnson's nomination was a heady experience. But the euphoria did not last long. Reality came when I returned to Iowa where I was running for a second term as governor. I was up against my attorney general, Evan "Curly" Hultman. Early polls showed me well in the lead and this is probably what made my opposition so bitter. For it was one of the roughest smear campaigns I have ever seen. I feel sure Curly Hultman had nothing to do with it himself. But I believe his campaign workers became desperate; and desperate people will pick up anything to throw at their opposition.

Hundreds of thousands of anonymous letters, including a scandal sheet about me, were sent out to people all over the state. Practically everyone I knew received one. Some even attacked my family with vicious lies that deeply upset my wife and daughters.

One man posted these stories in large type in a store window in a town about fifty miles from Des Moines.

At night I would sit alone in our library after everyone had gone to bed, sick at my stomach, wondering why this kind of thing had to happen. To smear me was one thing, but to hurt Eva and my daughters was more than I could bear.

"Don't worry about it, Harold," said Park Rinard in one of our late evening talks, "everybody knows it's untrue." I tried to forget the filth being spread around but it began to eat into me, consuming me with anger.

Finally, I was able to commit it all to God, the effect of the stories and the people responsible for them. Moreover, I was able to place Eva and the girls in His hands and trust that their spirits would not be harmed.

Then the *Look* magazine article poured gasoline on the fires of our campaign.

Some time before, the magazine had contacted me for an interview. The magazine was owned by the Cowles publishing company which also owned The Des Moines *Register* and *Tribune,* and I felt something of a kinship with its Iowan heritage. I was a bit uneasy about the article coming out in my reelection year, however, because I knew it would mention my alcoholism. Until then there had been very little comment about it in the press, beyond a comment here and there in columns. I had never ducked the subject in interviews but until then it had never really become widely known.

However, millions of readers throughout the United States would know about it if I went ahead with the article. I did a lot of soul-searching, sitting up late one night in the library thinking about it. As I meditated, I felt an immense gratefulness to God for saving me from eternal hell. Because of this I made up my mind to do the story. If it helped some men and women sick and dying of the damnable disease, then it all would be worth it.

From out of the darkness came a question: "Even if it means ridicule and criticism?"

"Yes, Lord," I prayed, not realizing what this was going to mean.

Since the story would be published in April, I figured that the months before November would give me enough time to recover from anything that might harm my chances for reelection. Thus I gave *Look* the go-ahead.

Fletcher Knebel, the *Look* writer, was a warm, scholarly man and I thought we had a good interview. His questions were incisive and we covered many phases of my life, including my alcoholism. I told him I had renounced alcohol and how my life had changed for the better.

Then I heard from *Look* that the April scheduling would be delayed.

In fact, as the summer months passed, I had almost forgotten about the *Look* article. In September I learned that it would be featured in their early October issue. I was stunned. Some thirty days before election day a national magazine would announce that I was an alcoholic. I worried about it until I again had to put the whole matter in the hands of God. If He wanted me to be governor, He would take care of it. And if He didn't, the *Look* article would make no difference anyway.

A peace came over me. When the magazine finally came out with the story, I prayed that it would help people who were as desperate as I had been. I thought it was a good article, though there were a few minor errors. For example, it placed the date of my last drink as 1952 when it was actually 1954. The wrong date could have very

well been my fault, but it seemed of little matter. I did write Fletcher
Knebel to set the record straight and then forgot about it.

In the meantime, despite the vilification I was receiving, my cam-
paign was going well. I thought how different it was from 1962 when
I had stumped the state on my own, speaking to sparse audiences.
This time I was covering the state by auto, bus, and airplane.

My campaign men still criticized me for speaking too frankly.
"Chief," complained Dwight Jensen, my executive assistant, after I
had talked to some folks in a town square, "did you realize you
told them to vote for your opponent?"

I chuckled. "Yes. I told them if they didn't think I was doing a
good job to vote for Hultman. But if they liked the way things were
going, vote for me."

"Dwight," I said, "if we don't think that things are going fairly
well in Iowa after two years of our party's administration, then we'd
better hang it up right now."

One thing I had then in far greater quantity than in my first
campaign was confidence. The Des Moines *Register* polls showed me
far ahead. Lyndon Johnson visited Des Moines on his campaign
tour. Some fifty thousand people lined the streets cheering as his
motorcade wound toward the Statehouse where he spoke on the
front lawn. Afterwards, he congratulated me on my lead in the polls.

Even the *Look* magazine article seemed to help. Instead of hurting
me politically, it turned out to have an opposite effect. Letters poured
in from people all over the nation congratulating me for my openness.
What really moved me were the letters from other alcoholics who
wrote how much my frankness helped them. Many said it gave them
renewed hope.

However, when The Des Moines *Register,* a statewide paper, re-
printed it, it rubbed salt in the festering wounds of my opposition.

One afternoon at my desk in the Statehouse I got a call from a
news reporter. He sounded frank and pleasant and I expected another typical query about my outlook on a bill in the legislature
when he hit me with the question: "Governor, we have information
that you were arrested on a drunken driving charge in 1954, two
years after you said in the *Look* magazine article that you had
stopped drinking."

I sat stunned.

"Do you have anything you want to say on this?"

I thought it best to say "no comment" rather than get into a lengthy explanation about a copy error and something that happened in my private life ten years before that had no bearing on the present.

I got together with Park Rinard, Dwight Jensen, Les Holland, Bill Hedlund, and my other advisors and we discussed it. Through some checking, we found that a disgruntled former chief of the Iowa Highway Patrol had fed the opposition the fact that I had been arrested in Kissimmee, Florida, in 1954.

Soon other news reporters called with the same query. Two came to the mansion one night to ask the question. Obviously, this item had been given to the press all over Iowa. However, not one newspaper, radio or TV station would disseminate it because I would not comment.

I prayed that that was the end of it.

On Friday, before the November 3rd election, the Des Moines Greater Chamber of Commerce held their usual pre-election luncheon at the Savery Hotel grand ballroom. It had become traditional for the two gubernatorial candidates to attend this luncheon for a public debate, which would be televised statewide.

It was a little before noon as I climbed the red-carpeted stairway to the large ballroom, already jammed with almost 300 civic and business leaders sitting at tables that overflowed into side rooms. TV cameramen were stringing cables to their equipment. A buzz of expectancy filled the air.

As I stepped into the corridor leading to the ballroom, I saw Curly Hultman standing at the side of the hall.

I thought how in so many ways our lives were similar, yet different. He had also attended the University of Iowa; only he was elected Phi Beta Kappa, was a two-year letterman, and had graduated. He had also gone overseas in World War II, only he had come out of it as a battalion commander. He was a Methodist, and also had three daughters.

The ballroom was abuzz with the chatter of diners and clatter of plates as waiters hurried about the tables. Music from a string ensemble provided a festive background.

As I started down the hall, Curly Hultman stepped up to me, a tense look about his eyes.

"Governor," he asked in a low voice, "could I have a word with you?"

"Why sure, Curly."

We stepped into a little alcove.

"I've got to ask you a question."

"Fire away," I said.

Was I drunk in Kissimmee, Florida, in 1954? he asked.

The noisy hotel suddenly seemed to become silent. I looked straight at him. "Yes, Curly, I was."

Was I convicted of a drunk driving charge there?

"No, I wasn't. But Curly, I'll tell you the truth. I *was* drunk in Kissimmee. I was picked up in my car drunk. I was put in jail where I spent the night. I posted bond the next day and left town. Since I forfeited my bond and didn't appear for trial, I was not convicted."

Curly stood before me; his eyes had the look of a desperate man, ready for a final fight.

He said he was sorry but that he was going to have to bring this up in the debate.

A knot developed in my stomach. "Well, Curly," I said, "you do what you have to do. You know there's nothing I can do to stop you and I'm sorry you feel that you must do it. But you do what you have to do."

I walked on to the speaker's table and sat down. A local banker waved at me from a nearby table and the knot within me tightened. I glanced out at the hundreds of other people looking forward to hearing their two candidates speak.

It would be a luncheon I would never forget.

17

The Way Out
Is the Way Through

AS THE LUNCHEON progressed I couldn't eat. I looked around the many tables of business and industrial executives. How many, I wondered, would be my friends when the luncheon was over?

Curly and I flipped a coin to see who would speak first. The little formality seemed strangely out of place at that moment. I sat down and Curly stepped to the podium. After adjusting the microphone, he began talking.

Why praise a man for sobering up, he asked, when no credit is given to another man for not getting drunk in the first place?

I sat frozen, my hand gripping the table edge as if it were the rail of a plunging ship.

Curly pointed out that I had claimed in the *Look* magazine article that I had not taken a drink since 1952. He halted a moment, glancing around the hushed room. Then, in dramatic tones he stated that he had evidence that I had been arrested in 1954 on a drunken driving charge. After going into the details of my arrest, he stated that if it had happened once, it could happen again.

The ballroom was still. Not a cough or clink of coffee cup broke the spell. I stared at my plate.

Curly said he regretted having to bring up this subject, but that I "had interjected this personal issue into the campaign" by allowing the publication of the magazine article. Thus he felt that the people of Iowa should know the truth about a man who was maintaining a stance of integrity when, in fact, the integrity wasn't there.

I looked at the sea of faces before me. Some were staring at me, others hung their heads in embarrassment.

195

"If there is to be an emotional appeal," he said, "I ask but one thing and that is that the record be made clear, that it be straight, and that . . ."

As he continued speaking about "deception," tampered driving records, and integrity, a sickness overwhelmed me; I wanted to get up and walk right out of the ballroom.

Curly finished his talk and sat down. In a daze, I forced myself to stand. For a moment the room of faces seemed to swim before me. Then everything came into focus. My prepared speech lay forgotten at the side of my plate.

"Well, ladies and gentlemen," I started, "I regret that the subject of my alcoholism has been brought up. But now that it has, I want to respond. The answer is yes. Yes, I was in Kissimmee, Florida." I fought to keep my voice from choking. "I did get drunk there. I was drunk driving my car. I was thrown in jail where I spent the night. I posted bond and left the city because there was no judge available the next day to appear in court. I did nothing to clear the files of the State Safety Commission. Whatever was on the records then is there today."

As I continued talking a Presence began to sustain me and I explained how I had turned in my old driver's license and had taken an examination for a new one.

"But I want to say one final thing and I'll never talk about it again." I began to choke up again. "And that is, I regret that my family has to continue to suffer because of my alcoholism. It is bad enough that I suffer but it's worse that my wife and children have to suffer because of it. I'm deeply hurt that they have to be dragged through this again."

I looked around at the faces watching me, some impassive, some sympathetic. "I am an alcoholic and will be until the day I die. But with God's help I'll never touch a drop of alcohol again. Now can we talk about the issues of this campaign?"

The meeting ended in a rising clamour of voices. I barely remember leaving the room. I paused only to answer reporters who besieged me with questions about the Kissimmee incident, shake hands with Curly Hultman who rushed up saying something about "It's been a hard campaign" and "May the best man win," and then, still stunned, step out into the cool November air.

That afternoon I was slated to visit a shopping center to greet people and pass out handbills. In the meantime news flashes about the luncheon seemed to be coming over radio and television every fifteen minutes.

I shrank from going to the shopping center. I didn't want to face anyone. Everyone, I felt sure, was wondering what sort of lying character I was. By now I just wanted to hide somewhere and get away from it all. Why did I ever go into politics, anyway? All I did was hurt my family.

Yet through it all I was conscious of that Presence which had sustained me through the luncheon. Along with His Presence were the people pressing close to me, taking my hand, and saying, "We're with you, Governor. Don't worry what they say about you."

The only way to meet this black cloud, I decided, was to walk right through it. And so I did go to the shopping center where I found a large group of women waiting to meet me; many helped pass out handbills as they walked with me. I saw some prominent women in the group and to my amazement, recognized some of them as Republicans.

What I had not realized was that Hultman's attack had backfired. Dwight Jensen said he heard that the Iowa Republican headquarters was deluged with angry calls, mostly from Republicans.

To me it was a lesson that if one is going to throw mud at another, he's bound to get some of it on himself. The next morning at the breakfast table Eva read an editorial that appeared in The Des Moines *Register* entitled "A Low Political Blow" in which it found the luncheon accusation "surprising and regrettable."

Eva read it aloud: *"It also is no secret that the Iowa Governor had the courage and fortitude to overcome the liquor habit. In our opinion, any man or woman who wins that battle and successfully puts the pieces of his or her life back together again deserves commendation, not censure."*

She put the paper down. "Don't worry about it, Harold," she said. "I think a lot of other people feel the same way."

A lot evidently did.

We won the election by a landslide.

Early Wednesday morning, after most of the returns were in, Eva and I sank wearily into bed at the mansion. Deeply asleep, I was awakened by a ringing of my private line telephone. As I reached for it half awake, I thought of the madman who had called me after my first election. But on picking it up I recognized the unmistakable Texan drawl: "Well, Governor, how'd we do out there in Iowa?"

I sat up in bed, excitement filling me. "Mr. President," I enthused, "I won by a tremendous majority, the greatest majority ever given a candidate in the state of Iowa. We elected practically everyone, got control of both the senate and the house. It's been the greatest Democratic election here since Franklin Roosevelt!"

Dead silence hung at the other end of the wire, then came the low measured words: "Governor . . . I meant, how did *I* do in Iowa."

Plummeting from my cloud, I snapped completely awake. "Oh, yes . . . Mr. President," I stammered, "you won by a great majority in Iowa, almost two hundred thousand votes."

"Well," he said, an easier tone in his voice, "I'm just calling all the states to see how everybody is doing. Congratulations, Governor, on a fine race."

The euphoric mood of winning soon dissipated in the daily battle of gubernatorial responsibilities. Some came raging in the form of storms. Others were more subtly complex. Always the answer seemed to follow the line I took at the Chamber of Commerce luncheon—that one can survive life's tempests by walking directly through them in faith.

Dark clouds gathered early in 1965 when a strike of the United Packinghouse Workers of America against the Iowa Beef Packers, Inc., produced violence. The center of it was the firm's Fort Dodge plant. Strikebreakers had been brought in by the company to run the plant and there was an explosion of anger as cars were bombed, tires slashed and bloody fights took place.

The plant had been shut down for a month, and strikers, armed with high-powered rifles, blocked roads to it. They vowed to destroy the plant if an agreement was not reached by midnight the following Thursday.

With the deadline only seventy-two hours away I found myself between bitter adversaries. I could not order the union to call off a strike to which they had the legal right. Neither could I ask the beef packing company to stop importing outside workers. I thought how each side honestly felt they were reflecting Iowa's motto: "Our liberties we prize and our rights we will maintain."

But everybody was hurting, the workers, the company and the public.

What I could try to do, I felt, was to persuade both sides to sit down and negotiate. At this, the company agreed not to reopen the plant until some kind of agreement was reached. For several days I first met with one side and then the other. When I thought they might be close to an agreement, I'd bring them together. Always these meetings ended late at night with shouting and cursing. On the evening of the final day, the men from both sides sullenly filed into my office. The word was out: If a settlement was not reached by midnight, the workers had vowed to destroy the plant.

I had driven past the plant earlier in the day; an ominous quiet had settled over it. Determined-looking company men with rifles could be seen stationed behind the high chain link fence. On the outside, armed strikers lurked behind cars and trees. There was a scent of blood in the air.

The meeting around the table that evening started out with tired, disgruntled men eyeing each other suspiciously. As they talked, it seemed evident that no agreement was forthcoming.

I glanced at my watch and thought of my adjutant general waiting in an unmarked car a few blocks from the Statehouse. He was there because it was my responsibility to uphold the law. We could not allow property destruction or violence. So earlier that day my adjutant general and I had come up with a plan.

Our decision was to alert a National Guard group from outside the local area, have them quietly assemble near Fort Dodge in full combat gear at a railroad siding where they would board box cars. Their commanding officer had orders to prepare to back the train right through the gates into the plant. If an agreement could not be reached by midnight, I would issue an executive order for martial law which would be immediately relayed to him through the adjutant general. Then the train would roll.

I fervently hoped that we would not have to do this. Though the troops would forestall the carnage of a full-scale riot, men were bound to be hurt or killed.

The conversation at the table waxed hot. Threats were made. At one point I felt the whole meeting would collapse. I kept watching the clock as it edged closer to midnight.

Finally, I interrupted the discussions. "Look," I said, "we've got to come to a decision or there will be bloodshed. I'm asking all of you to give what you can, to sacrifice, to come together for the sake of the workers, the industry, the state.

"I want to tell you all that I will enforce the law. The workers have committed themselves to violence and I'm committed to stop it. There is no alternative. So if you fellows go to the wire without a decision, some people might die; certainly many will be injured."

There was a momentary lull in the rapid-fire conversation. Then the men continued wrangling about pay scales, fringe benefits, insurance plans. Now the hour had passed eleven o'clock.

I felt helpless, as if I were watching some giant herd of steers stampeding out of control toward us. Then I thought of the one great Mediator. As the men continued talking, I sat back and quietly prayed.

"Father, You know that somewhere between these men is fair agreement, satisfying both sides. Please sit in on this discussion, enter the hearts of the men around this table so they can reach that agreement tonight to avoid violence."

The talking went on. But as it continued I sensed something new in the atmosphere. The men seemed to be listening more to each other. One man's face relaxed momentarily as he said: "Well, maybe we can work *that* one out." As the hour hand crept toward midnight I continued praying inwardly.

A miracle seemed to be happening. The men slowly began to work their way through issue after issue. They did not agree on all areas and there was more negotiating to do. But there was enough of an agreement so that the plant could resume regular production, while details were ironed out.

I relayed the information to my adjutant general, and then looked at the clock: it was 11:50 P.M.

God, I felt, had in some way touched the hearts of the men at the table. I felt sure that without prayer—mine and probably thousands of others—the evening would have ended tragically.

Prayer was becoming more and more vital to me. Eva and I had much to be thankful for. Our first grandson, Jon, was born September 14, 1965. His mother, Connie, wrote us often and I would read and reread her letters in the evening. Later, I would find myself seeking the Lord in the living room of the mansion after everyone had gone to bed. I'd love to light a fire and listen to a symphony on the stereo as I let the tensions of the day drain away. I'd read the Bible, and then as the embers glowed, I would seek the Lord's guidance for problems of the morrow.

One night, after long meditation, a vision began forming in my mind. I was on top of a mountain in a crystal clear stream tumbling downward. I seemed to float with it to a seashore and then into a large bay. The water became murky and foul. Then it became a river again, a dark polluted river. I seemed to be in some eastern city and was given the impression that it was Washington, that it had a destiny for me.

I shook my head, and fastened my attention on the flames guttering in the fireplace. Washington wasn't on my mind. Something else was—another stormy problem, right at home. It was a problem that had been going on for some time between the state and an Old Order Amish community at Charity Flats in the northeastern part of Iowa.

These plain, simple people had been sending their fifty-three children to their own little schools. However, state officials had decided the children must attend public schools, particularly since they did not have state-accredited teachers. But when the big yellow community school bus groaned up to their houses, the little boys in black wide-brimmed hats and girls in long country dresses scattered and hid in the cornfields.

Bearded fathers, wanting their children taught in the old Amish traditions, went to jail and dutifully paid large fines with liens placed on their property. Finally in frustration, state officials entered one of the Amish schools to drag the students into busses, only to retreat in embarrassment before wailing children and mothers praying on their knees.

In November 1965, I recommended that we halt the battle and have a moratorium to see what could be done. Again, it meant walking right through the problem with a lot of prayer and back-and-forth communication. Finally it was resolved with a compromise. The Amish parents would keep their children in their own non-accredited schools but would employ state-certified teachers. A bill allowing this arrangement was passed in the next legislative session.

It was an exception. And there were many arguments against it. But as I told those protesting, it was sometimes wiser to bend laws rather than people.

Even so, people continued to be bent all over the nation. Despite the passage of the Civil Rights Act in 1965, a bitterness was growing everywhere. A riot occurred in the Watts district of Los Angeles. No one would have believed it could happen. The thought of thirty-four people killed in it stung my soul. And along with Martin Luther King I dreamed ever more earnestly of an America where black and white children would walk together as brothers and sisters.

Not only would I soon find myself facing racial problems in Iowa, but I would shortly walk through my own personal fire. It happened while I was in Yucatan, Mexico.

Yucatan officials had invited me because of our mutual interest in agricultural production and marketing. Their economy was based on producing sisal-fiber twine that Iowa farmers had consumed in tremendous quantities for baling hay. Not long before, however, a new synthetic fiber had replaced their sisal. And we wanted to work out some projects to use their natural fiber in different ways. We also wanted to develop some youth exchange programs and scholarships for Yucatan students at Iowa State University.

An old friend from Ida Grove, Dr. Norman Kinney, a veterinarian who was on our state's Conservation Commission, was one of those going with me. Yucatan livestock raisers wanted his advice on breeding and disease control. The trip was arranged to take place during the recess of the Iowa Legislature and I looked forward to it. The Yucatan official suggested some hunting in the jungle.

However, a week before I was to leave, Mother and Dad came up to visit us. Dad's little greenhouse business in Ida Grove was going well and being late winter, he felt he could leave it for a while. He had had an eye cataract removed in November, and was suffering from a lot of angina pain; I was worried about him. I noticed him wince as he hobbled out of the car at the mansion. However, we had a good visit, sitting around the supper table. We talked about the good time we had enjoyed when the whole family had assembled for Thanksgiving dinner a few months before at the mansion. Then I told Phyllis how we used to sing "Red Wing" in the old days. Dad, who was wearing a patch over one eye, lifted his head in interest at this and sang a few bars. I tried to sing along with him but had a lump in my throat.

I thought about calling off the Yucatan trip. But Dad's doctor in Iowa City urged me to go ahead.

"No one can know for certain on these things," he said. "Your dad could die tonight and he could live for ten years."

However, I thought it would be best if I had Dad checked in at the hospital for another exam. A limousine would take him to the University Hospital in Iowa City.

We said goodby that morning. Tears welled up in my eyes as the graying 74-year-old man stepped into the car. I wanted to put my arms around him and tell him how much I loved him. But at the time I felt it was not a manly thing to do.

I shook hands with him, and said, "I'll see you when I get back." As the car pulled away, he turned to the window and waved.

That afternoon we left for Yucatan. It is a peninsula state protruding from the lower end of Mexico into the Caribbean. Part of it is still in equatorial jungle and some days later I was in the dark rain forest hunting. To find game one must follow dim trails at night. On Saturday night an ancient Mayan Indian with leathered face was leading me down a trail through the thick bush. He spoke no English but somehow we communicated through that mutual love of God's creation that outdoorsmen seem to share. Even though I could not see the trees in the jungle night I could feel their overpowering majesty. The atmosphere was beautiful, thick with the scent of verdant greenery and calls of night animals sounding through the towering trees.

Suddenly, shortly after midnight, the jungle seemed to hush for a moment. It was then I sensed a powerful nearness of my father. It was almost as if he were walking beside me. I couldn't help thinking of the many times Dad and I had gone hunting and fishing together. How he would have loved to be with me now, I thought. That beautiful poignant presence of my father stayed with me all night.

By morning I found out why.

As we were preparing to move deeper into the jungle, a radio message came from Merida saying that Dad had passed away. I couldn't help noting the time he died: 12:15 A.M. It was the same time I felt his presence.

We called off the hunting trip and headed back to Merida where Pan Am would hold a plane for us to Miami. From there we flew to Iowa.

We buried Dad in a March snowstorm in the Ida Grove cemetery. Gray clouds scuttled against a pewter sky as our little band followed his casket up the hill. As white snow crystals settled on raw clods of earth at the grave, it all seemed to symbolize the starkness of our family's life. I looked at Mother, her frail body trembling in grief, eyes desolate as she stared at Dad's casket lying next to Jesse's grave. Years of trial and sadness had worn her down like the gullied hills around us.

"What is man that Thou art mindful of him . . . ?" Wayne Shoe-maker's words were almost lost in the sighing wind that whipped the undertaker's canvas canopy, twisting and tugging at the guy ropes.

I gripped Eva's hand, squeezing my eyes against the tears. I wanted to hold all of my family close to me. Life was so fragile, so unpredictable.

18

Moments to Remember or Forget

MY CORNER OFFICE in the Statehouse with its tall windows over-looking Des Moines was becoming a busy place. And not all the events came as crises or raging tempests. There were special moments of satisfaction that I shall always remember; most involved helping people.

One afternoon at four o'clock, Ruth Yauk, my secretary, came in with a puzzled look. "There's a lady with a real problem outside." She described a black girl, about twenty-one years of age, with three little children.

"What is it?" I asked.

"They've evicted her, put her furniture on the sidewalk. Her husband has left her. And she doesn't know what to do."

She smiled at me. "You've developed a reputation for helping people, Governor," she said, "and so they come here as a last resort."

I had one of our staff call the Salvation Army to make sure the mother had a place to stay and that her furniture wasn't stolen. But the incident got me thinking. So often people came to me because they didn't know where else to go, yet state help was often available. However, even if they could reach the proper department, they often weren't able to make themselves clear, or they got lost in red tape.

One morning I called Ruth in and told her I was starting a new program. Each Wednesday, beginning at 8:00 A.M., anyone who wanted to see me was welcome to come to my office.

"You mean announce it openly?" her face blanched.

"Sure," I laughed, "how else will people know about it?"

So we announced it once in the paper. The following Wednesday morning the reception room was wall to wall with people. The press was there, too, just to make sure I meant what I said.

"How are you going to handle them all?" asked Ruth.

"Easy," I said, showing her an egg timer I brought from home. "Each one gets five minutes."

So when a person came into my office, I would set the timer where he or she could see it. We never had any trouble. We did have every problem in creation brought to us, from relatives in prison and wives not being paid child support to people needing a job or medical help.

Usually I was able to pick up the phone, call the proper state commission and tell them I was sending a man or woman there with a problem they ought to be able to handle.

Every Wednesday thereafter I acted as sort of an ombudsman for people who couldn't find help otherwise.

And some didn't need help.

One man came in, sat down at my desk, and smiled.

"What's your problem?" I asked.

"Nothing," he said, "I just wanted to visit with you for five minutes."

"Well," I laughed, "put your feet up on the desk and let's talk."

I also learned that in trying to help others, you can be too permissive. There was the case of the prisoner who had escaped from Fort Madison prison. He had been serving a ten-year sentence, got on a road detail and simply walked off.

One day he wrote me a letter stating that since his escape he had married, had two children, and established a small business in Canada. He wanted permission to come back to Iowa to visit his elderly parents.

I sat at my desk holding the letter for some time. I knew the escape charge would add an additional five years to his sentence. Yet, here was a man who in full trust had written to me expecting help and compassion. It was my responsibility to try and get him back into prison; yet he indicated that he had repented for his wrongdoing and was restored.

What could I do?

That night in front of the fireplace, I told Eva about it, then threw the letter in the fire and said, "I'll just not reply. When he doesn't hear from me, he'll never come back to Iowa and that'll be the end of it."

The letter continued to haunt me and in time I realized how morally wrong my action had been. As governor, I had the responsibility of enforcing the law. "I should have him extradicted from Canada," I told Eva later. "With his good record, the man could have been pardoned and been free for the rest of his life. Now, he'll be living under the shadow of the law for the rest of his days."

Eva nodded. "I guess," she said, "by not facing it squarely, you could call that misplaced compassion."

Compassion. Sometimes it was difficult to know how and where. I faced this not long after Mother came to live with us following Dad's death. I thought that in the mansion Mother and Eva would get along well. However, Mother was strong-willed and domineering. She had her own ideas on how things should be done and though she thought she was being helpful, it naturally irked Eva.

"Pack," said Eva one night as we were preparing for bed, "I don't know how much longer I can stand it."

I put it out of my mind, hoping they'd find some way to get along.

One afternoon my secretary called me out of a staff meeting: "I'm sorry," she said, "but it's your wife and she says its urgent."

I picked up the phone to hear an anxious Eva say that my mother was prostrate on the floor. "We had some words, Harold," Eva said in a tremulous voice, "and now she's lying there and won't get up. Will you please come home right away?"

I groaned, but soon was in the limousine racing out Grand Avenue. Why, I wondered angrily, does my day have to stop because of this? I was irked with Eva. Couldn't she understand Mother was an older woman, set in her ways?

I sighed and leaned my head back on the seat. Out of my memory came a Bible passage: "For this cause" said Jesus, "shall a man leave his father and mother, and cleave to his wife; and they twain shall be one flesh."

Inside the house, I found Mother flat on the floor. She threw her arms around me, moaning, "Oh, Harold, my son. I have no one left. Dad and Jesse are gone and I'm all alone."

I picked up Mother and carried her into her bedroom. Pulling up a chair to her bed, I sat down. "Mother," I said, "Eva and I love you and we are happy to have you staying with us. But I have to tell you something."

She quieted down, and looked at me.

"You must understand that Eva is the head of this household when I am not here. If you ever force me to make a decision, it will have to be for my wife."

Mother turned her head to the wall and cried: "I have no reason to live anymore. I just want to die."

I put my hand on her quivering shoulder. "No, Mom, you don't want to die. But I want you to know that this is the only way we all can live happily together."

Mother then calmed down. From then on the household tension eased.

An unexpected and happy occurrence took place for Mother not long after that on a hot Sunday morning in July. The doorbell at the Mansion rang and Eva answered it to find a kind-faced, gray-haired man and woman standing there.

"How 'do," he smiled, "I'm Harold Everett Jones and this is my wife. We understand that Mrs. Lewis Hughes is living here. We're driving through town on our way west and thought we'd stop in to say 'Hello.' "

Eva came to me and gasped: "I can't believe it; it's *him*."

Mother and the man after whom she named me had a wonderful visit catching up on old times. This happened on her 75th birthday and she said she couldn't have had a finer present.

Harold Everett Jones was a high-school principal in Mount Clemens, Michigan. And we all kept in contact with him after that.

Whether at home or office, I continued to find myself involved in one-to-one relationships. Despite my Wednesday "open house" invitations, there were still those people who came unexpectedly at other times of the week. Ruth came to my desk one Friday to say: "There's a man who's been sitting in the outer office an hour now and hasn't even come up to my desk. He's wearing an old pair of overalls, needs a shave and looks like a bum. But I'm afraid to have the guards move him because he might be someone you know."

I laughed. "Thanks for the compliment. Can you find out his name?"

She returned in a minute: "He says he's Bud Jenkins and that he knows you."

Old Bud, I mused. I knew him well from Ida Grove. He had spent seventeen years in the army, was one of the best soldiers our country ever had. He had been wounded three times, earned the Silver Star and was commended twice for courage. After leaving the army he became a master carpenter. But booze had gotten him.

Ruth brought Bud in and we talked. He said he had no place to live and needed money.

"Well, Bud," I asked, "why don't you go to the Soldiers' Home in Marshalltown? You're at an age now where they'll take you. It's a comfortable place."

"No," he said, shaking his head, "I don't want that."

"Well, what are you going to do?"

"Pack," he leaned forward, his watery gray eyes pleading, "if you could loan me a little money for old times sake."

I was tempted to reach for my wallet. "No, Bud," I smiled. "You'll spend it on liquor. Let's face it; you're an alcoholic."

He straightened in his chair. "I am not an alcoholic!"

"Yes you are, Bud," I said. "Don't forget, it takes one to tell one." My heart cried for him. "Look," I pressed, "I'll make all the arrangements for you to get into the Soldiers' Home. They'll care for you the rest of your days."

He thought for a minute, scratching his head.

"You go get something to eat and think it over," I said, naming a nearby restaurant. "I'll call up the place and they'll be expecting you."

He returned in the afternoon, picking his teeth in satisfaction. "Well, Pack," he said, shifting the toothpick in his mouth, "I've thought it over. If you'll give me the money for a bus ticket, I'll go up to that Soldiers' Home in Marshalltown."

I knew immediately what he'd do with the bus money. Putting my hand on his bony shoulder, I said, "That's good to hear, Bud. I'll call up there and make the arrangements."

Then I got in touch with our highway patrol. The patrol captain came to my office and I took him aside. "This man is going to try and con you before you get to Marshalltown. Now if he even wants to go to the men's room, accompany him; don't let him out of your sight."

We finally got Bud into the Soldiers' Home and though he ran off a few times to get drunk, he always returned. He grew to like the place.

It was because of men like Bud Jenkins that I felt impelled to develop a state alcohol program. Though there had been an alcohol

210

THE MAN FROM IDA GROVE

commission which met periodically, had discussions and issued some press releases, nothing really effective was being done for the alcoholic. All an alcoholic could expect was to be committed to a state mental institution as an inebriate, as I had almost been.

In our new program we started training people to work closely with alcoholics, utilizing every medical and psychological tool. In reaching alcoholics directly where they lived and worked, we were often able to help them before they reached rock bottom. In addition, we sponsored Alcoholics Anonymous programs within state institutions.

I met one of the first men to be rehabilitated under this program. As I watched him walk away, shoulders straight, body firm and in control of himself, I wondered if this was one of the reasons why God had led me into politics.

More and more I found myself being led by Scripture in my work; there were passages applying to every problem. Two of them "Thou shalt not kill" and "Vengeance is mine . . . saith the Lord" guided me in my fight against the death penalty as I stressed that capital punishment defeats the ultimate will of God that every man is redeemable, whether he is a murderer, rapist or whatever.

Finally in 1965, legislation ending capital punishment in Iowa passed in the second session of the legislature. I asked that the shackles used in the executions be brought to my office, thinking they would serve as an effective reminder of an inhuman past.

They were delivered and placed on my desk. Leo Figura had been the last man to die in them. Thoughts of that memorable letter he wrote me filled my mind as I looked down at the heavy leather straps with steel bands that had shackled his arms behind him. Another set had gripped his ankles. They lay on my desk like hideous coils of dead snakes. When I touched them, I could almost smell an aroma of evil exuding from them. "Take them out of here," I said. They were delivered to the state historical museum.

Not long after that another evil object was placed on my desk. On the surface it was an innocent-looking plain white envelope delivered by a man who had come to discuss a legislative matter. There was something about the smug way he walked into my office that raised my hackles.

"Governor," he said, "there's a bill now in a senate committee that my business associates want to see reach the floor for debate. If it does, we feel sure it will pass and become law."

He named the bill. "It will be good for the state and for the people, but there is a problem in getting it out of committee.

I knew the bill. It was controversial. Though it was not one I had proposed, I was open to it. As yet I hadn't decided what I would do with it if it passed the legislature.

He sat there for a moment, studying me, then pointed to the envelope. "There's a key in there. If you will get the bill out of committee and onto the floor, the key is yours. It's to a locked box in a bank in Omaha. In the box is $50,000 in small bills." That was almost three times my annual salary.

I sat for a moment, anger and disgust rising in me. I stood up, trying to control my rage.

"Take that envelope and get out," I said levelly. "If I had a witness to this conversation I'd have you prosecuted."

His face whitened, he stood up and snatched the envelope.

"And I'll tell you one more thing," I said as he retreated from the room. "I wasn't opposed to that bill when you came in. But now I know there must be something wrong with it. I can assure you I'll study it quite thoroughly."

The bill never did get on the floor. It seemed innocuous enough on the surface, but on examination it was loaded with hidden elements not in the public interest.

Eventually I found myself getting casehardened to all the various ways that individuals and groups sought to influence a governor. I had my weaknesses, but taking bribes was not one of them. Yet I was still very much the naive midwesterner when it came to national politics—and dealing with presidents.

My relationship with Lyndon B. Johnson, for example, was becoming far different than during my early days as governor when my calls to the White House usually ended up on a presidential aide's desk. Whether it was because of our party's landslide election of 1964 or the generous treatment I was getting in the national press, I found myself growing closer and closer to the president.

This was highlighted when I went to a White House state dinner in 1965, concerned about the desperate need of Iowa farmers for increased support of corn prices and other products. I was to see the president afterwards, but the dinner was a lengthy one and many people stayed on to chat with him.

Finally, around midnight the room emptied and I was able to approach him. "I'm sorry, Mr. President, that we haven't had an opportunity to talk," I said, "but it's late and I'm sure you're tired. So I just wanted to say goodnight and thank you for a great evening."

Concern filled his face and he draped his big arm around my shoulder and said, "Why don't you come upstairs with me, Governor? It takes me a while to relax anyway before I go to sleep." So we walked to the small polished brass elevator, just off the state dining room, which lifted us to the second floor.

We walked into the president's huge bedroom which was furnished with a large plain bed, two heavy leather platform lounge chairs and some western paintings on the walls. I was impressed by the elaborate communications console at his bedside with several telephones which I knew gave him direct communication with our military and diplomatic posts around the world.

A stack of papers rested on the bedside table. He pointed to them. "They give me a briefing on the Vietnam situation every night." The morning newspaper had reported he was sending 20,000 more men to that area.

He waved me to one of the chairs. "Sit down, Governor, sit down," he urged. "We'll chat as I get ready for bed." Being a rancher, Lyndon Johnson enjoyed talking about cattle and hogs. As he talked, he punctuated his statements by tossing his tie, shirt, and trousers onto the back of a chair, then his shoes and socks under the bed.

In his underwear, he strode about the room, talking about the national farmers' organizations, Farm Bureau, Grange and Farmers Union, and their stands. Still gesticulating, he hesitated for a moment to extricate a lanky leg from his undershorts. Then throwing them into the growing heap of clothes on the chair, he continued talking, pacing back and forth across the room in the same condition as when he entered the world one cold Texas morning.

I tried to concentrate on agricultural price supports and marketing problems, but the humor of the scene was getting to me. Without missing a beat in the conversation, he climbed into bed, pulled the sheet up to his chin and leaning back on two pillows with hands behind his head, continued talking.

Suddenly, he decided to phone another governor. It was now 1:00 A.M. but oblivious to this fact, he had the White House operator get the man on the phone. After a sluggish start, the telephone conversation sputtered along for another ten minutes.

Then he hung up and we returned to the farm program. I started to rise, saying, "Well, Mr. President, I'm sure you're tired and . . ."

"No, no Governor," he pressed, waving me back to the chair. "It's just impossible to get those farm associations to agree on policies, principle, or need," he continued. "How am I supposed to pass a farm bill when they're fighting one another? I can end the war in Vietnam easier than to get them to agree on anything."

Finally, he signaled that we had exhausted the subject. As I was leaving the room, he leaned over to pick up the pile of briefing papers. It was nearly two o'clock.

I had no idea that the subject on which we touched so briefly—the Vietnam war—would soon not only begin to poison the spirit of our nation, but would also cause this homespun man I liked so well to turn on me in a blind rage.

19

Lightning on the Horizon

IN MY BOYHOOD when we'd sit on our front porch on a summer's evening, Dad would comment, "Storm's coming up."

I'd look up into the soft violet night and wonder how he could tell. Fireflies sparkled in the warm darkness and it seemed like a good time to sleep on the porch.

Later I'd catch a flicker of light on the southwest horizon and that night I'd be jolted awake by lightning exploding in cannonades and rain pounding the roof.

In 1965 another kind of lightning flickered on the horizon.

Of the men attending the National Governor's Conference in 1965, there was only one who voted against our country's Vietnam policy. He was Mark Hatfield, Governor of Oregon. Along with the other governors, I supported Lyndon Johnson's position and the buildup of American troops in Vietnam, believing there was light at the end of that jungle tunnel. Under our pressure, I felt that the Viet Cong could not continue and we'd reach a stabilized agreement and peace in the near future.

Yet, something nagged me. Hatfield, I knew, was a good governor, a highly moral man. Why was he fighting such odds?

In 1965, however, I was too engrossed in my own battles in Iowa to engage in any soul-searching about an Asian involvement which I honestly felt would limit the spread of Communism.

One of these domestic battles was reapportionment of our state's voting districts. From the day Iowa had joined the Union in 1846, the state had remained under the control of rural legislators despite the growth of large cities. Some said our state assembly represented cows and cornfields more than people.

Finally, we fought through a plan in my second term in which the entire state was redistricted. The new districts, based on population density, gave each voter fairer representation in his government. The result was a legislature more people-minded, more interested in the needs of the poor and those suffering other incapacities.

If I needed any reminder of the latter, I had only to think about my back. Not long past it had started paining me severely. Every time I moved it felt as if gravel were grating in my spine. After X-rays, the orthopedic surgeon at the University Hospital called me into his office.

"Looks as though you had some kind of back injury some years ago."

"Yes," I said, "I slipped on the ice when I ran a cream route."

"Well, you should have had surgery then," he said. "Your spine was injured and has been deteriorating. Now there is some calcium buildup."

He didn't recommend surgery; instead, I was given a special brace to wear. Every time I put it on I was reminded of those days in Ida Grove when I couldn't afford to take time off from work for proper treatment. Such memories helped spur our endeavors to improve state medical facilities and bring medical care within the reach of more people.

Another inheritance of my past brought me into state mental institutions to work with alcoholics. I was repelled by the filth and mistreatment of patients. We learned that such institutions couldn't pay adequate salaries and thus attracted employees unable to get jobs elsewhere, often resulting in cruel, brutal treatment. We also discovered patients who didn't belong in these institutions at all—retarded people, or children whose families simply didn't want them. These unfortunates didn't have anyone to fight their battles.

We also had to weed out the perverts and sadists, such as men with twisted sexual appetites counseling young boys in state institutions. When our police picked up a state psychologist in a Des Moines bar wearing women's clothing and high heels, I called in the director of the state health division.

"Well, what's so bad about that?" asked the director, blank-faced.

"My God," I retorted, slapping my forehead, "no wonder we have problems!"

As with all states, Iowa's problems with homosexuals in prisons were no different. We had aggressive men who built harems. Every new man entering prison was vied for by these gangs and the resulting fights ended with stabbings and small riots.

Finally, we had all homosexuals segregated into one cell block, which was against mental health concepts at the time. But there was no other way; we had to break up the gangs. When we felt we had the situation under control, we fed the homosexuals back into the inmate population. We kept close watch, letting them know that if they got out of line they would again be separated.

All of this wrought tension and sometimes when the pressure seemed about to swamp me, relief would come through gubernatorial problems of another sort.

One started with an emergency phone call to my office in the Statehouse. "It's your daughter, Connie," said my secretary. A tearful Connie was on the phone to say that my two-year-old granddaughter, Tracy, had locked herself in the bathroom. Connie had tried to tell Tracy how to turn the little knob on the inside of the door but Tracy couldn't figure it out.

"I tried to call Mother, but the phone was busy," wept Connie.

"Well, I'll call for some help," I said. "In the meantime keep Tracy occupied by pushing pictures under the door."

I called the fire department and a rescue crew was dispatched. Attracted by the commotion, Eddy McCarthy, a neighbor boy, volunteered to help. He climbed a ladder to the bathroom window, removed the screen and wriggled through. Tracy had been happily playing with the Christmas cards Connie had been pushing under the door.

The next morning's headlines were: *"Hughes Helps Liberate Child Trapped in Bathroom."*

And then there was my early morning caper with Mike, our Irish setter. It started when Eva had taken him out into the yard at the mansion. Hearing the call of the wild, he slipped his leash and ran away. Eva came into the house all upset. I threw on a smoking jacket over my pajamas and dashed out into the cold gray dawn.

About a block from the house I spotted Mike across a ballfield. He was happily chasing pigeons and treeing squirrels. I took off after him across the muddy field and lost my bedroom slippers. Mike saw me, turned his ruddy head and with tail flying galloped down the street.

By now I was exasperated. As I plodded after him, barefoot in my bathrobe, I saw a milkman and newspaper boy staring at me curiously. A car drove up alongside. It was Eva.

"Harold," she said, thrusting Mike's leash at me, "take this. I don't want people seeing you out on the street in your bathrobe without a leash in your hand."

Eva drove off and after another fruitless half hour combing alleys and bushes, and stepping in the evidence of Mike's emergency stop, I walked home muttering invectives about man's best friend. Phyllis had awakened by now. "Daddy, why don't you blow on your hunting horn to call the dog."

I was ready to do anything. Taking it off the shelf, I stepped to the back door and sounded off. As the echoes bounced off the houses, and lights winked on in them, Eva came up and scolded me. "What will the neighbors think?" she said. "You'll wake everybody!"

It may have had some effect, for now Mike suddenly swept past the back door, tongue flying, eyes exhilarant.

I had an idea. Mike loved bones. In the refrigerator, I found a ham bone, tied a string to it and laid it in the backyard. Holding the string's other end, I crouched inside the door awaiting Mike's next swoop, at which time I'd pull it in, luring him inside.

In a few minutes he galloped past again, completely disdaining my lure. Suddenly it dawned on me. If anyone saw the governor of Iowa trying to catch a dog with a ham bone on a string, there would be impeachment proceedings for sure.

We had a hurried breakfast with Phyllis weeping in her cereal. Then in twenty minutes there was a scratching at the door. It was the prodigal dog, exuberantly muddy.

I put him in the basement, muttering. Then, while rushing to dress to be at my office at eight, I banged my shin against a bedstead. Ten minutes later I limped into the office.

It was a morning of complete frustration, publicized in full detail when newspapers all over the world printed the story, with Mike getting the glory.

In the meantime, another dog lover was being sorely tried. President Lyndon Johnson was facing more and more protest demonstrations against the Vietnam War. Rumblings against his decision to become further involved in Southeast Asia were building, not just among college youths, but men in his own party.

When Senator Robert Kennedy criticized the President's handling of the Southeast Asia situation, I quickly spoke up. "I'd support the Vietnam position taken by any president, be he Democrat or Republican," I emphasized to reporters, adding that such statements as Senator Kennedy's "dishearten our soldiers."

When I was about to begin a three-week mission to Europe with over one hundred business and agricultural leaders to develop foreign markets for Iowa products, Lyndon Johnson invited us to stop at the White House on our way. He was his usual folksy self, praising Iowa farmers for developing a special variety of corn used successfully in our Southeast Asia foreign aid program.

Then he looked at me and winked: "Keep an eye on Governor Hughes here. He likes to get up early in the morning and jog in his bathrobe. I'm afraid some foreign dog will do him in if you all don't protect him."

We all had a good laugh and I thought again how much I liked this tall genial Texan.

Later that summer, Lyndon Johnson flew to Minneapolis to address the National Governor's Conference; afterwards, he asked some of us to accompany him back to the capital to discuss the Vietnam situation. As a result, ten of us, going to Japan on an exchange visit in the fall, agreed to include in our itinerary an on-site inspection of Vietnam.

As I leaned my head back in the cushioned seat while the giant jet soared across the Pacific, I thought about the side trip I would be making in Japan to Kofu, the sister city of Des Moines. Kofu is the capital of Yamanashi, Iowa's sister state.

Our relationship had started in 1959 when a typhoon had destroyed much of the area. Iowans had sent thirty-six breeding hogs and fifteen hundred tons of corn to help Yamanashi agriculture get back on its feet.

After we landed in Tokyo, I left the other governors for the two-hour train trip to Kofu. Arriving at the station, I found myself amid a sea of little children waving American and Japanese flags. Some five thousand people were there for a tumultuous welcome.

I toured the farms, including the hog barns which are enhanced with fresh flowers in vases every day. "For the benefit of the hogs," said my Japanese guide. When he pointed to thousands of swine and said, "From Iowa," I remembered the Japanese friendship bell recently installed on our Statehouse grounds and thought how some twenty-odd years before we were deadly enemies. I glanced at my guide and estimated him to be my age. If I had been sent to the South Pacific, we could have killed each other.

What is it, I wondered, that makes people feel they have a God-given right to eliminate each other and then, a few years later, express their love?

The question resounded in Nagasaki.

It was a gray day and a cool sea-sharpened breeze swept in from the bay as I stood beside the giant Peace statue marking the explosion center of the second and last atomic bomb set off in anger.

The beautiful, modern city extending around me seemed oddly out of place in this ancient land of old structures. Then I realized something: the old Nagasaki had ceased to exist that summer day, August 9th, 1945, when seventy-five thousand people were instantly obliterated by an atomic bomb.

I looked up at the huge stone man sitting above me, his finger pointing to the sky where the explosion had occurred. And I felt tears running down my cheeks in the cold wind.

For the first time, I found myself questioning what we had done as a people in unleasing nuclear fission on the world. Would mankind ever have used it, if we had not? On the other hand, perhaps mankind, on seeing its awesome destruction, would never use it again.

Questions plagued me as the wind from the bay became cooler and I drew my coat around me. Couldn't we have just dropped it on the ocean or a military island to demonstrate its power instead of wiping out two cities? I realized that, at the time, our leaders did what they felt best. No one really knows what went through the minds of those making the decision.

I turned away from the silent statue and walked toward the waiting car. The city had assigned two plainclothes detectives to accompany us. I wondered if this was because of latent bitterness on the part of the people. If so, I could fully understand it.

Before stepping into the car, I turned back to the statue. The sky was darkening. The impassive stone giant sat in the dusk, arm raised, finger pointing to the sky. No, I would not forget.

We left Japan for Hong Kong where military aircraft flew us to Saigon. I donned G.I. fatigues and combat boots, feeling strangely at home in them, and then visited various battlefronts via helicopter.

I asked to see Iowa men everywhere I went. As I listened to youthful prairie accents and looked into fresh faces, my heart wrenched. Many of the boys, it seemed, should have been in a 4-H group, rather than facing death in the jungles. We talked about home and had our photographs taken together, which I promised to send to their parents.

A lot of the men expressed resentment at the anti-war demonstrations they'd heard about at home.

"The demonstrations have been blown up all out of proportion," I assured a group of Iowans at Cam Ranh Bay. "One staged against the war effort was a miserable failure in Des Moines," I added, stating that "the folks back home are 99 percent behind you."

We continued on, being shown what we were meant to see. I was struck by how the wounded were treated in this new war. Helicopters airlifted men directly from battle to the base hospital, where they were operated on immediately. It was a wholly different war than the one I had seen in 1944, where one was fortunate if just one first-aid man was nearby.

Men who would have died in my war now lived. Yet, because of this very reason, so many were returning home terribly crippled. I ached inside for the young Iowans standing before me as I told them: "Believe me, men, you are fighting on the front line of democracy. If the aggressor is not stopped here, we might well have to face him at home in the years to come. The Mississippi River could well be the front some day."

As I stood before these earnest young men, a vision of the stone man at Nagasaki hovered before me. And a new thought entered my mind. Do American soldiers really belong in this far eastern land? I shook it off.

But later when I sat at the bedside of the young soldier from Sioux City, I could not bring myself to talk about our commitment in Vietnam or the domino theory. Instead, we talked about hunting, while I had to avert my eyes from the flat sheets where his legs had been.

A gnawing ache grew within me as we continued our trip. It was intensified one afternoon in a helicopter taking Governors Phil Hoff of Vermont, Tim Babcock of Montana and me to the Vinh Long Province in the Mekong Delta area to visit some Vietnamese schools.

"Don't worry," said the young sergeant, helping us inside the olive-drab chopper, "there are steel plates under your seats in case of enemy fire."

But what about the rest of me? I wondered.

As we roared along, I mused at the verdant green jungle slipping by below. Suddenly, a ,U.S. fighter jet flashed past, diving at a grove of trees. I exclaimed at it and our pilot called back from the cockpit that it was an aerial strike.

Two more jets swept past wing to wing, and converged on the target, firing rockets. I began to wonder about the thickness of the armor plate below us and couldn't help thinking of the little metal-covered Bible my mother had given me twenty-three years before.

Less than a generation ago, I thought. It was true. No generation of our country has ever been without a war. I wondered about Jon my grandson and prayed that his would be the first generation to break the pattern.

The frenetic pace of our trip continued and the next day a group of us was flown to the U.S. aircraft carrier *Ticonderoga*. Our Navy plane landed with a neck-snapping jolt as the arresting cable on the carrier's deck caught the plane's hook. Then we watched fighter planes shot by catapult from the deck in dizzying succession. Later the fighters returned, with empty bomb bays and near-dry fuel tanks, impatiently circling to land. I squirmed with each plane as it kissed the carrier's deck, some missing the cables and roaring off to try again.

A sense of urgency seemed to fill everyone on the ship and I wondered how the pilots could maintain their equilibrium day in and day out. One of them, Jim Hise, a young naval lieutenant from Des Moines, was assigned as my aide during the visit. I mentioned the aerial strike I had seen from the helicopter and his eyes widened.

"I was one of the pilots!" he exclaimed. He told how they had held off the attack for a moment until our chopper was out of danger.

My sorrow for him and all the military men I had met grew daily. Vietnam was a combat zone in toto; one day's safe road was mined the next and one never knew where an enemy attack might be launched. At that time, there was little dissension in the forces. The narcotic epidemic hadn't yet started and everyone seemed to feel he was there for a purpose.

Supporting this general feeling of rightness were briefings given us by General Westmoreland and defense intelligence, plus the receptions by the military and meetings in which we were indoctrinated into the Vietnamization process. And yet, somehow, I sensed a dangerous lightning on the horizon as if we were poised on the threshold of something no American could yet imagine.

The feeling of unease grew within me on our way home. The

presidential plane landed on a large island for another briefing. There I learned the field was a staging area for B-52 bombers. Until that moment I had not been aware that we were launching raids by those giant ships from that distance.

As our homeward jet thundered through the night, a disturbing kaleidoscope of scenes filled my mind: Japanese men, women and children welcoming us in love, pictures of charred corpses at the Nagasaki museum, the bodies of American boys stacked in rubber bags at collection stations.

I could not sleep, and moved forward in the cabin where I found a young State Department official who had accompanied us. I sat down in a cushioned armchair across from him and said I had something on my mind. He was polite and willing to listen.

"Why don't we sponsor a world governors' conference?" I suggested. It would be one in which we could bring men at that level together from all over the world, where we could get to know each other and discover that we all share the same hopes and aspirations.

Out of these men would arise the leaders of nations, I said. And whether they surfaced as presidents or dictators, at least we would know each other and have an ability to communicate on a personal level. There was certainly no communication of any sort then between the leaders of North and South Vietnam.

The young State Department man nodded and agreed that it was a good suggestion. Other men joined the conversation and they, too, liked the idea. However, as dawn brightened the wings outside the cabin ports, our thoughts turned to home and the problems waiting for us on polished mahogany desks in Statehouses across the country.

20

The Wrath of a President

EARLY 1966 FOUND me wondering about running for a third term as governor. No Democratic governor had ever been elected to a third term in the history of Iowa. I wondered if I shouldn't step down, though, especially since many advisors were suggesting that I try for the United States Senate.

One morning at the breakfast table, Eva read an item from the newspaper: "There are indications that the Johnson administration in Washington would like to see Governor Harold Hughes run for the U.S. Senate in 1966. Hughes rates well with the president."

Eva looked up from the paper and nodded to me. "However, some state officials," she continued reading, "would rather see Hughes, a potent vote-getter in 1964, run for a third term as governor. Hughes has not yet made up his mind what to do."

I laughed. "I can only agree with that last sentence."

As weeks went on I felt considerable pressure to make an announcement one way or another.

"A number of people are waiting to see what you do before announcing their own plans," an aide argued. Many in my party wanted me to run for governor again.

Finally, one Saturday afternoon at a crowded press conference in the Statehouse office, I announced my decision to run for a third term.

"There are still jobs to be done, programs we want to see reach fruition," I said. One of the big issues facing me was taxes. In particular, they loomed as a campaign hurdle. For we had a $100 million treasury surplus that year. Iowa legislators either had to appropriate it for state improvements or refund it to citizens by reducing taxes. The latter was a sure vote-getter. However, the money offered a more far-reaching opportunity and we battled to keep the $100 million for state needs ranging from public education to homes for the elderly.

There were other signs that it was not going to be an easy campaign. By then there was a growing discouragement throughout the country over Vietnam. Conflicting reports on the war from the president and some of his cabinet were eroding confidence in the administration. The president was giving little support to gubernatorial and congressional candidates. And by mid-October, most of us started to see the ground give way under our feet.

I faced a strong opponent in Bill Murray, the distinguished professor at Iowa State University with whom I had shared the speaking platform that hot summer afternoon in Rock Rapids eight years before. This tall gray-haired man and I had become friends through the years. However, I was convinced that he was wrong in his economic projections for the state and attacked them vigorously. When the returns of the November election came in, I had won.

However, the national returns reflected the voting public's growing dissatisfaction with the Johnson regime. The Democratic party was hurt all over the nation, losing legislative and gubernatorial seats everywhere.

Neither was it a Democratic landslide in Iowa. Though my victory margin was a substantial 100,000 votes, it was much less than my previous election. Moreover, we lost half of the state offices to Republicans, including control of the House of Representatives. We barely managed to hold on to the Senate.

Further comeuppance followed the election. After getting into the budgeting process, I discovered that Bill Murray had been right in his economic projections. I learned that he was getting better economic information from his university than I was out of my own state government. As a result we decided to start double-checking state projections on revenues and economic trends with the university.

But something deeper than Democratic election losses around the country was bothering me. Even though I had been called to Washington several times for briefings on the Vietnam War with Dean Rusk and Robert McNamara, I found myself becoming more and more concerned about the money and men we were sending to Vietnam. Particularly, the casualties.

As chairman of the National Democratic Governor's Conference, I was being increasingly called on to defend the president's policies. Each time this happened I found myself with a lot of questions of my own. Privately, I wondered why he pledged no build-up of American troops before the 1964 election, and then after he won reversed this decision.

Questions seemed to be on everyone's mind and in the winter following the election we decided to hold a National Democratic Governor's Conference on December 18th at the Greenbrier Hotel in White Sulphur Springs, West Virginia. It would be strictly a "work only" conference with no social functions, or wives attending. It would also provide an outlet for a number of suffering Democratic governors to vent their feelings about an administration they felt was responsible for the election debacle.

In view of this, I stopped off at Washington on my way to White Sulphur Springs to apprise the president of the climate. His appointment secretary said I could have fifteen minutes. But when I walked into his office, I never had the chance to give my message. Instead, an agitated president paced the oval office for over an hour, raging about the war in Vietnam, talking about "my tanks, my airplanes, my bombings."

When I left, I wondered if Lyndon Johnson had begun to lose touch with reality.

At White Sulphur Springs on the night of December 18th, some twenty Democratic governors sat down around a large oval table in a closed-door session. There was a dark mood in the room. We decided to go around the table and give everyone five minutes to express his opinion on what went wrong with the election.

To the last man every one said the same thing. It was the fault of the president, Secretary of Agriculture Orville Freeman, and just about everyone else in the administration that we lost so many races. They pointed to certain statements made from the White House which were later denied. It became an emotional outpouring with governors unloading complaints, from not being permitted to take adequate part in federal-state affairs to Lyndon Johnson displaying to press photographers his operation scar.

As we neared the end of the meeting, I knew that reporters were waiting outside the door. "What do you want me to tell the press?" I asked.

"Tell them the truth," one governor said. Others echoed agreement.

"You mean you want me to tell them that Democrats took a

severe setback across the nation because of the ineptness of the president of the United States, the secretary of agriculture, and other people in the administration?"

"Yes, that's what we mean."

"Well," I said, somewhat dumbfounded, "I want a show of hands to see how many of you really mean this."

Every man's hand shot up.

"All right," I said. We adjourned the meeting. And as the governors hurried out of the smoke-filled room, dodging reporters with "No comment" and "Talk to the chairman," the press flooded in.

I gave them the consensus as cameras flashed, then went upstairs and wearily climbed into bed.

The news went out like a blast from hell.

An hour later the phone rang. "What the hell do you mean it was my fault we lost the election?"

"Well, Mr. President, I'm just reporting what the men felt. They asked me to tell the truth."

The next morning I got a call from an old Iowa friend, then a legislative assistant to the president.

"I'm going to resign," he moaned.

"Why?"

"My God, the man who recommended me for this job has come out in total opposition to the president. How do you expect me to stay in the White House?"

I tried to assure him everything would be all right. Then knowing how close John Connally, governor of Texas, was to the president, I called his room at the Greenbrier. He asked me to join him in his suite for breakfast.

As the room-service waiter set steaming cups of coffee before us, I said: "I guess the president is really going to hate me for this."

John slowly stirred his coffee, then looked at me: "No, I don't think so. If there's one thing the president admires, it's guts." He lifted his coffee, sipped it, and put it down and smiled at me. "Don't worry; he'll cool off in a few days."

John was wrong. My blunt report to the press backfired like a defective 4th of July skyrocket.

Word began filtering back that some of the men so stalwart in their opinions the night before, were now backing down. One man told reporters that I had spoken only for myself, not for the Democratic caucus. Others watered down their comments and some absolutely refused to discuss anything. On top of that several governors who hadn't been at the meeting the night before flew in to the conference the next day and the press landed on them at the airport. Outside of one man, Warren Hearnes, governor of Missouri, they repudiated everything I had said, or avoided comment.

.This is politics. Many were afraid of possible action taken against them by a president ultra-sensitive to criticism. Some had local government projects they didn't want to see torpedoed. I could understand this.

That night at a gathering, some of the governors and I were standing around a table of refreshments. "Well," said one, spearing an hors d'oeuvre, "nobody could accuse you of being diplomatic." He popped the stuffed olive in his mouth and grinned. "By God, I've always heard you were candid, honest and blunt—and all three adjectives fit!"

As I was going to my room, another governor stopped me in the hall, clapped me on the back and laughed: "Well, you and your wife can count on never being invited back to the White House as long as Lyndon Johnson is president."

He was right.

However, Lyndon Johnson did ask me and other governors to meet him at his Texas ranch early in January 1967. Few governors were eager to face him but finally twelve of us agreed to go.

We flew into Austin where a smaller plane took us on to a landing strip at the ranch. As we flew over the sparse, windblown country, I could see how much this man related to the lean and rugged land.

I thought about the Texan whom I had admired more than any other president since Franklin Roosevelt. I admired his courageous leadership in civil rights, his compassion for people in his war on poverty, his concern for the elderly, the sick, the street kids who would never have an opportunity otherwise. I felt a deep kinship with Lyndon Johnson. And I felt terribly torn inside. For I knew that in his eyes I had become an enemy.

The limousine pulled up before a large and unpretentious frame house. An amiable Lyndon Johnson, in shirtsleeves and Stetson hat, greeted us. We twelve governors, feeling somewhat awkward in our business suits, walked into the expansive living room where he waved us to chairs. He then sat down in a huge black leather chair which dominated the room like a throne.

"All right, men," he said, "let's hear what you want to say."

Again, I found myself the spokesman of the group.

"Well, Mr. President," I said, my throat tightening, "all I can do is repeat that we feel the reverses in the election happened because of the ineptness of a few men in your administration. There were some press statements made which were untrue, and later denied by you. But the press later proved that the plans as reported had been laid by your people, apparently with your approval."

I wiped my brow. "Frankly, Mr. President, the last four weeks of the campaign were like quicksand for us. I personally was losing ground so fast I was scared to death, not because of local conditions in Iowa but because of what was coming out of Washington."

The president sat there looking very calm. Then, like the school teacher he once was, he went around the room, pointing his finger at each governor, giving them their say.

When every man had spoken, he retained his calmness, denied much of what we said, adding that any misstatements had not been planned or that anything else was done intentionally.

We then broke for lunch and as the men began to gather in the dining room, the president took me by the arm and led me into his bedroom. It is strange what one notices in moments like this. I couldn't help thinking how plain his quarters were, not at all what one would associate with a man as wealthy and powerful as he.

He stopped and faced me, his eyes blazing, and proceeded to tell me that I had hurt the party and the president of the United States by washing dirty linen in public. He advanced on me, jabbing my chest with a large forefinger, "You had damn well better back off before you get yourself in a pot of trouble."

Fury filled me as he continued to hammer my chest. I wanted to haul back and punch him in the jaw.

"Mr. President," I said, struggling to stay calm, "I'm sorry you feel that way, but I'm not going to change what I said. I told the truth and if that's wrong, then it's wrong."

A call for lunch broke the tension and we joined the others in the dining room, where there was a stack of ten beautiful western paintings by a famous Texas artist whom Johnson and Connally had commissioned. They had cost several thousand dollars each.

Placing them against the wall around the dining room, the president asked our opinions on them. It was a pleasant relief from the morning. And we governors joked with each other as to which of us had first choice.

"Who gets first choice?" asked the president, turning to Connally. "You do," he said, "you're the president."

"No," said Johnson, somewhat bashfully. "You go ahead, John." Finally they agreed to flip a coin for the privilege.

I sat bemused by two men flipping a coin for paintings worth thousands of dollars when I couldn't afford to buy a corner of one of them.

That afternoon the president put on a business suit and he and I went to the landing strip hangar where we appeared before the press corps who had been waiting anxiously since morning for some statement.

As spokesman for the governors, I explained that we had made peace and expressed strong support for the administration. Though I could not bring myself to withdraw my statement made at White Sulphur Springs, I pointed out that we all had agreed to be together for a common purpose.

The painting which was everyone's first choice at the luncheon that day was a plains scene of a violent storm gathering over the distant mountains. The colors were dark, somber and threatening. Down from the foothills trailing a small herd of cattle, rode a little band of weary riders hunched on tired horses, heads down against the rising wind. Lightning streaked across the mountains and the storm was almost upon them.

In a sense it was prophetic of what lay ahead for all of us.

21

The Least of These

BY MID-1967 THE Vietnam War had escalated to frightening dimensions. The number of our troops there had expanded to 500,000 American men. Almost half of our combat-ready divisions and our airpower, plus a good part of our naval forces, were committed.

I was concerned about the intense bombings, the free-fire zone in which everything living in the area was killed, the defoliation of forests in which villages, human beings and animals were incinerated.

From reliable sources I began to learn that there were often differences between what actually happened and what was reported in military news.

Corruption seemed to be spreading throughout the South Vietnamese government. No longer did our involvement seem to be an honorable fight for democracy. More, it appeared to become a fetish of pride on the part of our national leaders who couldn't seem to admit that somewhere, something had gone wrong.

Of deep hurt to me were the increasing number of young Iowans coming home in military caskets. Over how many graves had the words been said: "Greater love hath no man than this, that a man lay down his life for his friends"? (John 15:13) Was it right, I wondered, that older men in frustration fought each other with the lives of youths?

Much of my evening prayer time was spent thinking on the war and Christ's admonition to love one's enemy. Could there ever be, I wondered, a just war?

Simultaneously with the mounting pressure overseas, was the increasing tension at home. Storm clouds, brewing for years, had

reached a head. Millions of people, sweltering in congested tene-
ments, and suffering from unemployment, built up pressures that exploded again and again, with bloody riots in Newark, Detroit and
other cities.

As I watched television news showing buildings burning, I found
myself thinking that Iowans had been spared because we had a small
percentage of minority groups and our few slums were concentrated
in a small number of cities.

Yet, as I sat at my desk in the Statehouse one afternoon, I thought
about the poverty areas in our own state that could not be ignored.
I stood up and walked to the tall windows of my office. Glancing
down I could see my limousine parked in the driveway. My eyes
swept across the broad green lawns surrounding the capitol and then
they hit the Southeast Bottoms.

Decaying buildings, some leaning crazily, were scattered across a
dreary landscape of debris-strewn streets and railroad tracks. People
of all races lived there, sharing the same poverty. I knew that there
were outhouses in the yards, as the area didn't have sewers.

As I stood at the window, I pictured a man heading across his
backyard toward the outhouse, looking up at the gold-domed Statehouse and thinking about the man sitting in the governor's chair
who rode around in a big Lincoln.

I started to turn from the window. A governor cannot put in
sewers. This was up to commissions and referendums. But something beyond that window had caught me. I felt I had to go to the
Southeast Bottoms and talk to that man who used the outhouse,
meet his family and neighbors, and hear what they had to say.

"How can we get into that area without dragging news reporters
and television cameras with us?" I asked my staff. "Otherwise it
will be just another political show."

A young woman federal worker was able to arrange the meeting
with some of the local Bottoms people. Thus, one hot summer night,
two staff men—Ed Campbell and Bill Hedlund—and I drove down
to the house where the meeting would be.

Broken glass crunched under the car tires as we moved past men
in undershirts slumped on doorsteps, and vacant-eyed women leaning
on window sills.

Dogs barked everywhere; I wondered how the poor seemed to
have so many more dogs than the affluent. Maybe it was because
they needed the company, I thought.

We walked into the house where the only room in which we could meet was the bedroom. I sat down on an old sagging steel-frame bed. The window was wide open, though no breeze ruffled the thin curtain. One glaring light bulb hanging from a ceiling cord added to the heat, already compounded by the dozen hot and perspiring bodies in the room. I could feel the sweat running down my legs.

But we talked. Representatives of the local people, black and white, explained their problems and what they were trying to accomplish.

They stood in the hall, quietly waiting. Each person had a specific problem in mind. One would talk about the lack of medical and dental care, and the inability to pay for it; another about the prevalence of hepatitis because of poor plumbing and sewage; another about the high crime and accident rate because of insufficient street lighting.

As the night wore on I shifted from the bed to a chair. My back was killing me, my trousers and shirt were soaked with perspiration. Finally, as the last person left, I looked at my watch; it was 2:00 A.M.

We held similar meetings in other cities around the state. The result was implementing a number of neighborhood improvement programs to remedy the problems.

I returned to the Southeast Bottoms some time later to dedicate a medical clinic which was opened in an abandoned theatre. The credit for it belonged to the compassionate staff of a school of osteopathic medicine in Des Moines.

But helping rehabilitate slums wasn't the only answer. The people needed jobs, particularly the youth when summer came. Out of school, these teenagers had nowhere to go but the streets where they drifted aimlessly, often getting into trouble.

However, again this was a problem confined to the larger cities. And some advised that getting involved in a minority issue like this wasn't politically expedient.

Most Iowans did live under fairly good conditions and suffered no discrimination. But didn't this mean we had an even greater responsibility for those who suffered?

To start the ball rolling, I called my old friends Wayne Shoemaker and Russell Wilson who were now administrators to Bishop Thomas, Methodist Bishop of Iowa. Imbued with the idea of helping the youngsters, Bishop Thomas contacted other churches, including the Catholic Diocese, plus the Rabbinical Council, and arranged a meeting in his office to see what could be done. We also contacted the business and industrial community.

The response was surprising. To alleviate summer idleness, the religious leaders opened their church camps and school facilities to kids who had never had a chance to attend before. Their playgrounds, basketball and tennis courts, maintained under proper supervision, were also thrown open to children who previously could only play in streets and bottle-strewn lots.

The country clubs joined in, making their pools available, with some even giving the kids swimming and diving instructions.

But the most critical problem—work for the thousands of teenagers —needed help from the business community, and this would cost money, lots of it. Several business leaders with whom I had become close agreed to help. One was Joe Rosenfield, a finance manager for two of my campaigns, and there was Bill Knapp, the large real estate developer.

The industrial and business community of the greater Des Moines area was invited to a special luncheon where we pointed up the need of youngsters on the streets who had no way to keep busy, no recreation, and no money to buy clothing for school. The men reached for their corporate checkbooks. And in donations averaging $1,000 each, we built a kitty that afternoon that reached $275,000.

When the work started, we faced more questions. Who was going to screen the kids? What about insurance coverage? How would they be transported to their work site? The firms loaned their own experts in insurance, employee relations, and transportation to iron out these problems. Since many youngsters were under eighteen, we also had to go to the federal government for special exemptions to bypass youth labor laws.

Through this program we also got the state, city and county to employ as many as they could. The program was so successful we expanded it to six major cities, and eventually hundreds of young people in all these cities did find jobs.

To cut bureaucratic red tape, we would go directly into cities with a task force of some twelve to twenty state experts and set up shop for a day. We'd locate in an auditorium, armory or city hall where people could come for firsthand assistance and information on jobs and other services. In addition, job fairs were held where we brought together businesses who had jobs and the unemployed who could fill them.

The high school dropouts particularly concerned us. John Ropes, who had developed a program to alleviate this problem, was the Republican whom I had defeated in my commerce commission race in 1958. However, I had known his excellent qualities and later hired him to run our State Manpower Commission. His plan for dropouts was compassionate and effective. If a student left school before graduation, we'd write him or her a letter offering help through vocational or technical training, and include a return post-paid postcard on which he could check his interests or needs. Then he would be contacted by state employment people with help. Often through counseling the youth would return to school.

There were many special needs which this survey revealed. Of particular concern to us was the girl who dropped out because of pregnancy. A typical case was Laura B., a blond fifteen-year-old high school sophomore from a farm family. She had her child and then gave it up for adoption. But she never returned to school. Our caseworker found that her parents, deeply hurt, had turned their backs on her. The school wouldn't allow her to return. And so Laura planned to go to Chicago to "find work." The caseworker counseled with her parents, the school authorities and Laura. Forgiven by her parents and assured of support by the school, she returned to classes, graduated and later married.

Time and again we were able to save girls in similar straits.

In much of this work with the disadvantaged, we were often criticized for advocating reverse discrimination. This really tore me, as it was illegal to discriminate in any way. In response, I had to point out that some reverse discrimination was in order to balance the ledger because it was obvious that over a period of years many people had not been hired because of their race.

But I was used to criticism by then. I realized that it was inevitable and, in a sense, welcomed it. For I had come to the belief that if I wasn't criticized, it was a sign I was not accomplishing much of anything.

So much needed to be done for the underpriviliged and such a great portion of our resources was being misused. The tremendous amount of manpower and money expended in Southeast Asia made me more and more convinced that our role in Vietnam was wrong.

I thought of our Lord's words: "As you did it to one of the least of these my brethren, you did it to me" (Matthew 25:40, RSV).

Were we as a country effectively helping "the least of these"?

22

Should I Run
For the Senate?

FOURTEEN MONTHS before my term expired as governor I faced a crisis of decision. Though there was no law against my running for a fourth term, no Iowa governor had as yet served more than three. And I wanted to quit as a winner. But the alternatives left me confused.

One hot Iowa night I came home tired and depressed. I had prayed for an answer to my future and lightning had not struck. Eva took my hand and we went into the kitchen for a bedtime snack. "Any new job offers?" she asked.

"Not today," I said, tossing my tie over a chair. "I'm still thinking about the old ones."

Several friends who were owners of major league baseball clubs asked if I would let them place my name in consideration for baseball commissioner. I said no, I didn't think I was qualified. But it started me thinking. Another offer was from a large firm with international interests. They were attracted by my experience in taking trade missions overseas to help build an industrial base for Iowa manufacturers. One dollar in every ten of our Iowa economy was an export dollar now.

"The business job would mean a lot of travel for you, wouldn't it?" Eva asked in a worried tone.

"Sure would," I said unbuttoning my shirt collar. I looked at her as she sipped her coffee and my heart melted.

"No," I smiled, reaching for her hand. "I've decided not to accept it." Her face brightened.

"In the first place," I explained, "they wanted me to leave the

235

governorship six months before my term was up. But, more important, I'm sick of being separated from you and Phyllis."

As we went upstairs to bed, I thought about the third reason. I
couldn't put it into words. But it had to do with that deep sense of
spiritual purpose which I had felt since a child. What was it? Where
was it calling me? All I knew for sure was that it had nothing to do
with any job in industry.

I turned to Eva, suddenly feeling exhausted. "I've been running
for ten years now, Honey, and I'm tired."

She put her arms around me. "That's why I worry when I hear
people talk about your running for senator."

"Yeah," I chuckled, "but that's one job you don't have to worry
about, Hon." I knew we both wanted to stay in Iowa.

"In the first place, Democrats haven't been very successful in
winning senate seats in Iowa," I said. "Look at Loveless and how
he lost. In the second place, after helping to put that tax bill through,
I don't think I could even bank on making it to the commerce commission now."

I gave Eva a playful push. "So you see—you won't have to join
that Washington drawing room crowd."

Late into the night, I lay awake wondering. What am I supposed
to do, Lord?

A few months later I had a visit from John McCormally, an old
friend and editor of the Burlington *Hawk Eye*. When he sat down I
saw pain flash across his face. A former Marine Sergeant, John
carried shrapnel wounds from World War II in his arms and shoulders. He pushed back a lock of graying hair, looked at me with
piercing blue eyes and said: "Well, Governor, I'm glad to see you've
caught up with the rest of us on the issue of Vietnam."

John had been against the war and expressing this viewpoint in
his paper for some time.

I grimaced. "Yes, and I think I lost a good friend in Washington
over it."

He leaned back and laughed. "I'll say you did!" He told about
attending an American Society of Newspaper Editors meeting in
Washington, D.C., during which he was invited to the White House
to visit with Lyndon Johnson. The president, knowing John was from
Iowa, asked him how the governor was doing.

"I told him I thought you were a good governor," said John, "and you know what he said?"

"I can guess."

John laughed and slapped his knee. "He narrowed those green eyes, poked me in the chest and snapped: 'As far as I'm concerned, he's a sonofabitch!' "

I spread my hands and smiled lamely: "The president wants everyone to agree with him. I don't. So what can I do?"

John leaned forward and said: "I'll tell you what *you* can do. You can run for the senate."

I shook my head. "No, John, I've been through enough battles. When this term is up, I'm retiring."

"From politics?"

"Yep. I don't know to what, but I've had about all I can take, old friend. I'm sure I'll find something. Besides," I smiled, "I want to stay in Iowa; I don't want to go to Washington and join that lace-pants crowd."

"But you're needed there."

We talked about Lyndon Johnson and how we agreed that he seemed defeated by the Vietnam War. "Somebody has to run against him in the next election," said John.

I glanced sharply at him. "Who can beat him?" I stared out the window for a moment, and then turned back to John, answering my own question: "Bobby Kennedy, that's who; he's the only one who has any kind of chance."

I had first met Bobby Kennedy in 1962. I hadn't liked the intense young man at the time. I thought he was too aggressive, too much a hatchet man for his brother. After he became a U.S. Senator from New York State, I had come to admire his strong stand on issues, his concern for people. Where I once considered his power drive sinister, I now felt it was motivated by a genuine compassion for the poor and underprivileged.

A few days later I answered my phone to hear his unmistakable broad accent on the line.

"I hear you're thinking of retiring, Governor."

"That's right, Senator."

"I think you should run for the senate," he said.

"In no way am I planning to take on that race, Senator."

His reply was terse and measured, "Governor, one more vote in here might make the difference on this war."

Something deep within me responded to those words. "Do you really believe that?" I asked.

"Yes," he said, "we're getting close to where we can bring some sanity back to our policies. We need you. The country needs you." And then a bit of the tone I recognized from his old days crept into his voice. "You don't really have the right to consider your personal feelings."

"Well, thank you Senator for your thought," I said, "but I've already made my decision. I'm not going to run for anything."

"Well, I wish you'd reconsider," he said. He was silent for a moment. "By the way, we're having the Empire State dinner in New York City on November 13th. Why don't you join us and we'll talk some more about it."

The Empire State dinner was a large fund-raising affair held at a big Manhattan hotel. It was attended by celebrities, entertainers and Democratic bigwigs that only the Kennedys could attract. I agreed to go. This would be a good opportunity to present my conviction to the senator that he should run for president.

The dinner was held on a Monday and I flew to New York a day early when Bobby called back and invited me for a personal conference Sunday afternoon in his room at the Plaza Hotel.

It was with much anticipation that I walked down the wide carpeted hallway to the Kennedy suite. The young senator met me at the door in shirt-sleeves, his white teeth flashing in a wide grin. "Come in, Governor," he said, shaking hands. "Ethel and the kids are down ice skating, so we have the place to ourselves."

He waved me to a chair, brushing back the ever-present cowlick on his forehead. His tie was off and I promptly shed mine. Bobby picked up the phone and ordered coffee. Then leaning sideways in his chair, a lean muscular arm draped across the back of it, he looked at me intently.

He had aged much since I saw him last. Lines etched his angular face. Many of them, I was sure, came from the loss of his brother. At an earlier meeting we had discussed the mutual sudden loss of brothers we had loved deeply. The senator seemed genuinely moved that I shared his experience.

Then we talked about Lyndon Johnson and his emotional involvement in the war. The senator's brow furrowed as he sipped his steaming coffee. He stated his opinion that Johnson neither could nor would end the war. I urged him to run against him.

"Somebody should do it," he agreed, impatiently ruffling his thick dark hair. He quickly stood and paced the room, hands in pockets.

"The war's a waste," he muttered, "and we're crippling our country by diverting our resources to it." He stopped pacing, and turned to me. "But I worry about further splitting the country. How can I come out against him without destroying our party?"

"I don't know, I don't know," he repeated, more to himself, pressing a fist into the palm of the other hand. He turned to me and laughed: "In October some of my advisers met here in New York to explore the situation. And even they couldn't completely agree on what I should do right now. And that included my own brother, Ted."

"The only unanimous recommendation they gave me was to get a haircut." He laughed. "They said I looked like a hippy. But something's got to be done," he added quietly, "this war has got to stop."

Shadows in the room lengthened as a winter sun began to set over Central Park outside the hotel. Its golden rays caught the window panes and Kennedy, eyes in deep thought, stood and strolled to the window. I joined him. An autumn-seared park spread out below us. Dusk gathered among the trees.

We talked about the dissension wracking the land, well-meaning people divided about the war, and its drain on the country.

"You know," he said, as we gazed out the window, "I like what George Bernard Shaw wrote: 'Some people see things as they are and say: why? I dream things that never were and say: why not?' "

For a long moment we stood there silently. Then Bobby said quietly, "Your reasons for my running for the presidency are the same reasons why you should run for the senate." His voice took on an intensity: "Somebody has to do something." He swung from the window toward me. "You can win your election, Governor, and your vote in the United States Senate could help make the difference in stopping this war."

His statement jolted me. I suddenly found myself reassessing the situation. "I frankly don't think I'm adequate," I said. "I'm not knowledgeable in foreign policy and certain national problems. I know my own state, but being a senator—well it awes me." I grimaced. "Besides, I'm in poor shape politically at home, not to mention finances. Something like that would take $350,000 to $400,000. I wouldn't know where to begin."

Bobby took me by the arm. "Think it over, Governor," he said.

eyes boring into mine. "Remember that I'll give you all the support I can, and feed you all the information you'll probably need."

I looked back into his eyes. "OK, Senator," I said, "I'll seriously consider it." Then I added: "And you consider running against Johnson."

The Empire State dinner was held in the grand ballroom of the Plaza and it seemed as if every big name in Democratic circles was there. I felt a bit awkward at first because light chatter comes hard for me. By the time I was seated at my table I felt relaxed enough to converse easily with my dinner partners who were older and obviously quite wealthy people.

We had been discussing the problems facing the country. The woman next to me tapped out her cigarette with a jeweled finger and sighed: "Oh well, fifty years from now it won't make any difference."

Something within me responded to her statement.

"Oh, but it will," I found myself saying.

She turned with a startled look.

"What do you mean 'it will'?"

I swallowed deeply, then plunged ahead. "I believe God put each of us here for a purpose," I said. "How we live this life determines what happens to us in the next."

"Oh," she smiled knowingly, "you believe in reincarnation."

"No," I said, "I believe that our reason for being here is to prepare for eternal life."

By this time her two companions—a man and woman—were now listening curiously. I went on to explain what Jesus taught us about eternal life. "He told us that *In my Father's house are many mansions. If it were not so, I would have told you. I go to prepare a place for you*" (John 14:2–3).

There was some discussion about what Jesus meant by "mansions" and their interest quickened. "What else did He say?" the older woman asked.

"Well, Jesus made a very significant statement to the repentant thief beside Him on the cross," I continued. "He said as they both were dying: *Today you will be with Me in Paradise*" (Luke 23:43, RSV).

The master of ceremonies was at the podium to introduce the speakers, so our dialogue came to an end. When the banquet was over I bid them goodby, wondering if they felt I was some kind of religious nut.

Following the banquet, I was invited to a reception at Averell

Harriman's Manhattan apartment to see his art collection. Many people thronged the sumptuous quarters, which seemed to extend endlessly from room to room. The apartment was more like an art gallery, with modern and traditional paintings filling the walls from floor to ceiling. The collection, I had heard, ranked as one of the country's most valuable.

The place was soon abuzz with the chatter of guests and clinking of cocktail glasses. Since I never felt at home in these social gatherings, I busied myself trying to make sense out of an abstract painting. As I did, I felt a touch on my shoulder and turned, surprised to meet the same three people who had shared my table at the dinner.

"We've been talking about what you said, Governor," said the man, "and we'd like to know more about your religious experience."

Were they serious? I saw a grand piano in a quiet corner of the room with a couch near it. "Let's go over there," I said. They sat on the couch and I, on the piano bench, proceeded to tell them all I knew about Jesus Christ and what He had done for me.

When I told them that I was an alcoholic, I noticed they became edgy about the drinks they were holding. "Please don't worry about it," I assured them. "I'm not tempted or offended. But fifteen years ago I might have been carried out of here," I confessed.

Then I told them how often I tried to overcome my addiction. "But the harder I tried, the more I failed," I said. "Not until I ceased striving and admitted that I was helpless was God able to help me. It was then I felt something happening deep inside me, a peace settled over me that I had never felt before."

"He was the higher power that you AA's talk about?" said the man.

"Yes. Before that my ego stood between God and me."

"Did God remove your craving for alcohol?" asked one of the women.

"No," I admitted, "but He did give me the strength to resist it. And He helps guide me through every day with the presence of His Son, Jesus Christ."

"You mean He talks to you?"

"Yes, in a way," I answered, "through little nudges, insights, inner guidance. He promised us before He left this earth that He would return to all who received Him as Lord."

The three were silent for a moment. The man said thoughtfully: "But I've made so many mistakes."

"So have I. But when we give ourselves to Him, He uses our

weaknesses and mistakes to His own purpose." I held his eyes intently. "The Lord reached down to the gateway of hell for me, and cared enough to say 'Come and follow Me.' I know He'll do the same for you."

As we parted that evening, I realized that we'd probably never see each other again on this earth. Yet, I had that deep-down satisfaction of doing what the Lord wanted me to do.

During my flight back to Iowa I thought about this conversation and my running for the senate. Somehow they were related and both seemed part of that distant destiny towards which I was being drawn. I was still pondering it when the plane touched down at the Des Moines Municipal Airport.

Perhaps it was walking on home soil again, but when the limousine pulled up to the mansion, I had a clearer feeling about what I wanted to do. Eva and I sat up late that night talking.

"I've been doing a lot of thinking about it, too, Pack," she said, "and if this is what you want, I think you should run. You'll certainly have enough people pulling for you."

One of those pulling for me was Park Rinard, who was now executive director for the Iowa League of Municipalities. Park and I still conferred together often, usually in my home, and he had prepared many speeches and statements for me as governor.

The more we discussed the possibility of my running, the more enthusiastic he became.

"OK, Park," I said, "I'll run on one condition: that if I win, you'll come to Washington with me. You're one of the few men who understands the issues and my relationship with them. Will you go with me?"

"All right, Pack," he said. "We'll win; we'll go to Washington together."

On Saturday afternoon, December 16th, I held a press conference in my Statehouse office to announce my candidacy for the U.S. Senate. It was a most difficult statement to prepare. A private poll I had taken in October showed Iowans to be generally hawks on the Vietnam War.

If I stamped onto the scene in flatfooted opposition to the war, I'd be lost at the starting post. And yet I had to stress that I was not in tune with the administration's handling of it.

It was one of the few times I read my announcement, not wanting anyone to misconstrue anything. After stating my intention, I drew a deep breath:

"I have serious reservations about where our Vietnam policy is taking us. My disagreement with President Johnson on Vietnam and other issues could grow deeper," I said. "I will speak my mind freely, as have other members of my party."

As it turned out, my announcement was but a ripple on a peaceful lake compared to the tumultuous events that were to follow.

23

A Rising Wind

ANGRY VOICES ROSE across the land from youth protesting the Vietnam War to blacks crying out against racial injustice. As Proverbs 11:29 said: "He that troubleth his own house shall inherit the wind . . ." and the wind was rising in Iowa.

Often I felt as if I were hanging on to a gale-swept deck of a ship plunging in a storm. Yet, perhaps because of growing up on the outside looking in and my own reoccurring nightmares from World War II, I found that I could understand and sometimes even sympathize with those making the clamor.

And this included the youthful demonstrators who were giving gray hairs to university deans and police captains in those tumultuous years.

My first confrontation came when I spoke at graduation exercises at Grinnell College. Located some sixty miles east of Des Moines, it is a medium-sized school which I had regarded as somewhat liberal. As I got out of my car on the pleasant, tree-shaded campus, two young students wearing black anti-war arm bands rushed up and offered me one.

A bit taken aback, I politely declined. Perhaps they were surprised at my not ripping them up and down. For later as I stood in the processional waiting to enter the auditorium, three other students slipped up and quietly let me know that they didn't want to upset me, but they were going to take over the microphone at the ceremonies.

"Just five minutes is all we want," a girl graduate whispered.

At that moment, the procession began and as we slowly marched up the aisle I wondered what to do. Finally, we ascended to the stage and as I sat down next to the college president, I leaned close and whispered: "There's going to be a problem. I just heard that a group of war-protesting students are going to take over the microphone."

He shot me a startled glance. "What should I do?" he whispered.

I hesitated. "If we give them the five minutes they want, I really don't think there'll be a problem. But it's your decision."

He studied his robe for a moment. Then as they started announcing the doctoral degrees, down the aisle walked three students, a barefoot girl and two bearded boys.

The girl stepped up to the microphone. "We just want everyone to know that this is a peaceful protest," she said, her voice quavering. "We plan no violence. But we want five minutes in which to state our point and we will leave peacefully."

Tension flashed through the auditorium. Two faculty members rose and shouted: "Get them out of here!" There was some booing from the audience.

The president stood and held up his hand for quiet, then motioned the girl to keep on talking.

Fighting back tears, the girl said she recognized that she was addressing not only her own parents in the audience but all mothers and fathers. She asked them to understand that she was refusing to accept her college degree as a protest against war and a society that would tolerate it.

She broke down sobbing, "I pray to God that you'll understand, Mom and Dad; I know the years of sacrifice that you have made in putting me through college. But I care more about peace than receiving this degree."

The auditorium was hushed as she concluded. The two young men stood up and gave basically the same message. The three turned and thanked us on the podium, then quietly walked out. I glanced at my watch; it had taken just five minutes.

The graduation exercises resumed and I thought how much controversy and trouble could be avoided if all our leaders could be as restrained and understanding as that college president had been.

It was a different situation, however, when I reviewed the ROTC units at the University of Iowa. As their commander-in-chief, this was my responsibility on Governor's Day.

As soon as I reached the campus, the student peace group asked to meet with me. I checked with the university president, Howard Bowen, and asked if he had any objections.

"Certainly not," he said. He seemed to feel secure in his position.

Tension filled the meeting room. The peace group committee announced they were going to break up the ROTC parade. As I looked at their determined faces, I knew there were several hundred additional sympathizers on the campus and felt sure they could break up anything they wanted. A number of them had stink bombs ready.

"Why break up the parade?" I asked.

"We want to protest the action being taken by the military!" was the cry.

"But you can't do it without resorting to violence," I countered.

The room was quiet. I continued: "It doesn't make sense, does it? How can you throw bombs to promote peace?"

For a moment no one said anything. Then a student yelled, "Well, how *can* we do it?"

I thought for a moment. "If you'll allow the Governor's Day ceremonies to continue unhindered, I'll stay and review your own parade if you wish. I'll address your group just as I will the military. But," I urged, "let them have their day."

There was some demurring, but they finally seemed to agree to it.

Even so, some officials wondered if it wouldn't be safer to have the police keep the peace group at a distance.

"No," I said. "I've given my word and I feel sure they'll keep theirs." I hoped I was right.

"All right," said the president, "then I'll stay on with you and review the peace parade, too."

We explained the situation to the military. They had their parade and review. The university president and I made our speeches. Then the ROTC assemblage left.

Just the president, his wife, Eva and I, and two other couples from the state office remained. Soon an undulating group of barefoot youngsters streamed before the reviewing stands, carrying symbolic caskets and throwing flowers. One of the girls scampered up to the platform, kissed the president and me and crowned us with a wreath of lilacs.

The spokesman asked permission for several of the group to make speeches. We relaxed and listened. After it was over, they left, leaving only strewn flower petals and wreaths around Howard Bowen's neck and mine.

Some months later, war protesters stormed the university offices. The Iowa highway patrol had been brought in and I told the sheriff that we didn't want anyone hurt. They maintained order, and must have developed a good relationship with the protesters because the next day, papers carried a photo showing the Iowa patrol captain dancing with a bearded student in the street.

It shocked some people. At my press conference the next morning, one of the reporters asked what I thought of a patrol captain dancing with the hippie in Iowa City.

"Did anyone get hurt?" I asked.

"No."

I said: "Well, hell, I'd dance with him, too!"

But there were no flowers or dancing amid the racial anger which smouldered in our larger cities. It was an issue that concerned me more than my senatorial campaign.

"But the blacks in Iowa are a half of one percent. That won't do you any good at the polls," argued an advisor. "Besides, getting involved in something like that could destroy you politically."

I didn't want to create an issue, but I sensed that, like in most northern states, the black-white problems were there just under the surface. When I turned to church leaders for help and suggestions, I learned that the local Des Moines council of churches and other religious groups had not met with the black ministers for some fifteen years.

In trying to learn why, I discovered that the white clergymen usually met on a weekday afternoon. Most of the black ministers had to work during the day. Since their parishes couldn't fully support them, they had to work at secular jobs.

I decided that the best way to get something started was for me to get together first with as many black Iowa pastors as possible. A meeting was arranged early in April in a church on the east side of Des Moines.

My aide, Ed Campbell, and I were ushered into the church basement where about fifty black pastors greeted us. After a delicious dinner put on by the church women, we had an informal discussion. As we talked, one could hear the faint clatter of dishes being washed in the kitchen. The pastors quickly voiced their concerns: lack of jobs, good housing and education.

One young minister got up and angrily said: "Black or white? I don't care if a man is polka-dotted. It makes no difference to me. But it sure seems to to your white brothers."

"I can't speak for my brothers," I answered. "I can only speak for myself, but I'm here because I want to help. I'm not going to promise you anything because I don't even know what to promise, but I'm going to try and break down these barriers and . . ."

The kitchen door opened and a matronly lady stepped over to my aide. Ed pulled me aside and whispered. "It's one of the wire services. They say it's urgent."

I excused myself and followed the lady to a small hall where the phone hung on the wall.

It was an Associated Press reporter. "Martin Luther King has just been shot and killed in Memphis by a white man," he said breathlessly. "Do you have a comment?"

I stood in the quiet hall, suddenly feeling sick. "I really don't know what to say," I replied. "It's a horrible tragedy." I added something about grieving for the dead man's family, that the nation had suffered a great loss and hung up.

I stood silently for a moment. I needed some place to think. I stepped into the kitchen where cheerful ladies bustled about and asked for the rest room.

Inside the little cubicle, I leaned against the paint-chipped wall trying to get myself together. "Oh God," I prayed, "tell me what to say to these pastors."

When I walked back into the meeting room, the men looked up with expectant smiles. One joked: "They sure keep you busy, Governor."

I stood before them, struggling for words. "Gentlemen," I said, "I have just been given some information that is shocking to me and I know it will be shocking to you. There is no way that I can lessen the pain of it. I have just heard that Doctor Martin Luther King has been assassinated in Memphis, Tennessee . . . he was shot by a white man."

I gave them what details I knew about the killing, then said, my voice breaking, "Since we are gathered together in God's house, I really think we should be called to prayer. Would one of you men please lead?"

What happened in that church basement is something I'll never forget.

There, with the terrible news hanging over us like a pall of doom, a black bishop got down on his knees and prayed simply and earnestly, appealing to God to have mercy on the assassin.

I stood rooted. This man's first thought was for the murderer? I knew that I could never have done it. Then he prayed for the soul of Martin Luther King, for his family, that the assassin be apprehended and brought to justice, but that God be merciful to him and whoever else was behind it.

The Bishop then asked the men to remind their people that injustice could only be righted through peaceful means in the spirit of Martin Luther King.

I promised to carry the same message to the white community. Then I asked if they would be willing to come to a meeting with white ministers, priests and rabbis to discuss our problems if one could be arranged. They said they would and we headed for our homes in the darkening evening.

The meeting of black and white clergymen was held some weeks later in a Des Moines Methodist church. Many pastors, priests and rabbis were there. As chairman, I pointed out that I knew of no other meeting like this in the history of Iowa. "At least we're all men of God regardless of how we approach Him," I said. "Whether we are Jews, Catholics, Protestants, black, white or chicano, we are here to reason together."

Immediately, a black pastor, fire in his eye, stood up. He angrily accused the white pastors of not living by Christ's words and applying them in their daily actions. He stated that they were contributing to discrimination and lack of opportunity.

The assembly exploded in heated rebuttal.

I wilted in my chair, feeling that the whole meeting was going up in smoke.

Then, a friend of mine, Irving Weingart, a highly respected rabbi, quietly got to his feet. Taking off his glasses, he cleaned them, and then looking about the room, said: "My people have been the most discriminated against in the history of the earth. We have been enslaved, and murdered in gas chambers. Our lands and property have been taken away and we have suffered every abomination that man can heap on his fellow-men." He spoke in modulated tones but his words seemed to thunder. "But we are still men of God," he continued, "and we still want to live with our fellow-men in peace. And that's what we are here for today, to learn how to do that. But as long as we hurl accusations at one another, we'll never come to any understanding of how we can begin with God as our teacher."

The tension and bitterness seemed to lift and soon there was a coming together. In a new spirit of fellowship, discussions started and before the meeting was over, black and white pastors had agreed to speak at each other's churches. They also decided to come together in groups for prayer, and began arranging for joint Bible study groups and dinners among their parishioners.

Similar meetings—called Crisis Conferences—were held in other parts of the state. It was a beginning and out of them gradually came a new understanding and better racial climate.

If I had to pick a turning point, it happened when a black bishop on that frightful April evening knelt down on the wooden floor of a little church and prayed for the murderer who had taken the life of the leader most dear to him.

24

A Traumatic Campaign

THREE LARGE FRIENDLY dogs bounded toward me from around the corner of the Robert Kennedy mansion on Hickory Hill in McLean, Virginia. It was January 1968 and I had gone to Washington to attend an Office of Economic Opportunity conference and meet again with the young senator.

The rollicking dogs made me feel at home. And when Ethel Kennedy greeted me at the door, I discovered I was the first guest to arrive. When she left to greet other guests, two more dogs rushed up to be petted.

The Kennedy children dashed in and out of the rooms and somewhere someone banged on a piano. I glanced around the living room; books and newspapers were strewn about. It was a relaxed and warm household.

And a fascinating evening followed. The main subject of conversation was the deteriorating state of the nation. The North Vietnamese had just launched the Tet offensive, their heaviest attack of the war, scoring surprising victories within American-held strongholds. Dissension over Vietnam had intensified in Congress and even among White House advisers. And this division was widening like an earthquake crack across the nation.

It was a tumultuous time to plunge into a senatorial race. Some people who had supported my campaigns for governor wouldn't come near me, usually because they felt I knew little about national and international issues.

But I was surprised by others who came forward to help. Some felt that my travels with trade missions to twenty-one different countries gave me an unusual insight into foreign affairs. Others were impressed by my deep involvement with national leaders, including three different presidents. I was also getting advice from experienced men such as economics expert Pat Dulurley.

Gene McCarthy had already entered the presidential race. In March Robert Kennedy announced his candidacy. As yet, I had not publicly given my support to any candidate, though Bob Kennedy knew that I was ready to come out for him whenever he felt the time proper.

The assumption that Lyndon Johnson would be running for re-election still kept the cover on the Democratic political pot.

Then on Sunday evening, March 31st, the lid blew off. I was watching the president make his statement on the Vietnam War on television. As he spoke, looking haggard and worn, I felt concerned for him and grieved the loss of our friendship. I hoped that one day we could forget the war and its problems. It was encouraging to hear him talking about limiting the bombings and inviting peace negotiations.

Then he talked of his thirty-seven years' service to the country, of division "in the American house" and "our people . . . must not now be lost in suspicion and distrust and selfishness . . ."

What was he leading up to?

He continued, "I shall not seek and I will not accept the nomination of my party for another term as your president."

It was a shock. But much greater shocks were in the offing.

The jetliner taxied up to the terminal area of Des Moines Municipal Airport and as the cabin door opened and the ground crew hurried a boarding ramp to it, a low murmur began to build from the crowd. When the tousel-haired man emerged from the cabin flashing his famous grin, the murmur exploded into a roar of acclaim.

Robert Kennedy had come to Iowa campaigning for delegates. He hurried down the ramp, embraced me and was swallowed up by the welcoming committee. I greeted Ethel as she followed him and said: "I'm really glad Bob's in this race."

She smiled at me: "You're one of the main reasons he's in it."

For the past weeks he had been racing back and forth across the country, speaking at colleges and universities, trying to snatch back much of the student support lost to Eugene McCarthy. He was also battling veteran campaigner Hubert Humphrey, who had announced his candidacy late in April.

My heart went out to Humphrey, a longtime friend who had often come to Iowa as vice president to support me in gubernatorial campaigns. Over the years we had agreed on almost everything. However, he seemed committed to his administration's position on the Vietnam War, and I felt he was too loyal a man to change.

In the meantime, over 4,000 delegates had gathered for the Iowa nominating convention at the Veterans Auditorium in Des Moines. A bitter three-way struggle began to shape up between backers of McCarthy, Kennedy and Humphrey.

With division imminent, I accepted a "favorite son" candidacy to help hold our Iowa delegation together until we got to the Chicago convention in August.

In May, Kennedy won the Indiana primary. Though a robust fighter, I marveled at how gracefully he walked the tightrope: he couldn't attack McCarthy too much or he'd lose the students' good will. Nor could he put down Humphrey as Johnson's man, for later he would need the Happy Warrior's support in the general election if he won the nomination.

He raced on to Nebraska, winning over both McCarthy and Humphrey and then on May 28th he lost in Oregon.

I watched him on television after the Oregon primary and was moved as he stated simply: "Well, I lost. We're going now to California . . ."

I wanted to come out for him right then. But my campaign advisors recommended that it would be premature because of the heavy pro-McCarthy sentiment among my supporters.

"You'll rip yourself up, Harold," they said. "Wait a bit, hold off until after California anyway." The Golden State, they said, would be the deciding factor.

The night of the California primaries Eva, Phyllis and I were at home watching the returns on television. Because of the two-hour time difference, it was quite late by Iowa time when he made his victory appearance.

It's settled, I thought, and knew I could now make plans to come out for him. Turning off the TV set, I yawned and Eva and I went to bed. Phyllis had already fallen asleep an hour earlier.

We had not been in bed fifteen minutes when the phone rang. It was a friend.

"Are you watching TV?"

"No, why?"

"Bob Kennedy's been shot!"

I called to Eva and we dashed downstairs and snapped on the set. He was lying there on the flickering screen amid shouting and confusion. Then they carried him away.

Word of his death came the next morning. I sat stunned, not believing it. Then I broke down and wept for the man who dreamed of things that never were. I wept for his wife and children at Hickory Hill where the shrieks of children playing and barking dogs would never sound the same again. And I wept for myself. For I had lost a good friend, a man whose heart I understood.

I stood, went to the window and looked into a gray sky. What plague of violence was attacking our country? Three good men shot and killed—John Kennedy, Martin Luther King and now Bob Kennedy. Why was God allowing it? Had the ultimate political instrument become a gun? How could our country be a beacon to the world when no man could seek its presidency without realizing he may never live through it?

Late in June, Senators McCarthy and Humphrey came to Iowa to address the State Democratic Statutory Convention. I made no statements endorsing either man. However, I was impressed by Senator McCarthy's theories of government, his foreign policy philosophy, and his understanding of current problems; many of his thoughts were reminiscent of Robert Kennedy's. With the proper people around him, perhaps he would make a good president, I thought.

One of his aides came to Des Moines in July to ask me about endorsing McCarthy. I thought long and hard about it; I realized the tall distinguished looking senator only had an outside chance of winning. But unless somebody stood beside him, he hadn't a chance at all.

I picked up the phone and told Gene that I would endorse him at the convention. He seemed pleased, and then surprised me by asking if I would give his nominating speech.

As the time for the Democratic Convention drew near, the Iowa delegates wanted to nominate me for president on a favorite son basis. I appreciated their loyalty, but told them I preferred that each person vote from conscience. I also felt that this favorite-son practice was more of an ego trip than anything else, that it consumed too much time. Much of the convention falderal was boring both the delegates and TV watchers.

I was pleased, however, to be part of an ad hoc committee which worked out two important reforms to be presented at the convention. These pertained to selection of delegates and their votes. A young lawyer, Geoff Cowan, headed the staff that did the research work and I was made chairman of the committee to handle the rules changes at the convention.

Many in our party had been concerned about the method of selecting delegates. In some states one man alone could appoint them; in others they could be named by an executive committee or even selected by self-styled representatives in small, unpublicized meetings. Too often the wealthy and powerful ran the show. As the political boss Jim Tate of Philadelphia once said: "I don't care who does the electing as long as I do the nominating."

We also felt that the unit rule requiring all of a state's convention votes be cast for the delegates' majority choice was unfair. Each person, we reasoned, should be able to cast his or her own vote.

With the Democratic convention just a few weeks away, we heard that protesters were converging on Chicago.

I told Eva one morning at the breakfast table, "We've made all the conventions together, but this is one time that I feel you and Phyllis should stay home." They agreed.

My worries intensified after I reached Chicago. The air was electric with tension. Yippies and other radical groups were congregating in the parks. Blood had already been spilled in heated battles with angry police burdened with the responsibility of protecting Democratic candidates in a year of assassinations.

But I was more concerned over the fresh-faced youths who had come from all over to support McCarthy. In a way Gene had become their folk hero. But what would happen, I wondered, if streetwise radicals led them into violent confrontations with police inflamed to where they would wade in swinging, not bothering to differentiate between the innocent and guilty?

Putting this worry in the back of my mind, many of us threw ourselves into getting the rule changes approved. A cadre of workers was organized to exhort delegates to vote for the changes. First, recommendations were approved by the Rules and Credentials Committees; then, after a bitter floor battle, they were finally voted in.

The abolition of the unit rule won by only twelve votes, with the state of Missouri casting the deciding votes.

These new rules would apply to the next convention in 1972. Not only would a delegate be able to vote for his presidential choice, but a delegation which did not fairly represent its state by sex or race, could be effectively challenged on the convention floor.

In time these reforms would be regarded as the most important achievement of the 1968 convention.

Meanwhile, I was actively seeking delegates for McCarthy. "He opposes the Vietnam War effort because he knows we can't win it," I argued. "The South Vietnamese government is not meeting its commitment. Many of our supplies are ending up in the South Vietnamese black market."

My final plea was made on nominating night. It happened in an interesting way. Mayor Joseph Alioto of San Francisco expected to nominate Humphrey at the start during prime-time television. However, Alaska, instead of yielding to California, yielded to Iowa. And thus I placed McCarthy's name in nomination at the very start of a long evening. The amphitheatre then erupted into a singing, shouting demonstration by hundreds of young people waving home-made placards, bedsheet banners and enthusiastically parading up and down the aisles.

In my nominating speech I called McCarthy "a different kind of leader. The political world of Gene McCarthy is lean, spare, stream-lined—strangely unlike the wheeler-dealer political world to which we are accustomed."

As I was speaking, streets around Chicago's lakefront hotels were teeming with battles between young people and the police. Radicals had mobilized the young into a mob, chanting: "Stop the war! Stop the war! Stop the war!" Blood spattered onto the asphalt of Michigan Avenue as rocks flew and police, overreacting in rage, flailed furiously with clubs as they drove beaten and bloodied youngsters into police vans or to flight.

The screaming of people and exploding tear gas grenades resounded to the windows of McCarthy's rooms on the twenty-third floor of the Conrad Hilton Hotel. Deeply concerned, he phoned me at his communications center in Convention Hall. In a voice choked with emotion, he asked me to remove his name from nomination. He had a withdrawal statement ready.

I couldn't believe it. "Look, Gene," I pleaded, "the violence in front of your hotel has nothing to do with your candidacy. The leaders are revolutionaries, yes, and some of your kids are caught up in it, but they're not leading it."

I pressed the receiver hard into my ear; the rising convention clamor was making it difficult to hear.

"If you withdraw now," I continued, "the kids may think that you were forced out, and no telling what will happen. At least let the delegates vote."

He wanted to think about it. By now word of his intention had reached others around me, and many McCarthy workers were weeping. His headquarters in the Hilton had already become a first-aid station for wounded kids.

I got him back on the phone. He was still adamant.

"Well, Harold," he said, "I think it's a farce to go on. All those people are being hurt out there, beaten and gassed. It's just horrible. Why should we go through with it with no hope of winning and everything getting worse?"

"It will get worse if you get out of it now," I stressed. "We've *got* to go through with it. You've been waging this battle for a year, you've spent millions of dollars. Now the convention is being ripped wide open. At least give your people a chance to vote. It will reduce the tension."

"Well," he said resignedly, "you're down there where you can sense things better than I right now. I can't even think clearly about it. I'll leave it in your hands."

Though we were soundly defeated, I felt the McCarthy challenge was a victory in the sense that it helped change our emphasis in the Vietnam War from escalation to searching for ways to peace.

When Humphrey won the nomination, I climbed up onto the platform to support him. I looked all over for Gene McCarthy; he wasn't there, nor had he issued a statement of support. The next morning I hurried over to his suite where we had breakfast together.

"I'll support him," said the haggard-looking senator, taking a sip of coffee and wiping his mouth with a napkin, "but I'm going to have to wait a few days to let things cool down. There are still a lot of kids here. I'd rather let them get out of town and let things dissipate before making an announcement."

However, McCarthy never did come out for Humphrey. I suspected he was badly in debt for campaign funds and beholden to people who would never approve his supporting Humphrey.

Back home in Iowa I wondered how I was going to pick up the remnants and get on with my senate campaign. There were only two months left before the election.

My campaign trail was full of roadblocks. I had backed Gene McCarthy in a state where many people thought he was some kind of kook. I was against the Vietnam War, which in Iowa was a controversial stand, and I had rammed through a highly unpopular tax bill in the previous legislative session—June 1967. We had rebalanced taxes to make them more equitable by siphoning off revenues from industrial-rich districts and feeding them into poorer areas. The bill also levied new taxes on newspapers and radio stations. Naturally, the bill was blasted by news media and businessmen throughout the state.

Moreover, I faced a powerful opponent.

David Stanley, age 39, seven years younger than I, was a state senator with an extensive background. He had served three terms in the Iowa House of Representatives, and was now in his second term as senator. He had already been campaigning for fourteen months, beginning long before me.

Leader of his graduating class at the State University of Iowa, he was intelligent, hard-working and was, as one assistant said, "a man with a computer memory who can catalogue and store hundreds of facts with almost perfect recall."

Not only that, but he had more funds than I. Some estimated that he had a million dollars to spend on television, radio, newspaper ads and billboards. All we could scrape up for this purpose was $158,000.

I also worried about my qualifications. "He has all that legislative experience," I told Park one day, "plus that schooling. I've only had a year of college."

Park lit his pipe, puffed on it, then looked up. "OK, Pack, but look at it this way: under your governorship, reapportionment has restored equality of voting rights in a state where one citizen's vote used to outweigh another's many times over; you wiped out the shame of the key clubs where any fifteen-year-old kid could buy a drink; you led the way to establishing vocational-technical education in the state and brought about the abolition of capital punishment."

He set his pipe down on his desk and rose from the chair. "Harold, you awakened the pride of Iowans in their quality as people and in their compassion for their fellow human beings."

Visibly moved, he stepped over to the window, looked out for a moment, then turned to me: "You've made historic gains for the well-being of the working people, promoted Iowa's first fair employment practice legislation, brought school aid up to record levels, and started a state scholarship program for kids of limited means. Do you want to hear more?"

"All right, all right, Park," I laughed. "You sold me."

Even so, my opponent was able to launch a formidable campaign. His repeated charge was that "Harold Hughes is spending the state into bankruptcy."

Though I was able to point out that our state treasury would have a surplus of close to ten million dollars, his charge was made so many times that I wondered if the voters didn't believe it.

A big issue in our televised debates was the Vietnam War. I called for an unconditional bombing halt as a step toward peace. He felt that bombing should continue to provide support for our troops.

I was accused of not having legislative experience on the floor, that I had shifted my position on the war from hawk to dove.

Sometimes my own advisors complained. "You use too many big words, Chief, like 'coalition,' 'unilateral' and 'demagogue.' Some of your TV spots won't be understood by the average person."

My response was that people were becoming more sophisticated; our academic levels were rising and public awareness of current events was increasing.

"Well, be that as it may," answered an aide, "do voters concerned about law and order really understand when you declare that 'law and order without justice is tyranny'?"

"I sure hope so," I answered. "Too many citizens who surrendered their freedoms for 'law and order,' such as in Russia and Nazi Germany, suddenly discovered that they were prisoners."

I sat up late at night in my study thinking on how best to reach the people. My view of America's future was based largely on my knowledge of Iowa and the strength of its people, and I had unlimited faith in the ability of our nation to attain new levels of greatness.

So when aides wanted me to "talk down" to people, I could only say that they were "good, honest folks who, when given sufficient information, will do the right thing." I wanted to be accepted as I really was and not allow public relations specialists to shape my image.

Responding to this were the young people who made up the bulk of my volunteer workers. They came from all over the country, some taking a sabbatical leave from college to work in the campaign. All they wanted was a better world and believed that I represented some of the viewpoints that could be a steppingstone toward it. One of them was my daughter, Phyllis, who had helped me in all of my campaigns since I had started the Iowa Better Trucking Bureau.

Volunteer workers, debates and television spots were fine. But I felt that nothing was as valuable as getting out and meeting people personally.

We visited every county in Iowa by camper bus. We spoke to groups ranging from a few merchants on a small town corner or men on a grain-elevator dock to hundreds of people crowding an American Legion or Farmers Union hall.

Our friend, Ramona Barry, scurried around the state in her sedan, springs sagging from the huge rolled-up aerial sign in its trunk announcing my candidacy. Driving up to a country airport, she'd help a pilot, Les Maynard, attach the sign to his biplane. Then, hair flying in the prop wash, she'd hold the sign steady until the little plane gathered speed to take off and trail it over a crowd of football fans at a university stadium or race viewers at a stock car track.

And so we continued, traveling from town to town, shaking hands, speaking to anybody and everybody who would listen. The state polls showed me a small percentage ahead of Stanley.

However, in Iowa, it was beginning to look like a clean sweep for the Nixon-Agnew ticket. The tragic debacle of the Democratic convention hurt our party everywhere. And even though Humphrey came out for peace as his own man in the latter weeks of the election, it was too late. Polls indicated a Republican sweep, with Nixon's coattails threatening to yank me off my feet.

Then near-disaster struck early in October when I became ill. I had been feeling dragged out for some time but kept going. One morning I couldn't get up. The doctor pronounced it pneumonia and ordered complete bed rest.

For ten days I lay in bed, hardly able to talk.

In the meantime, my opponent took advantage of my absence to fire a barrage in the mass media. When I was finally able to watch the television set, I found myself labeled as the man who was "spending the state into bankruptcy" and one who, along with the Johnson-Humphrey administration, was responsible for a general increase in "lawlessness." Television scenes of burning cities were interposed with statements lifted from my speeches to make me seem to condone violence, followed with: "Do you want a man like this representing you in the United States Senate?"

When the doctor finally allowed me to return to the campaign, I told Ed Campbell: "If the election were held today, I would lose."

However, as November 5th neared, I relinquished the whole result to God. And despite the clamoring telephones and the anxious faces of my staff, I found myself relaxing.

Under my opponent's relentless television campaign, each poll showed me losing more ground: some analysts predicted an upset.

As the weekend before the election approached, I wondered if I should make a last-ditch effort in the counties where I was falling behind. However, I was still weak from my illness and had the feeling that I had done all I could. Besides, I had a curious peace about the outcome of Tuesday's voting. I didn't dare mention this to my aides; they were already fussing about my "mysticism."

Sunday afternoon found me at my desk in the mansion working on our personal bills. I had let them pile up for a few weeks and now felt I might as well use the time to write checks.

Eva, Phyllis and I would go to Ida Grove the next day, where the local folks planned a dinner for us. As our voting registration was still there, we'd go to the poll booths in the armory first thing Tuesday morning, then return to Des Moines.

I pulled out the bundle of bills, and sat down at the desk. Before starting work, I lit a cigarette, waved out the match and placed it on my ashtray. It was a small square receptacle made of dark glass. There was a sharp snap as I touched the ashtray. I stared at it in amazement. It had separated into two pieces. I picked up the pieces, studying them. It hadn't been the heat of the match; it was dead when I placed it on the tray. Nor was there a defect in the tray.

There was something odd about the shape of the break that intrigued me. I heard a step in the hall. It was Phyllis. I called to her.

"What's wrong, Dad?" she asked.

"Nothing, Honey, but look at this ashtray." I explained what happened. "What do you make out of it?"

She studied the pieces. "It's a map," she said. Going to the book-shelf, she took down the atlas and opened it. Placing the two pieces on a page, she carried the book to me. "Now you know there's no doubt about the election, Dad," she smiled.

I looked at the two pieces of glass lying on the page. The square fit the outlines of the area perfectly, the break following the shape of the Potomac River.

It was a map of the District of Columbia.

25

Hughes From Iowa

THE LIMOUSINE'S TIRES sang on the wet pavement as we bore down George Washington Parkway toward the Capitol still illuminated ivory against the midnight blue sky.

My first day as a senator, I thought, and it has to end like this. What an incredible series of events! First the senate chamber with the glow of swearing-in ceremonies quenched by the intoxicated senator cursing me. Then our Finnish bath when my aides and I were locked out of the house naked in the cold. And now, all this topped off by my present mission to Capitol Hill to visit this same abusive senator at midnight. Was this some kind of divine joke? Was this why God wanted me here, to counsel with a drunk?

As I thought back over the events of the previous months, I had to admit that it was through no overwhelming mandate of Iowa voters that I was in Washington. I had won the senatorial election by a slim margin of only 4,200 votes, less than a vote and a half per precinct. The Nixon-Agnew landslide had swept Republicans into office all over the country.

In vivid reminder a car shot past on which a NIXON'S THE ONE bumper sticker reminded me of who would shortly be in charge. The limousine driven by the senator's aide who had picked me up peeled off the parkway and soon we were crossing the Potomac River which glistened darkly below. After a few minutes driving through deserted streets strangely bright under powerful lights, we pulled into the garage beneath the Senate Office Building, and the senator's aide escorted me inside.

Our footsteps echoed hollowly in the marbled halls. We reached the senator's office, the aide unlocked the door and ushered me in. For an instant I stood transfixed. I was seeing myself seventeen years before. The senator slumped at his desk, hair plastered in moist strands on his forehead, tie askew and clothes disheveled. The sweet-sour odor of bourbon filled the air. He stared vacantly at an empty glass before him.

My heart went out to him. From my aides, I had learned something about the burdens of this tragic man.

Looking up at me through swollen, blood-rimmed eyes, he struggled to rise, apologizing for bothering me. Assuring him that it was no trouble, I sat down beside his desk and said I understood exactly how he felt.

It all poured out of him, a flood of frustration and bitterness at what he felt were unfair accusations by his peers and betrayal by a trusted aide.

His aide caught my attention and took me aside. "Senator, would you call his wife and tell her he's all right?" he asked quietly. "She's worried about him."

I stepped into an adjoining room, picked up the phone and dialed the number given me. The voice on the other end of the line was fearful, tremulous. "Oh God," I thought, "how many times had Eva sounded like this."

"He's all right," I assured her, "don't worry." I tried to encourage her and said her husband would be home soon.

I was wrong; we talked for three hours. As usual, I found counseling with a sick alcoholic demanding, requiring every ounce of my attention and concern. He wouldn't admit he was an alcoholic and began cursing me.

Finally, he slumped back in his chair like an empty sack. "Killing myself is the only way," he muttered. "I have a gun at home and nothing anyone can do will stop me."

"I know," I said, "I felt the same way once. But you know something, Senator? You're already killing yourself and don't know it. Keep on drinking like this and you'll be in a grave in about sixty days."

I put my hand on his thin shoulder and felt the perspiration through his suit. "If you want to quit, friend, you can. You can rebuild your life."

"Look at me," I continued. "I've broken just about every commandment in the book. But I was able to come out of it."

He broke into tears. "But I've always been a man of high moral principles," he wept. "I've never been untrue to my wife. I've been loyal to my country, faithful to my church, and look at me . . . betrayed by my friends."

"Senator, we all really have only one Friend." I felt strength from another source beginning to build in me. "God loves you and will help you if you want to get sober. All you have to do is trust Him."

I touched his arm. "Would you like us to pray together?" I asked. He broke into convulsive sobbing, shoulders heaving.

Kneeling down beside him, I prayed that God would comfort him and give him the strength to keep away from alcohol.

Finally, his head rose; he seemed to be more at peace. I noticed by my watch it was 3:00 A.M.

"Look," I said, "we both need some sleep. I think you should stay home tomorrow and get yourself together; we need you in the Senate."

His hand tremored as he said good-by. "I still don't know what I'm going to do."

As I walked out with his aide who would drive me home, I advised him: "Make sure someone stays close to him. You can never dismiss the fact that he may attempt to kill himself. He's thinking about it and may well do it."

My first day in the Senate ended at 4:00 A.M. that morning when I fell into bed exhausted.

My fellow senator returned to sessions relatively sober. He seemed fine for a week and then his aide called me: "Senator, he's got a bottle somewhere and is drinking again."

When we assembled in the Senate, I glanced over at him and my heart sank. He was obviously intoxicated. I berated myself for not staying close to him. He couldn't stay on the senate floor in this condition. Another senator and I helped him into the Marble Room just off the Senate floor, sort of a sanctuary where senators can rest, read newspapers and chat with each other.

We helped the senator into one of the plush chairs and he began cursing me. Finally, holding him between us, we half carried, half walked him past the marble columns and stately mirrors into the hall, down the elevator and to the portico where his limousine picked him up.

We kept in touch with him through his wife and sons, and finally were able to get him hospitalized. He came out of the treatment in fairly good shape and seemed to remain stable.

In the months that followed, I came to know the senator quite well. I found him to be a sage man with a wealth of experience from his many years in the Senate.

He rarely slipped again and in the few times he did, he had help available. I think that is what helped sustain him, knowing that there were others around who really cared and wouldn't condemn him.

We'd often get together for a chat. We never mentioned his unorthodox greeting when we first met. I had long since forgiven it and felt that it was his only way of crying out for help. In turn, the senator was of great help to me. In our talks I learned much about the Senate that I could not have learned in any other way.

"You can't know everything, Harold, and so you have to hire specialists to keep you posted," he said, filling me in on the ins and outs of hiring technical help.

He also guided me with protocol about applying for various Senate committees. In all, he helped me overcome many of the problems a freshman senator faces and I greatly benefited from this veteran's wise counsel.

In the meantime, I was able to arrange for Eva and Phyllis to move east and finally our house in McLean became a home. Phyllis was then a junior in high school, Connie and her family lived in Illinois, and Carol and her husband had moved to Virginia.

Mother couldn't make it with us to McLean. By now she needed special care. A few days before leaving for Washington, I drove her to Friendship Haven, a lovely Methodist retirement home in Fort Dodge, Iowa. Wayne Shoemaker assured me he would stop by regularly to visit her.

My heart was heavy as we drove up there that gray December day. She was all that was left of the family into which I had been born. I remembered from boyhood, her standing healthy and strong at the table kneading bread dough and telling me stories as I worked the butter churn. Now she was a frail wisp of a woman reduced to one suitcase and a cane.

It was difficult for Eva, Phyllis and me to become adjusted to life in the Washington area. There was the loneliness without the rest of the family.

Everything was new—the land, the people; even the weather was mild and bland compared to the bracing bite of Iowa's climate.

There was also a sharp contrast between the lifestyle of a governor and a freshman senator. My permanent suite in the New Senate

Office Building was at the far end of a side hall and consisted of four rooms, and a reception center. From my window I had a good view of a side street.

When I stepped out of the Statehouse office, it was "Governor this . . ." and "Governor that . . ." For in essence a governor is the chief executive, the president, as it were, of his state and is provided with a mansion, servants, limousine and an airplane.

But when I stepped into the long hall of the Senate building, I was just one of one hundred senators, and at the bottom of the totem pole at that.

The answer was not to look back but to get immersed in my work. For close communications with my constituents, I set up offices in three different cities in Iowa. And I began to learn why few senators appear on the Senate floor in session. Usually there's a subcommittee meeting going on somewhere. Also, if one stays away from his desk too long, the letters and phone calls pile up. Later, a little loudspeaker was installed in every senator's office that transmitted all the floor activities directly to him.

The Senate then had sixteen standing committees which covered areas of national interest from agriculture and forestry to labor and public welfare. Before a bill, issue or proposal reaches the Senate floor for discussion and vote, it is first referred to the pertinent committee where knowledgeable senators and their staffs study it. Often, these studies involve special investigations, and hearings in which outside experts in the field are called in to testify. The House of Representatives had twenty-one similar committees. And all often have subcommittees to investigate more deeply various facets of bills.

Thus, when a bill finally reaches the floor of the Senate or House it has gone through quite a workshop, providing the congressman with a wealth of background information on which to effectively form his judgment.

Senators can request assignment to committees on which they feel their talents and experience can be most effectively used. However, since seniority rules, one usually takes what he can get.

Because of my stand against the Vietnam War, I wanted placement on the Foreign Relations or Armed Services committees. This did not work out right away, but I was assigned to three which served the needs of people: *Labor and Public Welfare,* which covered health, education and labor mediation; *Banking and Currency,* which included loans to small businesses, public housing development and mortgage-interest rate controls; and *Veterans' Affairs*.

One of these committees, Labor and Public Welfare, I particularly sought. I felt it would lead me into an involvement with fellow alcoholics that would be broader and more far-reaching than any previous relationship.

26

Prayer
In the Halls of Power

ANOTHER KIND OF senatorial meeting came to my attention during the first week of the Ninety-first Congress. I received an invitation in the mail from Senator John Stennis, a Democrat from Mississippi, to attend the Senate prayer breakfast the following Wednesday morning in the Vandenberg Room of the Capitol building.

I had heard of this prayer breakfast, but suspected that most of those attending were southern conservatives like Stennis, rabid hawks on the Vietnam War who stood at the far end of the pole from me politically.

Yet since I had been depending on prayer for years, early the following Wednesday morning I found myself at a white-linen covered table in the marbled Vandenberg Room. As I looked around the table, my misgivings seemed to be confirmed. Except for Mark Hatfield from Oregon, most of my prayer breakfast companions, Republicans and Democrats alike, were arch-conservatives.

We opened with a prayer. Then, as waitresses soundlessly hovered about us, refilling our coffee cups, talk at the table covered everyday problems, the war, campus riots, crime on the streets. One of the men led a discussion on a Bible topic; there was some sharing. Then we stood and joined hands, closing with a short prayer. But the prayer and Bible study was all too brief, I felt. And as I walked out of the room, I doubted that I would return.

A few days later my secretary, Jo Nobles, announced a visitor. "His name is Doug Coe and he'd like to talk about the Senate prayer breakfast."

"Sure," I said, "send him in."

A tall dark, curly-haired man breezed in, his brown eyes radiating friendliness. He introduced himself as being involved with the breakfast groups in the United States and other parts of the world.

I waved him to a chair.

"I just wanted to see what you thought about the Senate prayer breakfast," he said.

I looked at him for a moment, weighing whether or not to be frank. Something about his open countenance encouraged me.

"Well, I've been to one . . . and I don't like it."

"Why?" he asked, his brow furrowing.

"They seem like a bunch of hypocrites to me." I said this, probing to see how serious this young man was about prayer. His eyes retained their friendly spirit, inviting me to express myself.

"Really, Doug," I continued, feeling more at ease with him, "I didn't think we spent enough time in prayer. I wish we could get involved with the Bible more and have some real spiritual discussion. Otherwise, I'm not sure I'll be back."

"If you come, Senator, you may help change it. We're all groping for answers." The tall husky man edged forward in his chair. "And if you want to pray, Senator, I'll meet with you."

"How often would you want to do it?" I asked.

"Whenever you want."

"'How about Tuesday mornings?"

He said he had prayer-breakfast commitments then; Wednesdays and Thursdays, too.

"Would you like to pray at 5:00 A.M.?" I asked, feeling this would really throw him.

"I'm free then," he said. He seemed sincere. "Look," he added, "except for the times I'm out of town, I'll pray with you anytime, anywhere."

"Well," I said, "let's pray right now."

We both sat there and prayed for God's guidance in our lives and his protection of our loved ones. Then he left, pausing at the door to ask: "You will come back to the prayer breakfast, won't you?"

"I don't know, Doug," I said, "let's see how it goes."

The next day he phoned. "I thought you should know that in my ten years on the Hill I have never met anyone so aggressive about praying as you," he laughed.

"Well, I've never felt aggressive about it," I chuckled, "but I am anxious to start praying with you regularly."

And we did pray together almost every day, sometimes on the phone at 5:00 A.M., and in person at other times whenever and wherever we could make it.

And I did return to the Senate prayer breakfast seeking the fellowship I felt so necessary.

However, when Doug invited me to discuss the prayer groups at a luncheon in a large home called Fellowship House, I balked. Doug persisted. Finally I agreed to come and one noon we headed up Massachusetts Avenue in his little sedan toward the gracious French Provincial residence on quiet tree-lined Woodland Drive Northwest, just off the busy Rock Creek Parkway.

I learned we were to lunch with Abraham Vereide, the man who inspired the prayer fellowship work in Washington and other cities.

Vereide had come to the United States from Norway as a young minister, settled in Seattle in 1935 where he worked for the poor and helped start Goodwill Industries. Seeing the need for a genuine religious revival throughout the nation, he began encouraging local Seattle businessmen to gather together for prayer.

"They were small fellowship groups meeting for prayer and discussion," said Doug. "The vitality comes when business antagonists and political rivals see each other in the light of Jesus Christ. This is the way that people with political differences can often become friends."

He explained that the prayer breakfasts began in Washington after Congress convened in January 1942 following Pearl Harbor. Vice President Henry Wallace and several senators agreed that it was important to start meeting for prayer. "The first Senate prayer breakfast was held soon after," said Doug. "Later the House of Representatives began one, and now there are prayer breakfasts all over Washington in practically every government agency."

Doug turned his head and grinned at me. "Do you know where the first prayer breakfast was held?"

I shook my head.

"It is recorded in the Bible, John 21, when the resurrected Jesus called to His disciples who had fished all night on the Sea of Galilee."

He stopped his car in front of a large residence, took out his Bible and read: *"When they got out on land, they saw a charcoal fire*

*there, with fish lying on it, and bread . . . Jesus said to them,
'Come and have breakfast.' "*

I liked the picture the Bible painted. How many times Dad, Jesse
and I had cooked fish just like that on the bank of a river early in
the morning.

As we walked into Fellowship House, Doug explained that over
the years this residence had become a place where men and women
from all over the world could meet for spiritual fellowship. "We
have no organization, Harold," said Doug, "no creed except a belief
in our Lord Jesus Christ Who can solve all problems and . . ." he
chuckled, nudging me, "even helping someone like you and John
Stennis understand one another."

"That will be the day," I grimaced.

It turned out to be a pleasant lunch with the kind and gentle Abraham Vereide; in him I sensed a deep rock-like faith that had obviously carried him through some rough times. He was interested
in learning that I was a Methodist lay speaker, as his own affiliation
was with the Methodist church.

He told me about the National Prayer Breakfast which is held in
Washington every January with attendees representing a cross section of the United States, including the President and his official
family, plus people from about one hundred countries. The breakfast
is sponsored by a joint committee of senators and representatives.

It began during President Eisenhower's campaign. Senator Frank
Carlson of Kansas invited Eisenhower to attend the Senate prayer
breakfast after the election. Nothing came of it until after the inauguration when the president phoned Carlson and invited him over
to the White House, saying, "Would you fellows please come over
for a visit? This is the loneliest house I've ever lived in."

During their visit that evening, the president said he'd like to
attend the Senate prayer breakfast. Then the Senators began to worry.
The little room in which they met wouldn't accommodate all those
who would show up when they heard the president was coming.

Hotel magnate Conrad Hilton saved the day when he offered the
use of the Mayflower Hotel dining room.

"That's how it started," said Doug, pointing out that the National
Prayer Breakfast continues to be supported by individual contributions, with no government funding.

In finding fellowship with senators whose political beliefs con-
flicted so sharply with mine, the story of Cornelius, the proud Roman

centurion, and Peter, the Jewish fisherman, was also helpful. They were men of different religious, social and political backgrounds, but it was clear from Scripture that each loved the Lord. If it could happen then, I concluded, it could happen today.

And sure enough, as we senators continued to meet for prayer breakfasts, I began to gain a new view of my brothers in Congress. One senator said: "Until I went to a breakfast group, I thought I'd never really know another senator personally. Usually we'd only pass in the hall on the way to vote."

One morning a man came to the breakfast in deep need. His wife had just undergone major surgery and was fighting to live. Until then our prayers had tended to be formal and general. But moved by the emotion of my fellow senator, I impulsively said: "Let's join hands right now and pray for her healing."

That night he called me on the phone to say that when he had returned to the hospital that day, a major change for the better had occurred and his wife would soon be discharged.

As our prayers became more specific and personal, I came to see how important this relationship was to each of us. A legislator's life is under a constant bombardment of pressures from his constituency and special interest groups in Congress. As one rejuvenated senator put it one morning as we left the prayer breakfast, "I feel like I can sort things out again."

Through this my own faith deepened. Eva and my daughters, too, were finding strength in the companionship of other Christians. Carol needed this help in particular. Her marriage had broken up and she had come home to live with us, a sad, suffering girl. Through prayer groups in the Washington area, however, she found much spiritual nourishment. One night she came home with shining eyes to tell Eva and me that she had been baptized by the Holy Spirit.

Then she became part of a fellowship meeting in a nearby town headed by a pastor named Derrel Emmerson. Eva, Phyllis and I listened with growing excitement as Carol told us of witnessing supernatural healings of both minds and bodies through prayer.

At that time close friends of ours had a six-month-old girl who had been blind from an infection since birth. Eva asked Carol if there was any possibility of her group praying for this baby. The child's parents had studied the miracles in the Gospels and were quite open to such a healing prayer. So one day Carol's fellowship group went to this couple's apartment.

It was Pastor Emmerson who later told us what happened. The baby lay quietly on the mother's lap while the group prayed and worshiped God. It was a quiet but holy moment. Afterwards, the group talked casually with the parents, stealing occasional glances at the infant.

"The light!" someone said. "The light from the windows seems to be bothering her." The baby was squinting, turning her face toward her mother. Pastor Emmerson then prayed, "God, show me that this is indeed a miracle." As he moved out of his chair, the baby turned her head to follow him. Eyes that had never seen before were seeing!

Moved by the experience and later seeing evidence of the child's vision ourselves, Eva and I joined Carol in meeting with this group which believed as we did that God can do anything.

Something special also seemed to be happening to Carol. Her faith and implicit trust in Jesus was obviously deepening. She began working in the insurance office at Fairfax Hospital and during her lunch hour she would pray with the patients. She reported wonderful experiences and said she had never been happier. And yet, it seemed to Eva and me that Carol's health did not match her buoyant spirit. She looked so frail. When Eva mentioned this out loud, Carol would just laugh it off. "A good night's sleep will always fix me up," she said.

My own prayer life was expanding. By now Fellowship House had become a retreat for me as I met there more and more for prayer, Scripture study and the sharing of problems with men I could be comfortable with and not feel that anything I said would be reported in the press the next morning.

One afternoon as I was putting on my coat to leave after a prayer meeting, Doug Coe stopped me in the hall.

"Harold, could we meet for a moment in the parlor?"

"Sure."

After we sat down in the quiet room, Doug leaned forward. "For some time now we've been talking about a group of men who'd meet together regularly and really pray together."

"Yes?"

"It's time we really get serious about it," he continued. "I'm thinking about a group of just three or four men who would really commit themselves to praying for each other, who would share each other's problems." He stopped for a minute. "I mean *really* share . . . not just ask help for a family situation, but tell it *all* . . . to bear each other's burdens, like the Bible says."

I sat quietly for a moment, reflecting on my own problems. How good it would be to share some of my concerns about Carol with someone who really cared.

And yet I wondered. How open could one be with another in Washington, where this year's friends can be next year's enemies? Outside my family, I had never really gotten close to anyone except a few political advisors. I wasn't sure I was ready to open my personal life to anyone. And I didn't want to make a commitment I couldn't keep.

This was unfamiliar ground Doug was describing. Would my fellow-walkers be trustworthy?

I looked up at Doug who was watching me intently. Certainly *he* was reliable. I had learned that to be true.

"Okay, Doug," I said. "I guess the only way to find out is to give it a try." It would be like testing a hot iron; if it burned my hand, I at least could pull it back.

A small number of us decided to meet regularly in the Capitol prayer room where I had often gone to pray. The first get-together didn't go well. Sitting self-consciously in a small pew, I felt out of place; we couldn't seem to agree on what form our meeting would follow. We continued to meet week after week, but I wondered if we would ever reach that moment of mutual trust that Doug had talked about.

Perhaps it was like breaking in a new pair of shoes: after a few weeks they begin to be comfortable. Slowly we opened our lives to each other, talking about things I never would have dreamed of sharing with anyone but Eva. We discussed our life styles and how we could change them to follow more closely Christ's teachings, how we should handle our possessions, even our relationships with wives and children.

We discussed the differences in each of our children, and how we could best relate to them. We discussed their individual gifts, handicaps and talents. I talked about Carol as I found myself becoming more concerned about her. The sadness in her life seemed to be behind her now. But still, for some reason I could not fathom, I felt a special poignancy about this middle child of ours.

Our little group ended up as four men: Doug Coe; Al Quie, Republican congressman from Minnesota, a six-foot-two outdoorsman who wore western boots; Graham Purcell, a tall, silver-haired former Democratic congressman from Texas; and me.

When we'd first meet, we'd politely shake hands. After we came to know and trust each other, the hand shakes became bear hugs. If I had known that this fellowship would lead to my embracing one of the most ruthless, hateful men on Capitol Hill, I would have become physically sick.

27

The Deadly Amenity

THE SEAT BELT light flashed on as our jet swung into its landing approach to Washington's National Airport. I gazed out the window at the jeweled lights in the black velvet landscape, thinking about the mission from which I was returning. I had been in a distant city where I had met a civic leader and his wife. An alcoholic, the man was about to lose both his family and his position. Joining us had been my old friend, Ray Harrison, a municipal judge from Des Moines and, like me, a recovered alcoholic. Finally, after much prayer and counseling, the civic leader had admitted that he needed help.

It had been only seventeen years since I had made the same admission. I thought of the hundreds of thousands of men, women and youngsters who never seem to find help, who live as derelicts or die tragically. The statistics were heartbreaking. Not only did alcohol rank with heart disease and cancer as a public killer, but considering the highway deaths it caused, it had become our chief public executioner.

Was this one of the reasons I was brought to Washington, to represent the millions suffering from addiction to alcohol and other drugs? When I saw the Health, Education and Welfare budget of only $4 million for community assistance grants for alcoholism treatment programs for the whole country, I was deeply troubled, especially since that $4 million was eliminated by the administration in a budget-cutting move.

How could we reconcile this puny effort with spending $25 million for one bomber, many of which were now being downed in Vietnam?

I learned that Senators Javits of New York, a Republican, and Moss of Utah, a Democrat, had been trying for the previous three years to do something about alcohol. They had even come up with a bill. But there was a disappointing lack of interest among legislators.

Somehow we needed to focus national attention on the problem. I prayed for some kind of guidance but all I got was a strange feeling that the ball was in my hands. Me, a freshman senator? Ridiculous!

About the only thing I could think of was that it related closest to the Labor and Public Welfare Committee on which I served. A thought struck me. Why not establish a special subcommittee on alcoholism and narcotics to dig into it?

I approached Ralph Yarborough, Committee Chairman, about it. He felt as strongly as I did but pointed out that Labor and Health didn't have the funds.

It didn't seem right that lack of money should stop us. "Senator, I'll make you a deal," I said. "If you will establish the subcommittee, we'll do what we can without any money. If we can get something going, maybe we can ask for some money a year or two from now."

Ralph Yarborough took me up on it and on May 20, 1969, he named a Special Subcommittee on Alcoholism and Narcotics under my chairmanship. Serving with me were Yarborough himself; Jennings Randolph, West Virginia; Harrison Williams, New Jersey; Edward Kennedy, Massachusetts; Walter Mondale, Minnesota; Jacob Javits, New York; Peter Dominick, Colorado; Henry Bellmon, Oklahoma; and William Saxbe, Ohio.

To help pay for investigation and travel, I accepted speaking engagements for honorariums.

To my knowledge it was the first congressional subcommittee devoted to alleviating the human blight of alcohol and drug abuse. Rather than attacking the problems from a law-enforcement view, we tried meeting them with a health approach, treating the victims as desperately ill, endeavoring to rehabilitate them, and trying to stop the spread of infection.

We didn't know the answers. For example, why are some people addicted to these drugs and others not?

We started by holding Senate hearings for fresh information on which to make decisions. The first hearing started Wednesday, July 23, 1969, in the New Senate Office Building. We committee members sat behind a long horseshoe-shaped desk that extended across the room. One by one the witnesses came forward to the microphone to give their testimonies.

I'll never forget watching my friend, Judge Ray Harrison from Des Moines, stand up and acknowledge that as a hopeless drunk in earlier years he had been confined to his own jail eighteen different times. Then a 41-year-old lawyer, his life had been turned around through the prayers of his wife and mother.

He spoke of one man in his court who had been arrested over 500 times for drunkenness.

"And you are convinced," I asked him, "that you have not yet met the man who could not make the grade under the right set of circumstances?"

"That's right," he said. "If we can say the right thing to him when he is in an acceptable frame of mind, he can get well, providing he has the desire."

We talked of the many advertisements showing men and women drinking in glamorous circumstances.

Judge Harrison nodded. "Yes, I thought I was like the handsome man in the whiskey ad standing by the rail fence with the fancy saddle next to him."

He went on to say that his court had a class for young people who had been arrested for liquor violations. In four sessions they were shown the grisly truth about drinking, the graphic deterioration of the body, the destruction of brain cells. "I found if you tell kids the truth about it instead of condemning them, they seem to benefit from it."

Another witness was a minister who confessed that after a drinking bout he found himself sitting in a strange car in a garage of a family he did not know. It was twenty miles from the place he had been drinking.

"How I got there I have not the faintest idea," he said. I shuddered as I remembered how I awakened similarly in a Des Moines hotel room years before.

In lining up the witnesses, we particularly wanted someone of stature willing to admit being a recovered alcoholic. But it seemed hopeless. Time after time we'd approach such a person only to be politely turned down. I couldn't blame them.

Finally, a friend suggested we try Mercedes McCambridge, Academy award-winning actress. I reached her by phone and explained the hearings. "Your appearance could hurt your career," I warned. I told her of the criticism I had received for opening the alcoholic can of worms, of abuse even from alcoholics who considered our investigation a threat.

"Well, how do you stay above it?" she asked.

"There is no choice," I said. "If one person lives who might have died, I feel it will be worth it. But I can't ask you to take that risk, and I won't blame you if you say no. I have to tell you that I've been turned down by a dozen other people."

The phone was silent for a moment. Then in that husky voice, "OK, I'll do it."

We met in my office before the hearing. I could see the strong spirit in her bright brown eyes. "If you have any second thoughts, Mercy," I said, "the door is open and no one will think less of you if you walk out." She answered me with a fiery look.

Later, in the hearing room, she sat down before the microphone, self-assured, and with an underlying current of emotion in her voice, confessed: "As I sit here, scores of women like me are being arranged on slabs in morgues throughout this country with tickets tied to their toes that read 'Acute Alcoholism,' or if they have been protected as I was, those tags may read 'Liver Ailment,' 'Chronic Bronchitis' or 'Massive Hemmorrage.'

"I did not know I had a terminal disease . . . a psychological and physiological disease. Psychologically, I knew there was something wrong with me; I was born guilty, because my 'first parents' got mixed up with a bad apple and my life was an atonement for that."

Chuckling inwardly at her description of Adam and Eve, I had no idea that this glamorous-looking woman was this spiritually aware of the basis of her disease.

"I had no doubt," she continued, "that it was merely a matter of time before the fires of hell caught up with me anyhow. I was convinced that my Maker was standing directly behind me with a whip in His hand. Finally I stopped running long enough to turn around and take that whip out of His hand, because I was the one who had put it there in the first place."

She went on to say how alcohol-oriented our society had become. "To go into someone's home and be greeted with 'How do you do? How about a drink?' or to sit down in a restaurant and be asked first off, 'What will you have to drink?'

"So I drank, like everybody else . . . this delicious chemical, this social amenity, this medicine that puts people at their ease because merely being together makes them uncomfortable. This medicine became my poison. The insidious, diabolical evil, the viciousness of my disease, is that the poison set up its own craving for more of itself.

"Nobody need die of this disease," she continued. "We are eminently salvageable. We are well worth the trouble. We are eminently equipped to enrich this world. We write poetry, we paint pictures, we compose music, we build bridges, we head corporations, we win the coveted prizes for the world's great literature, and too often, too many of us die from our disease, not our sin, not our weakness."

When she finished, the room was quiet. Senator Yarborough broke the silence. "Miss McCambridge," he said, emotion in his voice, "I vote you another Oscar, this time for public service!"

We had other enlightening statements, from housewives and young people to such leaders as Marty Mann, founder of the National Council on Alcoholism.

One statement that burned into me deeply was by Bill Wilson, co-founder of Alcoholics Anonymous. At the time, before his death, he could only be identified as Bill W., since he preferred to stay in the background and let the light shine on what this wonderful organization could do for the hopeless.

He told our committee how he felt Alcoholics Anonymous had its start in the office of a famous psychiatrist. "I refer to one of the founders of modern psychiatry, Carl Jung," said Bill, "who in the early 1930's received an alcoholic patient from America, a well-known businessman named Roland who had run the gamut of all known cures.

"Roland came to Jung and stayed with him almost a year. He grew to love this learned and wonderful friend. During this period the hidden springs of his motivation were revealed. He felt then that with his new understanding he had really shed this strange illness of mind, body and spirit."

Bill stopped for a moment, glanced at all of us, and continued. "After leaving Jung, Roland was drinking again in a matter of a month. He returned to Jung, broken and dispirited: 'Carl, what does this all mean?' he asked."

Bill glanced over at me and said: "Jung then made the statement which I think led to the formation of AA. He said, 'Roland, I thought you might be one of those rare cases who could be made to recover by the practice of my art. But like most who will pass through here, I must confess that my art can do nothing for you.'

" 'Doctor, you are my last resort,' exclaimed Roland. 'Is there no other recourse?'

"The doctor said, 'Yes, there may be. I am speaking of the possibility of a spiritual awakening; if you like, a conversion.'

" 'But,' said Roland, 'I am a religious man. I used to be a vestryman in the Episcopal Church. I still have faith in God, but I think He has little faith in me.'

"Jung slowly shook his head. 'No, I mean something that goes deeper than that. I am talking about a transforming of spirit that can remotivate you and set you free from this.

" 'Time after time alcoholics have recovered by these means,' Jung continued. 'The lightning strikes here and there, and no one can say why or how. All I can suggest is that you expose yourself to some religious environment of your own choice.' "

As Bill spoke, I knew exactly what he was talking about. Bill went on to say that Roland joined a group that brought him close to God, had a transformation in his life and was released from his hideous compulsion.

And then Bill told how this businessman passed on his discovery to an alcoholic friend, who in turn was the man who had come to Bill's rescue when he had given up hope.

"Out of this eventuated a very sudden spiritual awakening in which I was released from this compulsion to drink, a compulsion on my mind morning, noon and night for several years," said Bill. "I was suddenly released from it." *

From this developed the Alcoholics Anonymous organization, as Bill and his friends began to help other alcoholics find what they called a Higher Power.

Later, I learned more about his spiritual awakening. Bill had felt that some of the people at the hearing wouldn't understand it. In 1934 he had been a stockbroker, confined in a New York hospital, completely defeated by alcohol. "I could not accept the personal God my friend had talked about," he admitted.

---

* Taken from hearings before the special subcommittee on alcoholism and narcotics of the Committee on Labor and Public Welfare, United States Senate, 91st Congress, July 23–25, 1969.

Later, alone in his hospital room, his depression deepened. "It seemed as if I were at the very bottom of the pit," he continued. "I still gagged on the notion of a Power greater than myself, but finally, just for the moment, the last vestige of my proud obstinacy was crushed. I found myself crying out, 'If there is a God, let Him show Himself! I am ready to do anything, *anything!*' "

Bill's deep-set eyes were alive. "Suddenly the room lit up with a great white light. I was caught up into an ecstasy which no words can describe. It seemed to me, that I was on a mountain and that a wind not of air but of Spirit was blowing. Then it burst upon me that I was a free man. Slowly the ecstasy subsided. I lay on the bed, but now for a time I was in another world, a new world of consciousness. All about me and through me there was a wonderful feeling of Presence, and I thought to myself, 'So this is the God of the preachers.' A great peace stole over me and I thought, 'No matter how wrong things seem to be, they are still all right. Things are all right with God and His world.' "

After the hearings I thought long and deep about what Bill had told me. Seemingly, all the detoxification centers and psychiatric help had no effect on the terrible bondage that alcohol had had on him.

Only God could help him, the same God Who had lifted me.

I found myself walking toward the capitol prayer room just off the rotunda. I had learned of it in my first weeks in the Senate and found it a restful place to pray and meditate.

I got the key from the guard and walked in. A simple room of about eighteen feet square with soft green walls, it was created in 1955 through a resolution by Senator Mike Monroney of Oklahoma and Representative Brooks Hays of Arkansas.

It was empty; I sat down in one of the small white oak pews and studied the stained-glass window glowing behind the altar. The words "This Nation Under God" surmounted a portrayal of George Washington kneeling in prayer. Around him was the first verse of the 16th Psalm: "Preserve me, O God, for in Thee do I put my trust."

I thought of the last verse in this song of David: "Thou wilt show me the path of life: in thy presence is fullness of joy; at thy right hand there are pleasures for evermore."

Certainly Bill Wilson's group was showing others the path of life. Why was it really helping people when all the statements and findings from government research only seemed to illuminate the problems? I thought of the many brochures and warnings I had read on alcohol; none of them ever stopped me from taking that drink.

There was an answer here that eluded me.

Part of it came later. I had been in New York City all day for a meeting which ended with a formal dinner. In the middle of dinner a waiter whispered that I was wanted on the telephone.

He led me to a phone near the kitchen. Because of the clamor I had to hold a hand over my other ear to hear the caller. It was Nick Kotz, a young reporter I had met in Des Moines and had tried to hire as an aide. We had kept up communication and now he was with the Washington *Post*. Nick was calling from D.C.

"Harold," he said, "the brother of a good friend of mine desperately needs help. He's in New York City right now and is at a crisis point. Can you see him right away?"

"Right now?"

"Yes."

"Where is he?"

"Bedford Stuyvesant," he said, naming a rough area.

"Nick," I said, "I'm right in the middle of a formal dinner. I'll get there as soon as it's over."

Nick's tone tightened. "Harold, the guy could be suicidal. His sister, the one who called me, is wrought up. He has so much to lose, a wonderful wife and family."

The word suicidal chilled me.

"Well, if you can get his sister to have him contact me, I'll have a better chance of helping him." I found myself hoping this would be the end of it.

Twenty minutes later the waiter returned to my table. There was a call for me. I went back to the phone. The voice was a bit incoherent.

"Can you come here to the hotel?" I asked. He said he couldn't.

I excused myself from my dinner companions, went down and hailed a cab. As it jounced over bumpy Manhattan streets toward Bedford Stuyvesant, a mixture of apprehension and self-criticism filled me. Why was I doing such a foolish thing? I didn't know this man. I'd been warned this was a dangerous section of town. The man must have friends there who could help him.

The cab pulled up in front of an ancient hotel. Men lounged against the building; an empty bottle clattered nearby. I hesitated, then forced myself out and walked up the crumbling steps of the building. I felt stupid entering the dim lobby in my tuxedo. The acrid odor peculiar to old buildings surrounded me as a creaking elevator lifted me to the fourth floor.

The eyes of the black man who pulled back the door had that lost, hopeless look I had seen in the mirror so many times.

As I stepped into the room, he slumped back on a rumpled bed, head buried in his hands. The sink in the corner was full of cigarette butts. I pulled a rusting metal chair up to the bed and sat down. In the light of the bulb over the sink, the man's body cast a vast shadow on the wall. I just sat there, not saying anything. His back began to heave as deep sobs rumbled from his chest.

Finally, he looked up at me. "I've got nothing to live for."

"Friend," I said, "it wasn't too long ago that I felt the same way."

Interest flickered in his eyes. I related how I had climbed into a bathtub with a shotgun but then had been given the strength to put the gun away.

"Well," he sighed, "you're stronger than I."

"Look," I said, "I didn't get myself out of that tub. It was God. The same God Who is in this room with us right now."

"Nobody cares about me, including Him," he said.

I noticed a glint of gold on the big hands clasped before him. "You're married, aren't you? Do you have a family?"

He nodded. "But they're all better off without me around."

I remembered the time I had said the same thing. For a moment there was no sound in the room except his heavy, sighing breathing. Down the hall, someone beat on a door and cursed.

Leaning forward, I took his arm. "You're obviously an intelligent man. God has a plan for your life and it doesn't include drinking your good brains out."

Perhaps it was because of a fellow human being's interest, but a thin wire of communication seemed to have been strung between us.

I told him how God had lifted me from the mire, but I still had problems. "I get angry easily, fall into dark moods, and women call me a male chauvinist," I said, "but when I fall down, He is always there to pick me up."

He leaned back on the bed and relaxed a bit. Some of the tenseness drained from his face. As we talked I learned that he had a master's degree and taught school.

"You have so much to live for," I stressed, "and there are people who will help you."

His face became grim. A dark force seemed to have come over the room again. "Oh, let's cut the crap," he said, "I'm not good for anything. I'm no good for my family. I'll start drinking again. Let's face it; I'm no good."

"Look," I said, putting my hand on his shoulder, "unless you love yourself, you can't love others. God made you a special person to help other people. But you must first accept yourself."

He leaned forward on the edge of the bed studying the worn linoleum floor.

"I can talk all night and it isn't going to do you any good," I continued. "I know one Person to Whom we can go and I'd like to talk to Him now." Then I got down on my knees before the chair and began praying for the man on the bed. I asked God to encourage him and reunite him with his family.

I glanced up to see his eyes closed, hands clasped. Something happened in that dingy room as we prayed together, as if another Presence was there. When I arose, the man looked up. There was a new light in his eyes. He took my hand and gripped it, not saying anything, just holding on for a long time. I looked deep into his eyes and knew that I wouldn't have to worry.

"Come see me in the morning," I said, giving him my hotel room number. Riding back to my hotel, I thought about that moment when another Person seemed to be in the room. It was as He said in Matthew 18:20: "Where two or three are gathered together in My name, there am I in the midst of them."

It was something of a shock to meet the man the next morning at my hotel. Well dressed and freshly groomed, he looked entirely different from the broken person huddled on the bed. Mercedes McCambridge, who was attending the same meeting, talked with him also. She was able to put him in touch with an Alcoholics Anonymous group.

I gained something far more significant from this encounter than knowing someone had been helped. The key to his renewal, I felt, was fellowship. Left alone in that lonely room he might well have taken his life. I thought of the desolate man in Iowa who had called me late one night before Christmas and then did kill himself. Satan works best when someone is alone. But when two or three are gathered in His Name . . . I remembered the man who hailed me on the Des Moines street when I was looking for a drink, the Alcoholics Anonymous friends who supported me in Storm Lake and Ida

Grove, and all the other men and women who had kneeled beside me in my time of need.

The key to it all, I felt, was fellowship on a one-to-one basis in the Spirit of our Lord Jesus Christ. We all are like starving beggars, each telling the other where to find bread.

28

A Very Dark Horse

"THERE IS NO reason that the Alcoholics Anonymous concept shouldn't work with drug addicts as well as it does with alcoholics," I said, as our subcommittee continued hearings on narcotics.

We had been listening to former addicts reveal their wretched existence. "Treatment for drug abuse is virtually nonexistent because addiction is not recognized as an illness," I added. "Under our law it is a crime.

"Research into the causes, treatment and prevention of drug addiction is pitifully lacking, for we're concerned with punishing people, not educating or healing them."

In endeavoring to develop drug therapy programs, I had been giving many talks around the country. People also began asking for my views on the Vietnam War, poverty and other crucial issues. As a result, I started getting national exposure on television talk shows such as "Today" and "We, the People."

After I returned from a "Meet the Press," appearance, Park Rinard looked hard at me. "Keep this up, Chief, and they'll be pushing you to run for president some day."

I laughed and said, *"That* will be the day!" But Park's words fanned that tiny spark that lies deep in the heart of every governor, congressman or senator. What if?

I quenched it at first. I knew that anyone in the running has his life opened to public view like a can of sardines. All my old problems would be brought up and hashed over. My family had suffered enough for my indiscretions.

However, the spark remained and was fanned brighter when

Averell Harriman, former U.S. peace negotiator, stopped at my office for a visit, impressed by my stand on Vietnam.

When more and more people began to focus on my running for president in 1972, I commented one night to Eva: "With our budget, we'd have just enough money to give everyone in Ida Grove a bumper sticker."

"Speaking of Iowa," she said, and handed me a copy of the December 14, 1969, *Des Moines Register*. A front page article was headlined:

"HUGHES DARK HORSE CANDIDATE IN '72?"

In part, the article read:

"Washington, D.C.—Just one year after taking office as Iowa's newest congressman, Senator Harold E. Hughes has acquired somewhat of a national reputation and is often mentioned as a dark horse Democratic candidate for president in 1972."

It went on to say that a New York organization of business and professional people, many of whom had backed Eugene McCarthy for president in 1968, had shown an interest in me.

"He is also attracting some of the same young people who were the driving force behind McCarthy's campaign," it continued. "Many of them now find McCarthy too aloof and are disenchanted with him. They consider Hubert Humphrey 'old guard' and Senator Edmund Muskie too much of an 'established figure,' so they are searching.

"Hughes is quietly pleased by the presidential talk, but is realistic enough to know that his chances are remote. 'If the lightning strikes, that's fine,' is the way one of his aides put it."

My heart beat faster as I studied the article. But then as I read the last paragraph out loud to Eva, I laughed, "Well, Honey, you won't have to worry about living at 1600 Pennsylvania. I've never been struck by lightning."

But lightning of another kind was building. As college students stepped up their protests against the Vietnam War, thousands of young people demonstrated in Washington, D.C. I believed in the freedom of peaceful demonstrations, but urged protesters to work through the democratic process. After the deaths at Kent State in April, 1970, I intensified my stand against violence.

"Do you believe in peace?" I asked a massive antiwar rally at

Madison Square Garden in New York City. Thousands stood and roared "Yes!"

"Then find peace in your own heart," I said. "If we are to bring peace into the world, we must love our brothers as we love ourselves."

I had to face these words in a very personal way when I got back to Washington. Among presidential appointments was a man slated as district attorney for the northern district of Iowa. The individual's name was submitted to the Senate Judiciary Committee for approval. In turn, they passed it on to me for clearance, since I represented Iowa.

The name came to me on a blue slip. I sat looking at it for several minutes. Evan Hultman. Again, Curly's face appeared before me as he met me in the hall at the Savery Hotel luncheon and said he was sorry but that he was going to have to bring my alcoholism up in the debate.

I could approve the appointment or kill it.

What was right here? As I thought about it, somehow I began to understand the Curly Hultman of six years before. Desperate, he was struggling as all men do in the political arena. But he was a good attorney and an honest man.

I signed the slip indicating my approval and sent it back.

Some days later, I was surprised to see Curly Hultman in my office. After catching up on each other's families, Curly said he hoped there was no ill will left over from the past.

I put my hand on his arm. "No, Curly, that's all dead and past. It's good to be friends." There's something about a reconciliation that warms one like a bright spring sun after a long cold winter.

Curly went on to become an excellent district attorney. And I went on with my work with the subcommittee. I knew that God was the Source of help for the alcoholic, but I also knew man had to do what he could to help alleviate this disease. *Faith without works is dead* has always been a Scriptural guideline for me. We reached a major milestone in 1970 when the Senate passed a bill I sponsored which funded alcohol treatment centers all over the nation and founded the National Institute on Alcohol Abuse and Alcoholism. The goal was to help millions of alcoholics recover and save thousands of lives on highways, reduce crime, decrease the welfare rolls and cut down the appalling economic waste from alcoholism.

It was also the kind of headline-making legislation that my supporters felt would advance my image as a contender for the presidential
nomination.

As Park Rinard said one day as we discussed the possibility, "Presidential candidates go through three stages: flattery at being considered, the let's-look-at-it phase, and then figuring out how to go
about running."

He lit his pipe and looked at me. "I figure right now we're about
phase two."

He was right about the flattery; I was already well-fixed on that
score. I was in the stage where I really wanted to look at it.

To do this, in late 1970 a small group of men rented a little green
townhouse at 41 Ivy Street, two blocks south of the Capitol. Using it
as headquarters, they began compiling information on key issues,
studying Democratic politics and exploring funding possibilities. The
latter was still a problem with us. Operation of this office itself was
costing around $5,000 a month. And most of that was coming from
three long-time friends and supporters, Joseph Rosenfield, the retired
retail executive from Des Moines; Bill Knapp, the Iowa real estate
developer; and Brinkley Smithers of New York, a philanthropist
who had dedicated himself to helping the alcoholic in any way he
could.

The lease for the Washington headquarters ran until September
1971. "By then," said Alan Baron, office director and former Sioux
Citian, "we'll need a bigger place or we won't need any place at all."

Contenders for the nomination already in the water were Senators
George McGovern, Birch Bayh, Edmund Muskie, Edward Kennedy
and Hubert Humphrey. When I joined the group, newspapers referred
to us as "the 6-pack." All of us were against the war, pollution, infla-
tion and unemployment. All of us were for realigning national priorities to help get the country together and move forward.

Soon I intensified my traveling, speaking at every opportunity. It
meant leaving Eva, Carol and Phyllis home alone more often. But I
told myself that I was doing it for them. What wife or daughter
wouldn't want their husband and father to be a presidential candidate
of the United States?

But there were many times when the truth of just how little known
I was came like cold water thrown into my face. At a banquet in
North Dakota, I discovered that the tickets read: "Guest speaker—

Howard Hughes." And posters on the campus of Fairleigh Dickinson University in New Jersey invited everyone to hear "The Honorable *Howard* Hughes."

"Well, I wish our campaign fund had *his* money," is all I could say to my aide, Ed Campbell. Ed did much for me on these trips, masterminding our schedule.

I had heard a horror story through Margo Coleman, writer for the Chicago *Tribune,* who told about another senator on the same kind of trip. His dress shirt studs had been left behind, page six of his speech was missing, there hadn't been time to eat, and the entourage arrived at the Waldorf Ballroom a half hour after it had been cleared —missing entirely a banquet where he was to be the keynote speaker.

Besides keeping this from happening, Ed encouraged me as I traveled places well covered by men better educated and more experienced than I. "Here's your secret, Harold," he said, reading from a newspaper:

"Plain people like Harold Hughes instinctively because he *is* them. He is magic with people who feel the whole world's a tuxedo and they're a brown shoe."

But my brown shoe was well scuffed, and some people worried about it. A Capitol Hill staff member, a heavy drinker himself, said: "How could you put a man in a high-tension situation who's had a drinking problem? Wouldn't you be afraid he'd take a drink?"

To which someone else answered: "I don't care that he'd drink. What worries me is that he might *pray.*"

A lot of people still called me a "mystic." "Sure, he has a basic faith," worried another. "He's a devout man and some of my friends put this down. Maybe we've come so far into the computer age that people with God are suspect."

However, the more I spoke to different groups, the more encouraged I became. At San Marcos, Texas, I addressed 1,500 students filling the gymnasium of Southwest Texas State University. I was not only in Lyndon Johnson's home territory, I was at his alma mater where sometime earlier eleven students had been expelled for merely participating in a peaceful antiwar rally.

When a student called from the floor asking what I would do in Vietnam if I were president, I told them I'd announce to the American people that we had fulfilled our commitment and then withdraw our troops. The gym filled with applause. And my ego, now well-nurtured, began to grow.

I was low in most of the polls, but not all of them. Eva looked up from the newspaper one morning and handed it to me with a wry smile. "Just what the girls and I have been telling you." I had been voted by fashion experts as "One of the Ten Worst-Dressed Men in Washington."

Maybe it even helped me. For my support grew as I continued to speak across the country. In northern New Jersey when I spoke to a group of iron workers, I overheard one burly worker say: "That guy's really got it. You can tell when someone's sincere."

It was all heady exhilaration. I felt even more flattered when people began forming local campaign organizations around the country.

As we moved into the summer of 1971, columnist David Broder described me as "a very dark horse, but the only Democrat around who excites the kind of personal enthusiasm the Kennedys used to generate."

As a dark horse, I now found myself galloping. I had again applied for an appointment to the Armed Services Committee, hoping to wield some influence on excessive arms expenditures and our conduct in the Vietnam War.

John Stennis was chairman of the Armed Services Committee and I felt sure he wouldn't want me on it. To my surprise, I received the appointment and relinquished my post on Banking and Currency.

In the meantime, our subcommittee on alcoholism and narcotics produced a bill to provide $1.7 billion to fight drug abuse; the Senate approved our proposal for an amendment to the draft extension bill that would protect drug-addicted servicemen from discipline and discharge if they turned themselves in for treatment and rehabilitation. That same year I was also named a delegate to an international drug control conference in Vienna.

But funding our fight against drugs and alcohol was always a problem. I blamed much of this opposition on those who surrounded President Nixon, men like Robert Haldeman, John Erlichman and Charles Colson, powerful, manipulative men whom I felt were careless of the forgotten unfortunate.

Yet I was to be accused of this same carelessness. It happened at one of our subcommittee hearings. A heavyset black woman in her middle forties was testifying about how she couldn't get the police to close down a hangout in her New York City neighborhood where addicts shot up drugs.

"Nobody cares about us down there," she snapped. "Nobody will come and see for themselves what goes on . . . and," she glared at me, "I'm sure *you* don't care either!"

"I'll come," I said.

"Well," she sniffed, "I'll believe it when I see it."

Senators Jake Javits from New York, Harrison Williams of New Jersey, and Richard Schweiker of Pennsylvania, traveled with me to Harlem a few weeks later. The lady who so bluntly testified at our hearing was surprised to see us.

"C'mon," she said, "I'll show you how easy it is to buy heroin."

Patting a small youth on the head, she pointed to a hamburger stand on the corner. "Give him ten dollars," she said, "and watch how easy it is for him to get a hamburger and five bags of heroin."

"Will he be safe?" I worried.

"Sure," she snorted. "He can pick out every pusher in the neighborhood."

I gave the youth ten dollars. He trotted off to the hamburger stand and soon came back munching a hamburger. Out of his pocket he pulled five bags of heroin.

"Now do you want to see the shooting gallery which I've been trying to get closed for two years?" She pointed to a basement entrance in a sagging tenement across the street where addicts shot dope.

"Won't we be attacked going in there?" I asked.

"You would," she said, "if you went in there alone. But if you all go with me and a couple of other blacks, nobody'll hurt you."

We followed the woman across the street and down crumbling cement steps into the basement doorway. When we stepped into a fetid darkness, I could see nothing. Then our guide pulled back a blanket hanging across a clothesline and in the light of two guttering candles, we saw six men. Three were lying on mattresses, three were sitting, "cooking up," each holding a spoonful of white powder over a candle flame. When the powder had melted to a liquid, they would tighten thongs around their arms, fill the hypodermic needle and inject the liquid drug into a bulging vein.

I was transfixed by the scene, appalled by the helpless misery of it.

Suddenly a bright white light flooded the basement. We had forgotten all about the TV cameramen who had followed us during the day and had, without warning, turned on their floodlights to film the scene.

The room exploded into screaming and cursing. One of the addicts, face contorted with rage, whipped a shining blade out of his pocket and lunged at me.

Instantly we all began falling over each other trying to escape. I dimly saw Ed Campbell trying to get between me and the knife-wielder, while I attempted to assure the attacker that we were not the police. It was no time for explanations.

We scrambled out of the basement into the street. Wiping my brow, I turned to our host: "I thought you said it would be safe?"

Breathing heavily, she replied: "Well, I didn't know the networks were going to make a TV special, either."

Police closed the shooting gallery that afternoon while steps were taken to provide drug treatment facilities at the local hospital.

However, as we traveled back to Washington on the plane, something that had happened in New York kept troubling me. When our investigation group was being interviewed by newsmen on the steps of the Tombs prison earlier that day, a reporter had asked, "Senator Hughes, isn't this trip a gambit to draw attention to your presidential effort?"

I shrank inside. Even though some newsmen always seem to attribute ulterior motives to anything a would-be candidate does, it continued to gall me.

What was happening to me? Had I been running so hard for president that every senatorial move I made would be looked at in this light? I didn't have any more time to think about it, however. The plane landed at National and I rushed to the office to prepare for another speaking tour starting the next day.

The momentum was building. But, as I traveled around the country and the campaign drums beat louder, a vague disquiet began to grow within me. More and more, I was finding myself confronted with doing things that would conflict with my conscience.

As we raced from reception to cocktail party to discussion group, it was always with the underlying purpose of seeking funds and support. Over five million dollars would be needed to finance any kind of presidential campaign. And contributions depended greatly on how I addressed the issues.

One hot July evening at a reception in a midwest hotel, a wealthy industrialist asked me what I thought of government-funded abortions. For a moment, I was about to tell him that I thought there were some arguments for this, as I knew the industrialist and his wife were pro-abortionists. Then I caught myself. Except for special situations I believed that abortion was wrong and I had to say so.

Later that night I stood at my hotel window looking at the lights of the city. How many times had I answered questions in such a way as to encourage prospective supporters? Had I begun to do this without realizing it?

I thought about the conversations on sensitive subjects when I had blurred the issues so that others wouldn't know how I felt.

I shrank from toadying up to important people. Once, after a cocktail reception, an aide complained: "Harold, your problem is that you'd rather talk to some college students than to men with money."

Columnist Mary McGrory perceived this. After a Democratic National Committee dinner she noted: "While the others were down on the floor slapping backs, Hughes sat brooding alone at the head table. He hates small talk. He likes a heavy rap. He talks about religion, and about drugs and alcohol. . . . He hated being trotted out to cajole financiers wanting to look him over before opening the checkbook. His staff had to prod him to call county chairmen. Hughes preferred a session with the kids at the local drug treatment centers."

Newsmen began delving deeper into my personal beliefs. A New York *Times* reporter accompanied me on a speaking trip during which we had long casual conversations which probed into the subject of life after death. I thought no more about it until one morning Park Rinard showed me a copy of the New York *Times* article. I read the story with astonishment. Hardly anything about my political thoughts but everything I said about life after death, and reported in such a way as to infer I believed in table rappings and crystal balls.

I looked at Park. "You think it's going to hurt?" He nodded, puffing his pipe.

How right he was. Letters poured in. One Iowa educator said: "When I came to Iowa all my new friends were enthusiastic Hughes' fans. I was impressed. But when that story came out, you have to ask yourself, 'What would the man do in a national emergency— contact John Kennedy through a medium?' "

Commented a Democratic colleague: "I didn't mind the God bit, but this eternity thing is too much for me."

What I had tried to say was that a Christian becomes involved with the supernatural the moment he prays for the Lord to guide his life. God often answers such prayers through planting thoughts in our minds—a type of communication which is always hard to explain to nonbelievers. Yet the Bible makes it clear we are to seek God's voice and then to act upon His instructions.

In our reach for Divine guidance, however, we can sometimes get sidetracked and our seeking can bring us into contact with the world of evil spirits who want very much to foul up our relationship with God.

The Lord warns us in Leviticus 20:6, "If a person turns to mediums and wizards, playing the harlot after them, I will set my face against that person, and will cut him off from among his people."

I have concluded that it is dangerous to try and contact the other world where spirits of another nature wait to entrap one through counterfeit manifestations, or other diabolical means. As my awareness of this danger has increased, I have asked God's forgiveness for anything that I have done wrong of this nature.

But trying to explain all this to reporters was very difficult. I believe that people today are receiving the gift of prophecy and that the fulfillment of the prophecies of the Old Testament is taking place in our world.

I believe God does heal people through prayer; my family and I had attended a Methodist church in Washington where healing was part of the service.

"There is nothing unusual about this," I've stated. "It means prayer is not empty; it means I'm not praying to a fictitious but to a living God. What are people seeking but supernatural healing when they pray for a sick child to get well? But that doesn't mean we don't go to the doctor for a regular checkup."

I have attended Kathryn Kuhlman's services. At first I was turned off by her affected voice and dramatic mannerisms, but when healings began to take place there in the auditorium, I sensed the presence of the Holy Spirit.

I wondered what the newsmen would have thought if I told them about when Miss Kuhlman and I prayed together for an alcoholic. She had called me from the audience. I had laid hands on the man and prayed for his deliverance in the name of Jesus. Miss Kuhlman then asked me to share my own experience with alcoholism.

Afterwards, she had laid hands on me, praying in the Spirit, and that's the last thing I remember. I seemed to float; I knew I was falling and didn't care, the sensation was so blissful. Eva, sitting in the audience, later said that I went down like a big tree with men running from both sides of the stage to catch me. I awoke to find myself looking up at the bottom of the grand piano, not caring whether I ever got up. Finally, I arose and was embarrassed to see everyone in the audience on their feet clapping and cheering. For about twenty-four hours after this the blissful sensation remained with me.

"I'm well aware that most people would regard my beliefs as unconventional," I've said to reporters. "And if my beliefs are a block to my becoming president, then so be it. I've left too many footprints all over the country to deny them even if I wanted to, which I don't."

Even so, the momentum of my campaign for the nomination continued. Instead of a few dozen people supporting me, it had become a few hundred, and then there were thousands. I began having a horrible feeling in the pit of my stomach that if I stopped, I'd be letting all those people down.

As the news reports increased about my activities and statements as a candidate, almost everything I said or did was now discounted as done with presidential motives. In an interview in Chicago at Malcolm X College, another reporter asked if I weren't using the drug problem to carry me to the White House.

It was disheartening. There was still a year to go before the Democratic Convention and much work to be done in the Senate. If I stayed in the presidential race, I could see that much of my legislative activity would be frustrated.

Moreover, I was worried about my family. I was hardly seeing Eva and the girls anymore, and I knew it would only get worse.

It all came to a head in a California motel room on a speaking tour. My associates and I had sat up discussing prospects just before I was to catch a late night flight back to Washington. Financially, we were in good shape. Iowans were funding our campaign at the rate of $20,000 a month. True, I was far down in the polls. Yet all around the country we kept hearing encouraging words of support.

"The heck with the polls," said Ed Campbell. "You have a vast untapped potential of people out there just waiting for you to be nominated."

Something interesting *was* going on, I had to admit. Just a few days before, two California businessmen had offered me $5,000 a month until convention time. They said they had never made a political contribution before; in fact, they had never even seen me before. They just knew what I stood for. All they wanted was my firm commitment that I would stay in the race.

"Just keep in there," advised another aide. "It's obvious your support is building every day."

After more discussion, I headed to the airport. As the jet climbed into the night, I sat in my seat perplexed, thinking about the California men awaiting my commitment. What if I did win the nomination and then the election? What were the decisions I'd face? Nuclear threat, armaments, relationships with Russia, Cuba and others.

All these conflicting thoughts swirled about me as I pondered in a torrent of emotions. Then I leaned my head back on the seat and asked God for guidance. As I prayed, a Scripture verse was emblazoned on my mind: *For what shall it profit a man, if he shall gain the whole world and lose his own soul?* (Mark 8:36).

I saw a vision of a red button. Pressing that button would launch an awesome nuclear attack destroying part of the world, its men, women and children, making it a wasteland of poisonous vapors and soil. Again I could see the huge stone man at Nagasaki, his hand lifted high in reminder.

As president of the United States, it would be my responsibility to press that button if there were a nuclear strike against us. I knew that I could not do it. A threat of doom hung over this world because of man's poor relationships with his fellow-men. Yet I knew that God had been gradually showing me something over the past years: man's relationships cannot be changed by political acts and alliances alone, but change must start in his heart.

To continue the race for the presidency I would have to make many compromises. Yet I knew I couldn't do that to get greater financial and political support. If I did I would lose my soul with every step I took down that road.

I looked out the jet window and noticed that we had climbed above the clouds. The sky was crystal clear and the stars blazed like diamond points.

The message in my heart was as clear as those lights. It had been growing there all along, but now I could face it. I could not continue in the race as a candidate for the presidency of the United States.

"What *do* You want me to do, Father?" I prayed. More than ever, I knew He had an assignment for me. It was out there, like some mysterious ship waiting in a harbor.

But He had no answer for me at that moment. Therefore, I would go on doing the work at hand that He had given me to do. And that was politics as I saw it, an honorable and important calling. For I believed that God-inspired political acts carried out by men of vision and compassion can help change the world. Now, unfettered by the ties of campaigning, I could give this work my very best.

Feeling free for the first time in months, I relaxed back and slept soundly until the giant plane touched down at Washington's Dulles Airport.

My toughest job was telling my aides of my decision the next morning. They had a difficult time understanding my reasons. Some were angry, some mourned, a few said they were not surprised.

I announced my withdrawal in a press conference in my Senate office on July 15, 1971. Expressing my appreciation to friends and supporters, I pointed out that "I am now convinced that my greatest value to my country and to my state is to pursue the goals to which I am committed as a United States senator, unimpeded by the label of presidential candidate."

Released from campaigning, I was able to devote myself again to the concerns of my heart: drug and alcohol legislation, the need to admit that we as a people were wrong in our war effort in Vietnam, the reform of Democratic party machinery to make it truly democratic.

A malaise seemed to be affecting the country, the Watergate burglary was about to blow up the Nixon administration, morality was declining in every phase of life. More than ever, I found myself turning to my friends in the Senate prayer group and at Fellowship House.

In some ways this was a paradox. John Stennis, whom I had once considered a conservative fossil, had become a warm and close friend with whom I shared many problems in these prayer sessions. We still battled on the Senate floor over divergent viewpoints on how our nation should best meet our responsibilities as a world leader, but we shared a common belief in the saving grace of our Lord Jesus Christ.

Wasn't there a lesson in this paradox, that the machinations of men alone will never solve our world's problems, no matter how hard we try? Wasn't my friendship with John Stennis a small example of how different viewpoints bathed in the Spirit of Christ could meet in reconciliation?

29

A Pacifist?

SOMETHING FAR DEEPER than giving up the race for presidential nomination had happened to me in that jet from California. What it was I did not as yet know. But I sensed a breaking and rending in my spirit as if it were being hammered into something new on the anvil of God.

I prayed that He would illumine me. I had given Him my will, my soul, my spirit twenty years before.

Meanwhile, I was led to continue my daily work. With guidance unclear, I was encouraged by a small quotation someone gave me. I do not know the source but it spoke for our Master:

As I prompt you—act.
When you have no clear guidance, then go forward quietly along the path of duty I have set before you. No fear, no panic, quietly doing your daily duty. This attitude of faith will receive its reward as surely as the acting upon My direct guidance. Rejoice in the sense of security that is yours.

And His guidance came, in strange and interesting ways. Doug Coe, several others from Fellowship House, a congressman and I went to New York City where our host had invited a number of Arab ambassadors to the United Nations for dinner.

Limousines with diplomatic license plates crowded the curbs at the high-rise apartment building and I looked forward to meeting the guests. But as we stepped into the drawing room where the ambassadors were gathered I sensed an atmosphere of resentment.

It definitely was not the relaxed air of a social gathering. As we were introduced around to the some dozen ambassadors, I caught antagonism behind bristling black mustaches, glints in Oriental eyes, and in deep Arabic accents.

However, I had forgotten it by the time dinner was announced. As we sat down, I found the ambassador from Egypt at my right and the Syrian ambassador to my left. All of the foreign representatives present were Muslim except one.

Again I felt the spirit of antagonism. All through dinner I sensed it in certain comments and word inflections. It was, I'm sure, because of our government's support of Israel and what these ambassadors felt was our insensitivity to Arab needs. As the barbs continued, I quietly prayed.

Before leaving home, I had been prompted to put on a pair of cuff links that carried Egyptian symbols. They had been a gift to me on a trip to the Middle East. As I reached for the salt, the Egyptian ambassador pointed to them. "Ah," he said, "I see some familiar symbols there; do you know what they mean?"

"Well, I know what they mean to me," I said. "But perhaps I don't know what they mean in your country. Tell me about it."

He eagerly leaned over and went into an interesting explanation of how the symbol representing enduring life dated back to the ancient Pharaohs. As I listened, fascinated, the tension at our table diminished.

When dinner was over and it came time for remarks from those present, I felt very much at ease. When it was my turn to speak, I looked over the room. Faces turned toward me expectantly. I still saw some antagonism but also open interest too.

I began talking about our common belief. "At least," I said, looking around at the men, "we all believe in God. This is our hope. As part of God's creation, we are brothers. And though I realize that my spiritual viewpoint is in the minority here tonight, I'd like to talk in the spirit of Jesus Christ. It is through His example that we can have some points of reconciliation, and we can begin in prayer."

I was encouraged to see Doug smiling broadly at me.

I told them about our Senate prayer group and how, though we strongly differed on many worldly viewpoints, we prayed together and discussed our varying views in an atmosphere of friendship and trust.

"We're trying to live more Christ-centered lives," I said, "hoping that what we are doing might help lead to reconciliation and peace

in the world. We'd like to see a similar group in the United Nations,"
I said. "I would hope that the Arab nations, whose people so strongly
believe in prayer, might lead the way."

A mood of good fellowship seemed to brighten the room as I
ended. The Egyptian ambassador stood up and talked about the long
history of Christianity in his country. Then the Lebanese ambassador,
a Christian, told us about the history of the Muslim religion in
Lebanon. We ended up with a round-table discussion about our
faith and how much we can really let God guide us.

"In our Senate prayer group," I said in closing, "we usually end
in prayer. With your permission, I wonder if we could all join hands
in a circle. We'll ask God's guidance for our countries and for us
individually. I do believe that He will hear us."

For a moment it was silent. Then with a shifting of chairs, all of
us stood up. We formed a circle and held hands. Again, it was quiet
while everyone waited for someone to start.

I looked across the circle at a handsome young ambassador with
black piercing eyes. "Mr. Ambassador," I asked, "would you pray
for us?"

Surprise filled his face and he said in a heavy Arabian accent, "I
. . . a . . . why, I'm the only man in this group who isn't a believer. I'm an agnostic." He looked around anxiously. "Every other
man here believes in God in some way and . . . I'm not sure there
is a God." His black eyes implored me. "And you want me to pray?"

"Mr. Ambassador," I said gently, "why don't you just bow your
head and say whatever is in your heart and we'll all accept it. After
all," I added, "we're here as brothers."

"All right," he said. We bowed our heads. For a moment he said
nothing. Then in his halting English he spoke. "Thank you, God, for
this meeting. We have different beliefs but tonight we have talked
like brothers. Go with us, God, so that we may continue to live like
brothers. Thank you." I have heard few men talk more personally to
God.

When it was over and we started to break up, I saw him stepping
across the circle to me. Embracing me, he said: "Can I call you
Brother?" His eyes were moist, his voice husky. "Something happened to me tonight, Senator. I really believe there is a God. I felt
His Presence." He went to others saying, "Can I call you Brother?"

Tears filled my eyes as I took his hand. "We are brothers, not by
our doing but by His."

The next day as we flew back to Washington, I found myself dwelling on why it had all happened as it did. And again I felt that strange harbinger of being called to something which as yet I could not discern.

Episodes such as this were momentary illuminations, like sudden spots of blue in an overcast sky. The clouds quickly closed over as I immersed myself in work. George McGovern became our party's presidential nominee in 1972. But it was a disastrous year for Democrats, including problems and mishaps.

I found myself wondering just how much the "dirty tricks" experts were involved in all that had happened. I suspected that Nixon's hatchet man Charles Colson was behind a lot of what went wrong for our party.

It wasn't only the campaign that was giving me qualms. It was our continuing military activities in the Vietnam War theatre. In 1972 the Paris peace talks were underway and everyone was hoping for some kind of a settlement.

Our government had an understanding with the North Vietnamese that our planes would attack only if they received hostile fire. However, the North Vietnamese were telling the world we were violating this agreement. And the administration was stating we were not.

Early in 1972 I received a letter from an Air Force sergeant, Lonnie Franks, an Iowan stationed at one of our Thailand air bases. His job, he wrote, was to write up reports from returning bomber crews. He was deeply disturbed at being asked to falsify reports by stating that planes had received hostile fire, thus "legalizing" their air strikes. Since his superiors were involved, he couldn't turn to them. In a state of moral confusion, he was writing me, since I was his senator.

He wanted to know where his ultimate authority was, and was this a correct practice for our Air Force.

I brought the letter to the attention of the Armed Services Committee, and the Pentagon made an investigation. They reprimanded the field commander, Major General John D. Lavelle. However, I felt it was more of a wrist-slapping action.

To find out how widespread our deception was, I asked our committee chairman, John Stennis, to hold official hearings under oath. He didn't feel it was necessary.

We argued about it again and again. Once, as we flew out to Montana to inspect a military base, we had a bitter confrontation in the plane over the disputed bombing missions.

Finally, John Stennis relented. The hearings were held in the fall of 1972 and the falsification of bombing reports was confirmed. Major General Lavelle, who was planning to retire, did not receive the promotion to lieutenant general.

It was sad to see a man in the last hours of his career receive this humiliation, particularly since he was an excellent military officer and had never before displayed disobedience. Even though he accepted the responsibility, I felt sure he was following orders that came directly from the White House. In addition, hundreds of other officers' promotions were held up because of the hearings.

And yet, I could not see the logic of lying to the world in the Paris peace talks about our air strikes against Vietnam while at the same time we were kicking young men out of the armed forces academies for cheating on exams.

One morning at our Senate prayer breakfast during these controversial hearings, I found myself wondering how John Stennis and I could still sit down together at the white-linen covered table as friends. I looked at the dignified silver-haired southerner across from me sipping his coffee and chuckled inwardly. I knew he considered me a bleeding-heart liberal who, if left unhindered, would soon send the country down the drain. By the same token I felt he was such a flinty conservative that if our country followed his line of thinking it would soon blow apart.

And yet I loved John Stennis as a brother in Christ and I was sure that John felt the same way about me.

I had other friends and fellow-senators who believed in the "just war" theory and who had also accepted Christ as their personal Savior. There was no anger or judgment in me about their opinions. I simply had to leave them in the hands of God and realize that He was indeed a Sovereign Lord over all men and knew what He was doing in this world. All I could do was follow the convictions that He and His Word had placed in my own heart.

I felt this to be even more vital as the tremendous 1972 Nixon election majority swept across all but one of the states. A poll showed that even a third of the Democratic voters had cast their ballots for him. Couldn't they see, I wondered, that much of what was wrong with America—the war, the forgotten poor—were being swept under the rug by Nixon and his henchmen?

And yet, something far deeper concerning my own path troubled me. Perhaps it had started when I saw firsthand the savage bloodshed of World War II. It continued when I stood at the foot of the Peace statue in Nagasaki and wept for the millions killed in all wars. It had come to the front when I struggled with the decision about the presidency and knew that I could not push that nuclear strike button. But as I traced back deeper into my feelings, I realized that the real turning point came when the Lord reached down and saved me from taking my own life.

The truth was—I had become a pacifist.

What did this mean?

Though I was living and working in the world, my home was not here. Jesus had called me to live in another world. The earth was Satan's world. I would live in it, but I could not participate in its hate and destruction and still love the Lord.

When people ask me what the United States should do if a violent nation attacked it, the answer is obvious. We are prepared to defend ourselves. The national policy has always been thus. But if we were really God's people and trusted Him implicitly, I believe our attitude would be different. The Scriptures show that God intervenes to defend His people.

If we Americans truly trusted God and believed in His divine protection, I am convinced that then He would take care of us in any and every circumstance.

I believe that I am to trust Him above all else. If God chose not to protect my mortal life, then I would depend on Him for my salvation and eternal life. If this meant my dying for the cause of Christ, then I would consider it glory, not loss.

"But what would you do, Harold, if you saw an enemy soldier or a crazed drug addict about to kill your wife and daughters?" asked a friend with whom I was discussing my beliefs.

I stopped for a moment. "Probably rush to their defense," I said. "But I really don't know what I'd do. Ideally my belief in God's love and protection should be enough for my family without violence on my part."

When everything else fails, should we kill? I've pondered this question so many times. It was certainly not a solution which Christ had given us. If God is love, then the taking of life by any name, whether it be murder, capital punishment, abortion or self-defense, is not a part of that Divine Love. We should want the very best for everyone. If we give ourselves to God, He will uphold us and keep us.

As this conviction grew within me, I worried about being a member of the Armed Services Committee. Was I being unfair to my fellow members?

Finally, I approached Senate Majority Leader Mike Mansfield of Montana who had helped get me on the committee.

"Mike," I said, "could we have some time alone?"

"Sure," he said, and took me back to his office and closed the door.

"What's the problem, Harold?" he asked, slipping into a chair across from me, the lines around his eyes crinkling as he smiled.

"Mike," I said, "I believe I have become a pacifist. My faith has led me to the conviction that I should never participate in or condone war under any circumstances."

The room was quiet and his thoughtful look invited me to continue.

"You know," I said, "I asked your help to get on the Armed Services Committee, and now ask if I shouldn't be removed from it."

I leaned forward, placing my hands on my knees. "I really don't feel I can sit there any more in good conscience, being against war, the creation of its weapons and the killing that results. I don't want to be dishonest with the Senate, with you or any of the members. I want you to know how I feel."

I sat back, feeling a huge weight had been lifted from me.

Mike sat quietly for a moment, pressed his fingertips together studying them, then looked up at me. "Harold, in the first place you have done a tremendous job on the committee. Your views have as much right to be represented on it as those of anyone else." He looked at me levelly. "I think you should stay."

"Even if I can't vote for a military budget?" I asked. "In fact, Mike, I'm not so sure I wouldn't be voting against everything."

"That's all right. I still think you should stay."

"Okay," I said, "if you don't think it's hypocritical, I'll stay and do the best I can."

I felt relieved, but as days went on I realized there was still a churning within me that did not involve committee appointments or Senate controversy but stemmed from my soul. It seemed to be a calling. I would hear it early in the morning during my prayer time, in the day as I sat at my desk in the Senate, in the evening as I meditated on Scripture passages. It was a calling that I didn't want to hear, for to answer it would mean throwing away every material success I had struggled for all my life. The thought was so ridiculous that I dispelled it from my mind.

But as I pressed my attention on Senate duties, I was reminded of the reality of eternal life compared to the gauze of daily living.

One morning in January as I walked into the Senate restaurant, I heard my name called. It was John Stennis breakfasting with a man from his home state. He introduced me to his friend and we had a friendly chat.

That same evening John Stennis was walking in front of his home when he was held up and shot by several young thugs. Near death he was rushed to the hospital where surgeons battled to save him. The news flashed throughout the capital; calls went to members of our prayer group. Like a chain reaction, the word circulated to churches and fellowships throughout the whole Washington area to lift the dying senator in prayer.

Senator Mark Hatfield, a Republican who had often battled Stennis over military expenditures and civil rights, rushed to the Mississippi senator's hospital. He stayed there throughout the night, maintaining a prayer vigil and answering questions on the constantly ringing phone. The next morning at the National Prayer Breakfast in the capital, some 3,000 people of one mind and spirit joined together and prayed for John Stennis' healing. Miraculously, his life was spared.

Through it all I couldn't help being reminded of Job's words: *Our days on earth are a shadow* (8:9, RSV). How fragile we were. How unsubstantial our earthly efforts, like messages carved into the sand, to be washed away by the next ocean wave.

30

In His Steps

TURBULENT WAVES WERE already washing close to the powerful Nixon administration. Five of the men implicated in the Watergate break-in had pleaded guilty. And in January, two of them,
Gordon Liddy, counsel for the Nixon campaign fund committee, and
James McCord, security officer for the reelection committee, came
to trial and were convicted. Even so, Judge John Sirica said he still
felt the investigation had not yet plumbed the bottom of the affair.

As with everyone, my family followed the Watergate proceedings
closely. But during that January of 1973 our interest turned to a
setting that would be vibrant to us long after Watergate gathered dust
in history books.

For years my family had dreamed of going to the Holy Land, to
walk where Jesus walked, to feel the wind that caressed His face, to
see the sun slant on the Sea of Galilee as He saw it. With a mixed
group of Jewish and Christian people from Des Moines, Eva, Phyllis,
Carol and I landed at the airport in Tel Aviv. While driving to
Jerusalem I was excited to see such Biblical landmarks as the town
where Peter healed the blind man and the valley where Samson was
born.

A surging Spirit filled my heart. After arriving that evening at our
Jerusalem hotel, Eva, the girls and I pored over Scripture together.
We had promised ourselves to read each day the passages that per-
tained to the areas we visited.

After this family time, I stepped out onto the balcony and took
in a scene which would forever be burned in my memory. Night had
settled on the Kidron valley before me. Across it wound the crum-

bling walls of old Jerusalem. Rising above them was David's tower and the domed mosque covering the rock where Abraham had prepared to sacrifice his son, Isaac.

It was quiet, broken only by low bell tinkles from grazing sheep and the distant cry of a muezzin calling evening prayers. A soft wind sighed across the valley bringing with it the pungency of an ancient city. Broken clouds floated past a low yellow moon. Phyllis joined me on the balcony. Suddenly I was overtaken with deep poignancy. This was the place and we were like pilgrims coming home. Overwhelmed with the presence and power of Jesus, I sank to my knees in prayer, tears streaming down my face, Phyllis kneeling at my side.

Our pilgrimage began the next morning as we stood in Pilate's court, meditating as we relived Christ's indignity. Then we followed His steps down the Via Dolorosa to the place of crucifixion. In the huge church festooned with flickering lamps and glittering hangings I found it difficult to pray, as hawkers waved candles, postcards and olive-wood carvings. In a way I knew how Christ felt when He walked through the temple and scattered the tables.

Then we came to His tomb. Again it was encrusted by a church building. Lines of people waited amid priests and monks anxiously selling prayer cards and candles. As we stepped back into the hot Israeli sunshine, I also wondered if there were any place where Jesus had walked that wasn't cluttered by commercialism.

We found it at the Garden Tomb. This was the site that General Gordon felt to be a logical place for Jesus' burial. As we stepped through the creaking garden gate, I had to agree with him. Glowering at us from the hillside were the cave eyes and rock-breakout teeth: Golgatha, the place of the skull.

The garden was empty except for a wizened Arab gardener raking winter debris. He looked up, his smile exposing broken teeth, and pointed to the pathway. In a few minutes we found ourselves staring at a tall wall of rock, the tomb, a black opening in it. We sat down on a small bench to rest a moment.

An afternoon sun warmed our backs. It was so quiet that we could hear the flutter of wings as birds twittered in the olive trees around us. For the first time in months I felt like putting my feet out and really relaxing.

Eva sighed and took my hand; Phyllis snuggled close; Carol pointed out tiny bright specks of flowers beginning to bloom around the base of an ancient winepress. I was glad to see her this light-hearted; she had looked so drawn and tired for several weeks. I leaned back and silently thanked Him for my family; it was so good to have them with me. In the press of my work we had been separated too often. I thought of Connie living with her family in Illinois. I hardly knew what my two grandchildren looked like.

We sat on the bench and talked about the crucifixion of our Lord, His burial and resurrection. Then we got up and went through the tomb entrance, stepping over the slanted runway where the giant stone had been rolled. Bending down, we entered the dark interior. Before us was the burial slab. Against the wall, a small stone bench. I visualized Joseph affectionately carrying his Lord's body in through the doorway. All of us sensed an overwhelming presence of Jesus in that tomb.

Reluctantly, we stepped out into the blinding white sunlight. I thought of Mary, coming from the city with her ointments and herbs, seeing Jesus in the early morning mist and not knowing Who He was.

Strengthened, we roamed the country. We looked down on the bright blue expanse of Galilee where legend says that on certain days one can see a lighter streak in the water marking the pathway where Jesus walked. Laughing and singing, we waded into the Jordan River where Eva and the girls were baptized again. In Capernaum we stood on the site of the synagogue where Jesus had healed the man's withered arm. While traveling down a narrow lane in Nazareth, not far from the home where Jesus was raised by Joseph and Mary, I glanced up to see a carpenter's shop. On its porch a boy was wielding a wooden plane over a plank while a bearded man stood watching him, occasionally giving direction.

But not all the sights were historical. At every bridge, machine-gun muzzles glinted in the sun. As we drove into the Negev Desert, a crackling thunder jerked our heads up to see Phantom jets streak across the blue.

Peace and war so close, I thought. The weakness of man and his hope, so mingled.

On our homeward bound plane, I faced up to a conviction growing within me. The walk had deepened my need to get closer to Christ. It had heightened a desire to become His disciple completely, to walk in His steps as He walked, to live as He did, to give up the world as He did.

And the suffering I might face? No way to avoid that, but I was given the assurance that He would walk with me through it.

31

The Decision

TWO WEEKS AFTER we returned from the Holy Land, Eva met me at the door one night after work, her eyes full of concern: "Carol is not well; she's having problems again, and her doctor says she needs some minor surgery."

My heart tightened. I knew doctors considered this procedure routine. But Carol had had so much surgery, beginning when she was operated on in the Des Moines hospital as a little girl. Since then she had had intestinal growths removed three times, always described as "nothing to really worry about."

We drove Carol to the Fairfax Hospital on the day of her operation. As we pulled into the parking lot of the modern red-brick building in a quiet residential area, Carol was in good spirits, pointing out the parking spot and entrance she used when she went there to work.

The doctor said he'd have a report right after her surgery, so Eva and I went to the waiting room. When the doctor finally appeared, he said reassuringly, "Your daughter will be able to go home tomorrow." Then he hesitated for a moment and a slight frown crossed his face. "I have to tell you, however, that I have come across something that doesn't look good. I'm sending a section of it to the laboratory for a report."

Eva's face whitened. The doctor put his hand on her shoulder. "I don't want to frighten you but you can understand how it is; we have to check these things out thoroughly."

A week later when I was in a Senate labor committee meeting, a secretary came in and handed me a note: *Your daughter's doctor is on the phone.*

I excused myself, and went out to the committee-office phone and picked it up. The doctor's voice was terse: "We've bad news about your daughter, Senator. The laboratory report has come back and . . . it's cancer."

I swallowed hard, feeling a weight building in my chest.

"How bad?" I asked.

"Not good," he said. "It's an adno carcinoma, and on the range of one to five in deadliness, I'd put it at 3½."

I chilled inside. She was only 30; I had heard cancer worked fast in young people.

"It's not the worst," he tried to soothe me, "but I'd recommend another examination immediately." He talked of surgery, radiation and chemotherapy, and gave me the name of a doctor at George Washington University Hospital.

I drove home sick inside. Carol hadn't come home from work yet, and I told Eva. She broke into tears. "I can't tell her, would you?"

When Carol came home, I asked her to join me in our living room where I did a lot of my meditating and praying. It seemed like the right place.

"I'd like to talk to you about the lab report on your surgery, Honey."

"What about it?" she asked, nervously smoothing the hem of her skirt.

"It's not good news." I got up from my chair and sat down next to her on the couch.

She looked at me apprehensively.

"The lab reports have come back and they indicate cancer."

Her face paled and her dark brown eyes filled with tears. She bit her lip. Fighting hard not to cry, I took her in my arms and she buried her chestnut curls in my shoulder.

She shook with sobs and for a minute couldn't speak. "How bad is it?"

"We don't really know yet." I explained the cancer diagnosis, that there was hope and that we should look at it optimistically. "There's one thing we can do right now, Honey," I said. "We can pray that God will heal you and believe that He will."

"Let's do that, Dad." Then she wiped her eyes and managed a little smile. In it I could see the strength of her faith.

After the family had gone to bed, I sat by myself in front of the fireplace in the family room. Snow covered the ground outside the house, glittering in the light of a full moon. A fire guttered on the hearth. I couldn't sleep; I felt shaken to my very core. Not until I faced the possibility that one of my daughters could be taken did I realize how much they meant to me.

In agony of spirit, I realized how often I had placed my political career before my family's needs. So often I had not been there when the girls needed me, from school problems to marital difficulties. This had to change. After God, my family from then on would come first. Kneeling at the sofa, I put this in the form of a promise to God.

Without my realizing it, He had inched me closer to a vital decision I would soon make.

To support Carol I developed a set routine. In between Senate sessions and committee meetings, I would go to the little Capitol meditation room to pray for Carol. As I knelt there one afternoon, a thought struck me. It was almost as if I were being asked a question.

Was it really true that I wanted to serve Christ fully in every possible way?

Yes, my soul cried out. Yes!

Then give up your position as Senator and serve Me full time.

The thought struck with numbing intensity.

No, I said, feeling that this word could not be from God. As a senator I had the position and leverage to do so much for Him. It would be foolishness to give that up.

But days went by and the thought persisted. If it were so foolish why couldn't I forget it? One afternoon I left the prayer room and walked to the large Capitol doors overlooking the mall. A February sun was coaxing out a bit of green in the grassy expanse which stretched before me to the pale spire of the Washington Monument.

I thought about the famous landmarks before me. Beyond the Monument was the Lincoln Memorial, to my right the White House and to my left the Jefferson Memorial. Suddenly I realized that I was standing at the foot of a great cross! The Capitol at its base represented the people, the Lincoln Memorial surmounting its top reflected the nation's unity; the Jefferson Memorial at the left of the cross arm symbolized the Declaration of Independence; and the White House at the right, national leadership. Soaring from the heart of it was the Washington Monument, a memorial to the father of our country, a beacon straining skyward.

God had His Hand in the origin of this nation, I was certain of that. He was in the hearts of the men who had founded it and guided it through the years.

I also knew that God raises nations and causes them to fall. And as I stood there looking across the mall, I felt that it had been God's will that our nation rise and be a symbol of hope for mankind. For what other reason would He bring together people from all over the world, giving them the greatest freedom that man anywhere possessed?

I also knew that the only way we could continue to win others to our way of life would be how we *lived* it, by demonstrating that racism dies here, that there *is* equal opportunity and justice for all, that compassion and care for the unfortunate is a national characteristic. Only then, I knew, would God continue to be our defender and advocate.

The approach of a group of tourists broke my soliloquy, and I turned and walked on past the marble statues of past statesmen in the echoing rotunda. I remembered looking at them as a freshman Senator, wondering if I could ever measure up to these men.

Leave the Senate? I shook my head. Where could I serve God more effectively than in my post here in Washington?

From an early testing of the waters, it appeared that I would be reelected Senator in 1974. According to newspaper reports, Iowans seemed to like me despite the fact that I fought for some causes they did not agree with.

Summer of 1973 came and the Watergate hearings were heating up. One night I walked out on the deck at the back of our house which overlooked trees and a stream. The stars were out and I stared at them pensively.

So much had happened since those boyhood days when I first looked up into His firmament. My memories ranged the years from when Jess and I followed our traplines along the Maple River, through the war, alcoholism, driving a truck, becoming a commerce commissioner, then governor of Iowa and finally to the Senate of the United States.

I was 51. If the Lord allowed, I should have at least twenty energetic years ahead.

Twenty years? If I ran for reelection, would I ever be able to quit? Would I go on and on like the elderly silver-haired men who had been senators for twenty-five and thirty years? For these men it could well be right, but for me?

Yet to give up everything? It was like being asked to walk a strange wilderness path at midnight without a light. What if there were a cliff? And the thought came: *yes, even a cliff,* followed by: *I will take care of you.*

But still there were so many concrete reasons why it would be difficult to walk such a path. One was money. Our financial condition was not good. We had some funds in government bonds and about $35,000 equity in our house. My mother was in a nursing home and we were also helping other family members. With Carol's medical costs and Phyllis' college expenses, money was tight. In fact, we needed my speaking engagement honorariums to help pay our household bills. If I served out another term as senator, I would be eligible for an excellent pension. If I quit it would be greatly reduced and I'd have little except Social Security for my later years.

Still the thought persisted. One evening, more to silence the notion than anything else, I stepped into the family room where Eva, Phyllis and Carol had been watching news on the Senate's Watergate investigation. It had ended and they had just snapped off the set when I walked in. I presented my thoughts about leaving the Senate. It would be very difficult, I said, particularly in view of our finances. But if I was expecting objections to bolster my own, I was surprised.

Eva continued doing her crocheting. "Whatever you decide to do, Harold, we'll know it's because you must." She pulled a knot tight, and added, "And you know we'll be with you." Phyllis and Carol agreed. So did Connie whom I phoned. By this time she and her family had moved to Virginia and it was nice to have them fairly close.

A few days later my fellowship group, Doug Coe, Graham Purcell and Al Quie, met at my house in the same room. I asked them as brothers to give me counsel and advice. To a man they felt that I should stay in the Senate. However, they reluctantly agreed I had to listen to my own guidance.

I talked to Mark Hatfield who had considered not running for reelection himself at one time. Since he had decided to remain in the Senate, I wanted his opinion.

"I know you're thinking, Mark, 'What if we all quit?' " I looked down at the floor for an instant, then back up into his clear blue eyes. "But I wouldn't feel as if I were quitting, only changing direction. That's why I so greatly need your prayers and God's guidance."

Mark, like the others, agreed it had to be a decision between God and me.

Summer waned, the oppressive Washington heat continued and the Watergate hearing seemed to be closing the net on Nixon and his associates. Vice President Agnew was close to resigning.

I wrestled with my own decision. Perhaps it would be better to delay it. To make such an announcement then might be premature, with over a year of my term to go.

However, as I sat on the deck overlooking our backyard one afternoon reading the Bible, I was struck by the men in the Gospels who had faced similar decisions. I reread the account in Luke 5:1–11 where Peter, James and John had just pulled in a record fishing catch. And yet, when the Lord called, they did not wait to haul that catch to market or sell their nets and boats. Trusting Him, *They straightway left their nets and followed Him.* In Luke 9:61–62 (RSV) I read of the man who was called by Christ but begged: *I will follow you, Lord; but let me first say farewell to those at home.* And looking sorrowfully at him, Jesus said: *No one who puts his hand to the plow and looks back is fit for the kingdom of God.*

I placed the Bible in my lap and looked into the trees. Their trunks glowed in the mellow afternoon light as the sun sank lower. Time passing. The night would come.

I knew I had to decide. Run for reelection or follow the leading that God had given me.

For me there was only one choice.

I told Doug Coe and, after discussing it, he suggested I share my decision with Al Quie.

I met Al in the little chapel off the rotunda. We prayed together at the altar rail. Al wanted me to be certain. "It will be a great loss to the Senate, your state and the country," he said, "but if the Holy Spirit is leading you, I know it's right." He was concerned about my future, and my family.

I thought to myself as we talked. Here was I, a liberal Democrat, sharing my innermost feelings with a conservative Republican. He could have destroyed me with the things I was telling him in confidence, but we were one in the Lord.

Another man who knelt with me in the prayer room was the tall sandy-haired Billy Graham. Though he said he'd like to see more devoted Christians active in politics, particularly in view of Watergate, he understood my desire to serve Christ full time.

I went to Mike Mansfield, Senate majority leader; Robert Byrd, Senate majority whip; Stu Symington, and the chairmen of the committees on which I served.

All tried to talk me out of it. "Stay in there, Harold," pressed Mike Mansfield. "You're serving your country, your state in the very best possible way. Why give it up?"

I tried to explain that I had reached the point in my thinking where I felt that the best way to approach the world's problems was through the hearts of men. We had to begin somewhere on this and I was going to see what I could do.

Park Rinard, with whom I had been discussing my decision along the way, was not surprised. He reminded me that we had to make a public announcement and clear the decks. The announcement, of course, would be made at home in Iowa.

On the night of September 5th, I called my staff together and made the announcement. There were tears and objections. "Well, you can't argue with God," said one of the secretaries.

That evening I phoned my political counselors and advisors and told them my decision. The next morning I flew to Des Moines. There in the Iowa Room of the Savery Hotel, where so much had happened to me, I made my public announcement. Under the eyes of television cameras and before a cluster of microphones I started talking as reporters took notes. "I have called this press conference to announce a decision I have reached after a long period of personal soul-searching and extended discussion with the members of my family.

"The decision is this: When my present term as a United States Senator is ended, I will retire from the Senate and enter another field of public endeavor." I went on to explain that I would work as a committed layman in connection with Fellowship Foundation in Washington, D.C.

"This work represents to me a new kind of challenge and spiritual opportunity in today's troubled world," I said as notes were scribbled furiously. "It is the kind of move I have long been motivated to take for profoundly personal religious reasons." I stressed that I would continue my efforts in alcohol and drug treatment fields, working for social causes and world peace.

"Why change jobs if the aims remain the same?" came the obvious question. "Why not remain a Senator and use the leverage that seat provides for God's purposes?"

My answer: "I have an intuitive, compelling commitment to launch out in a different kind of effort that will be primarily spiritual rather than political. This new work will cut across political and religious creeds; ethnic, and language barriers; and will, I hope, reach into other countries of the world to further international understanding."

These words expressed my heart, but, as I expected, few people understood them. "One social worker more or less means relatively little," lamented David Rudgers in a Washington newspaper, "but a liberal senator is an important asset to those who wish progressive reform."

A businessman protested: "For God's sake (and ours), please reconsider. We need you a lot more than God does right now."

The comment that pleased me most was from Ernie Brenden who ran one of the typesetting machines at the Ida County *Pioneer Record:* "Didn't surprise me a bit," he said. "Pack's a man of strong convictions and I think he can do more good outside politics than in it."

One thing was certain. As I stepped out of the hotel onto the bustling downtown streets of Des Moines that morning after the announcement, I was outside of politics. Around me were so many memories: the apartment building where Eva and I had set up housekeeping, the old hotel in which I had awakened one evening not knowing how I got there, the downtown street where a friend had hailed me, saving me from what could have been a disastrous drink.

Now there would be changes. No longer would I be a member of what has been called the world's most elite club. Many of those who sought me out before would now pass me by.

But there was One Whom I could count on. He had been with me since the beginning of time and would stay with me through eternity. Deep in my heart I had His assurance that I had made the right choice.

32

A New Beginning

I HAD NO IDEA that the Lord would test my commitment to a new life so soon.

For a while after announcing my decision, life seemed to settle on an even keel. I had even stopped worrying about Carol. Radiation treatments seemed to be helping her and she was looking much better and continuing in her job.

Then in late September a phone call came one Saturday morning from Doug Coe.

"Harold," he greeted me in his usual good-natured way, "we have a brother in Christ I want you to meet."

"Who is it?"

"Chuck Colson."

I swore.

Thoughts of this arrogant, cruel man who would do anything for his president choked me.

"I really think he's had a conversion experience," said Doug. "It would be great if you could meet with him."

I thought of the philosopher's statement that religion is the last refuge of the scoundrel. "No, Doug," I said. "I don't believe him and I don't want to meet him."

Silence.

"That isn't a very Christlike attitude, is it?" Doug said at last.

"My God, Doug, do you realize what you're asking me to do?"

"Yes, Harold. I'm asking you to meet a man who's met the Lord. Does it make any difference *who* he is?"

"I'm sorry, Doug," I said, "but this is going too far." I hung up.

And then I began to wonder. What would the apostles Peter, James or John have said if someone phoned to tell them about the miracle God wrought with Saul on the road to Damascus? Wouldn't they have been just as incredulous? But if God had touched this man, how could I turn away?

I picked up the phone and called Doug back. "I doubt very much if it has really happened, Doug, but I'll meet with him."

"I have to tell you something else, Harold."

"What's that?"

"No one else wants him."

"Can you blame them?" I asked. "But I'll tell you one thing, Doug, I'm going to have to ask him some mighty tough questions. And I'll not be easy to convince."

Doug said he'd make the arrangements. A few days later he picked me up in his car. We stopped at Charles Colson's office in downtown Washington and Doug went in to get him. I watched the two come out of the door. The husky bespectacled man with the cherubic face didn't *look* any different. We drove out to Al Quie's house, none of us saying much. The stocky man in the back seat acted pleasant enough, but I knew only too well that some of the worst men could be the most ingratiating.

Our fellowship group was there with their wives, except Eva who was home with a bad cold. Patty Colson drove directly from home to be with us.

We had a strained chit-chat. Gretchen Quie seemed overly anxious, asking me three times if I wanted cream for my coffee. Al set out chairs for us while Graham, Doug and their wives exchanged pleasantries with the Colsons. I studied the couple, still harboring a chill wall of resentment. I had to admit that Patty Colson seemed warm and down-to-earth with none of the affected facade so many Washington wives seemed to develop.

Colson himself seemed hale and hearty, which somehow bothered me. The man who supposedly had led him to Christ was Tom Phillips, president of the Raytheon Corporation in Massachusetts. Raytheon was one of the largest manufacturers of weapons in international warfare. I had discussed national defense and international warfare with Phillips and we were miles apart.

Yet I knew that I had to respect a man's relationship with God, whether or not we agreed on worldly problems. It was up to God, not me, to choose His disciples. But now looking at Colson I wished God would pick people with whom I could feel compatible.

As we finished our dessert, I felt we'd better get down to the point of this get-together.

"Chuck," I said, leaning forward, "tell me about your encounter with Jesus Christ."

The room quieted. With some hesitation at first, he told about his visit with Tom Phillips who had stressed to Chuck that the missing factor in his life was Jesus Christ. As Colson talked, his voice caught at times and I sensed how difficult it was for him to share his experience, knowing my skepticism.

He went on with his story, speaking slowly and self-consciously picking a bit of lint from his slacks. He told how he was beginning to overcome a lifelong dependency on pride, that he was ashamed of his arrogance and that he was now struggling against doubts. "It all fitted into place," he said huskily, looking up at me, "when I was able to see Who Jesus was."

My heart suddenly knew that what he was saying was true, yet my mind wished it were not. Then came the extraordinary discovery that my own hostility toward this struggling human being was being washed away by a tremendous sympathy.

"That day in Maine I gave my life to Him," he said, looking around at each of us, his eyes misting behind his horn-rimmed glasses. Then he added: "I'd be grateful for any help you can give me."

I sat there feeling the presence of the Holy Spirit in the room. My God, I thought, it really happened. I didn't have to ask the hard questions. It didn't make any difference anymore. I knew in my heart he had been forgiven through the blood of Jesus Christ, just as I had been forgiven.

I stood up from my chair, walked over to him and put my arms around him. "Brother," I said, my voice choking, "obviously you've had a confrontation with Jesus Christ and the Holy Spirit and I for one will stand with you, walk with you and be with you wherever God takes us for the rest of our lives."

Words are easier to come by in the flush of emotion, I found. A few days later when Doug and I were talking together at Fellowship

House, he hit me with another difficult question. "Do you feel we should invite Chuck to join our prayer group?"

I checked the "no" that was on my lips and pondered the question. Our little four-man group had been meeting for three years; it had taken that long to develop the trust to share our lives with each other. I thought of the men whom I had come to love despite our political differences . . . Al Quie, an honest conservative; Graham Purcell, in many ways more conservative than Al, even though he was a Democrat; and Doug Coe. There I was in the middle of all those conservatives, and now another one. But though I no longer questioned the integrity of the men in the group, I still wasn't completely sure about Colson.

At that time the Nixon Administration was beginning to come unglued, the president had fired the chief Watergate investigator and most of the nation was in an uproar. My family and I were so concerned that I had seriously discussed the best possible escape route to a friendly foreign embassy if the president were to suspend certain rights of American citizens.

As Doug stared at me I looked out the window. I felt certain Chuck Colson was headed for trouble. There was already talk of his being brought into court. Were we going to love him through it all, no matter how deeply he was involved? Would we stand with him if it turned out he had engineered the whole Watergate mess?

And yet wasn't this judging him on a worldly level? I looked back at Doug. "I'm for it, Doug," I said. "Since he's a brother now, what else can we do?"

So there were five of us who met every week in the parlor at Fellowship House for prayer. When word came out about this new relationship with Chuck, I was roasted a bit by Senate colleagues who were certain I was either misled, used, or confused.

The press corps, taking a gallows interest in Colson, wanted to know the intimate details of his confession. One asked: "Why hasn't he made a public confession of all his sins in the White House as a result of his conversion?"

The reporter had his answer some months later when Chuck voluntarily confessed that he had tried to smear Dr. Daniel Ellsberg who had released the Pentagon papers on Vietnam to the press. For this law violation Chuck was sentenced to from one to three years in prison.

He was disbarred as a lawyer in Virginia and the District of

Columbia and suspended in Massachusetts. To top off his misery, Chuck's son was arrested for drug possession and his father died while Chuck was in federal prison. Through it all my former enemy held steadfast to his faith in Jesus Christ. The four of us met weekly, suffering with him; any one of us would have taken on his prison sentence if it were possible.

After his release from prison, Chuck Colson added strength to our prayer group. Certainly we continued to have disagreements. Sometimes it took one brother going to another in private with whom he had difficulty and frankly expressing a resentment; sometimes one of us would bring two others back into a loving relationship by counseling both. Under the influence of Christ, our disagreements were always settled.

I needed the strength of my brothers because Carol was waging a losing battle against the cancer in her body. Eva brought it to my attention one night after Carol had gone to bed. "Harold, she doesn't feel like doing much anymore; she's even missing her prayer meetings." Visibly tiring more each week, Carol finally gave up her job at the hospital, though she would return whenever she could to pray with the patients.

There was something ethereal about Carol at that time, as if she were living both in this world and the next. Her ever-deepening love of the Lord, along with the joy she gave others, while concealing her own suffering, heightened our own family's spiritual life. I was so grateful that Connie and her family lived nearby. For the first time since entering politics, I had all my family close with me.

Late at night after long sessions on the Hill, I'd come home to find Carol asleep, with only the sound of her soft breathing in the room. Kneeling by her bed, I would place my hand on her moist forehead and pray for her happiness, for her complete healing.

One day Eva found Carol in her room, extremely weak. She was rushed to the hospital where Eva stayed with her. The next morning at 3 A.M. Carol called me at home. I picked up the phone, my hand shaking.

"Dad?" her voice was so distant, so weak.

"Yes, Honey."

"Dad, I know I'm going. And I want you to know I've been looking forward to it. Please," she faltered, "please tell everyone not to pray for my healing anymore." The line was still for a moment, as if she were gathering strength to talk. "Please don't feel bad about it, Dad," she continued, her voice getting weaker. "I want you to go on with your work."

That evening Mark Hatfield, Doug Coe, Dick Halverson, pastor of a large Presbyterian congregation in suburban Washington, Eva, and I stood at her bedside praying. Tears dimmed my eyes. She was only 32. "Oh, don't feel sorry for me, Daddy," she whispered, raising a slender pale hand. "I'm so happy to have you all here." Her face, wreathed by chestnut ringlets on the white pillow, seemed to glow and I felt that she was already in His presence.

We men walked out of her room quietly. In the hall, Dick Halverson took my hand: "Harold, I feel as if we've been in the presence of a saint."

A miracle then took place in that hospital. Carol did not die. When her vitality returned in the days that followed, nurses and doctors were amazed. "A remarkable remission," said one. Carol returned home and I was convinced that she was healed.

All of us had a most joyful celebration that Christmas of 1975. For the first time in years, our three daughters were with us, including our grandchildren, Tracy, 12, and Jon, 9, who added their own merriment.

Carol went to work at Fellowship House. There we spent many hours together talking and praying, as my decision not to return to the Senate was still causing me much soul-searching. Carol seemed to understand my feelings. "I feel that the length of our lives here on this earth is not important," she said. "It's what we do with our lives that matters."

A poignancy of parting touched my last year in the Senate. Free from the next election and yet not sure of just where my future lay, I submerged myself in the work at hand. While helping to bring about the Institute on Alcoholism, I found myself becoming more and more involved with American Indians, whose susceptibility to alcohol problems is high.

Since I have Indian blood myself on my mother's side, dating back several generations, I have become very close to these people. Shunted to reservations, almost forgotten by the government, cheated and denigrated on every side, they seemed to have little support.

I did what I could to help clarify and establish their rights. Some of us were able to establish prayer fellowship groups for Indians in the capital and encouraged the formation of similar groups on reservations. Through legislation we appropriated funds to begin pilot programs to reach Indian men and women alcoholics and help them start on the road to recovery.

For this work I was invited by the Indians to attend a special pipe ceremony in Utah. The ceremony of the pipe signifies a sacred covenant between God and man. Though differing in some aspects, it is a sacrament basically common to all tribes. Men representing the Cree, Seneca, Winnebago, Black Foot, Sioux, Cheyenne, Apache, Kema, Ute and others, were there. Mark Small, a Northern Cheyenne, welcomed me.

The site of the pipe ceremony was a pole lodge next to a sparkling brook high in the mountains. Far below us we could see the city of Salt Lake. Pointing to the Mormon Temple dimly seen in the distance, the men then turned to their lodge and said, "We have our temple here."

As the medicine man blessed the lodge with burning sweet grass, I was reminded of the ancient Hebrews sanctifying their temples with incense. Everyone said a prayer to begin the ceremony. Then each man shared his hopes for his tribe. The pipe was then offered to God, and then it was passed around to each of us to smoke. At the close of the ceremony, the pipe was offered to God again.

The silence was awesome. Even the wind seemed to still. One tribesman told me that the animals stay quiet when the pipe ceremony is conducted.

Pointing out that the ground on this spot was now hallowed, the leader placed his hand on my shoulder and said, "You are now our brother."

I felt such kinship with these people that I was reluctant to catch the plane back to Washington, a city now convulsing in the last throes of Watergate. And once again I would soon be faced with another deep inner conflict and a difficult decision of conscience.

The issue was President Ford's use of his right to pardon law violators—in this situation the resigned Richard Nixon, plus the use of the pardon for other Watergate offenders. I had met Richard Nixon only a few times. First in 1952 when he ran for vice president and I was a delegate to the Iowa Republican convention. In 1974 I was invited to his office for the signing of the Hughes Bill (widening and extending alcohol treatment programs) but couldn't bring myself to attend, since his administration had fought it every inch of the way.

However, in the midst of the Watergate turmoil, I had sent Nixon two letters on behalf of the brothers in Fellowship House offering to pray for him and with him in regard to the crisis of his presidency. I wrote the letters by hand, since I did not want anyone to know what was in them; they were delivered through a responsible source. I knew that they reached him but I never received an answer.

In September 1974 he was out of the presidency and a defeated man living in seclusion in San Clemente. When President Ford pardoned him, an angry cry rose from the Congress, and the Senate proposed a resolution declaring that there be no more pardons for anyone accused of Watergate offenses.

The vote came up quite quickly and we had little time to consider it. I sat in the Senate cloakroom for ten minutes thinking it over. My emotions were all for it, but my inner spirit told me something different.

When the roll was called, I voted against the resolution. I personally felt that the Senate had no right to imply to a President of the United States that he doesn't have, in his own wisdom and conscience, the final decision to pardon. It is a right guaranteed to him by the Constitution.

Only a few of us voted against the resolution. Many people criticized me, including members of my own staff; I explained that in my opinion a president's right to pardon went back into history and came from divine inspiration to those in authority.

Some months later I stood alone in the now silent office where I had spent most of my Senate career. My view was still on the side street but I had come to like this suite. Being at the end of the hall, it was secluded and quiet.

My desk was empty and my belongings were packed in boxes. I had said good-bye to my people, many of whom would be joining the staff of John Culver, the Iowan who had succeeded me. He was a good friend whom I had known for years.

My secretary, Jo Nobles, stuck her head around the door. "There are more people out here waiting to say goodby."

"I'm sorry, Jo," I said, "I can't do it. They'll understand." Jo saw the tears in my eyes and nodded. I opened the side door of my office, stepped out into the hall alone, closed it behind me, and walked out of the building.

If I had expected to find a quiet life after leaving the Senate, I was very much mistaken. The appearances, speeches, meetings on social concerns continued, though I could be more selective. No longer representing a constituency, I felt released to speak openly about what the Lord had done for me and to invite my audience to follow Him.

Even so, an echo from the past still resounded in comments from audiences: "Senator Hughes, many of us still feel that you could be far more effective for God if you stayed in the Senate."

Though I answered as best I could, I could not tell the whole story. For when I closed the door of the Senate, I discovered new doors opened to me. They were doors into the confidence of men in high places who felt they could share their deepest thoughts and problems with a man who was not beholden to any political office.

I received further confirmation of my strange new role one night from an old friend—Paul, the Apostle. He had often helped me in the past with his incisive discernments. While reading First Corinthians, Chapter 9 (TLB), the old tentmaker's words seemed specifically directed at me:

If I were volunteering my services of my own free will, then the Lord would give me a special reward; but that is not the situation, for God has picked me out and given me this sacred trust and I have no choice. Under this circumstance, what is my pay? It is the special joy I get from preaching the Good News without expense to anyone, never demanding my rights.

"How right you are, old friend," I thought. Paul continued with these words that gave me a very special support: *And this has a real advantage: I am not bound to obey anyone just because he pays my salary; yet I have freely and happily become a servant of any and all so that I can win them to Christ.*

This, I believe, is God's call for me now. *A servant of any and all.* If He ever wants me back in the political arena, I feel sure that He will make this clear. Politics for many men can be the place where God wants them. And I believe that a man in public office who practices the teaching of our Lord, *without holding back,* can affect the world.

Since leaving the Senate I have found fulfillment in sharing His love and compassion with other needy men and women. In the process I learned how much I and my family needed it too. This was particularly so in July 1976. Instead of attending the Democratic National Convention that year, I had to enter George Washington University Hospital for prostate surgery. Shortly before the operation, Eva came in, her face unusually strained.

"What is it, Honey?" I asked.

"It's Carol," she whispered. Eva sank down beside my bed weeping. "She completely collapsed at home. We called the ambulance and had her brought here."

Stunned, I couldn't believe it. Carol seemed so well the day before when I had left for the hospital. Shaken, I went to Carol in her room. She looked up at me from her pillow and tried to smile. As I reached out and touched her thin, pale face, I remembered the cherubic brown-eyed baby with dark ringlets I so proudly held in my arms that long-ago summer day when I had returned from overseas.

But Carol ministered to me instead, speaking words of encouragement and with such love and warmth that I could see Jesus Himself in her luminous eyes.

After my surgery, I was in terrible pain, unable to leave my bed. Carol came to my room. Again, she comforted me, praying for my recovery. Several days later I was able to hobble down to her floor for beautiful short visits in which we read the Bible together.

"You're looking so very much better, Honey," I said one morning, buoyed up by the improvement in her. She had gotten up and was sitting in a chair by the window. "We'll both go home together."

She managed a little smile and squeezed my hand as I bent down to kiss her. "Yes, I'd like that. I'd like to go home."

One gray evening a few days later, I felt greatly encouraged. It was July 27th. Carol had been out of her bed four times that day and looked exceptionally well. Eva was sitting at her side as I turned to leave the room.

"Honey, I'm going to call Connie to tell her how much better you are," I said. "I'll be right back."

Carol smiled, waved, and then turned to Eva.

In a few minutes I returned to Carol's floor. Her doctor, a woman, stopped me in the corridor. "Senator Hughes?"

"Yes."

"Your daughter has just expired."

What did she mean? I rushed into Carol's room. Her mother sat at her side, holding Carol's still hand. "She's all right," whispered Eva. "She has gone to be with the Lord."

God in His infinite wisdom had arranged my presence in the same hospital with Carol during those days and I shall always be grateful to Him for it.

Memorial services were held at Fellowship House in Washington, and at the United Methodist Church in Ida Grove with my old friends, Wayne Shoemaker and Cliff Isaacson speaking. They asked me to say a few words. As I stood at the pulpit looking down at Eva, Phyllis, Connie and her family, a wave of emotion surged through me. It seemed I could see Carol as she was in her white stockings and little black patent Mary Jane shoes when she watched me stand in this same pew 24 years before to give my first sermon.

I felt her presence close to me and I was able to speak of the job of trusting Christ Who promised we could all look forward to that grand reunion when we'd be together again.

For some months a vision had been slowly building within me, a picture of a quiet country setting where national leaders could come together for worship, Scripture reading and prayer, a place where they could relax and discuss the spiritual issues of the day.

One morning as I prayed in our family room in McLean, I was directed to write down the ingredients of such a place: recreational facilities, land to grow food, a place to practice soil conservation. The location seemed to be on Chesapeake Bay.

The next day I took the list to our Fellowship group and shared it with them. Al Quie was astonished.

"I've just been to a place that exactly fits that description," he exclaimed. "And the owner wants to sell." He described a 21-acre parcel of land on Chesapeake Bay near Easton, Maryland, with two houses, office, lodge and recreational facilities.

We investigated and though the buildings needed repair, the place coincided startlingly with my vision. It was called Cedar Point. Step by step we set about purchasing it, praying each step of the way. Financing was largely on faith.

In September, 1976, through support of the brothers at Fellowship

House, we moved in. It is continuing to take much hard work getting the buildings and facilities in shape. We also had to overcome some local misunderstanding as to what kind of place it would be.

Some of the members of a local Alcoholics Anonymous chapter became interested in what was going on at Cedar Point and came out to help with the work. They painted buildings and shingled roofs. Then they asked for regular meetings in which we could share our experiences, study the Bible and pray together.

Soon all kinds of people—oyster men, barbers, body-shop workers—began coming regularly to Cedar Point for a deeper understanding of God.

The other evening I walked out onto our dock which extends into the mouth of Broad Creek and watched the sun set over the Chesapeake. Mike, our old Irish Setter, nuzzled me as the sky flamed a brilliant crimson, the promise of a beautiful tomorrow. And I thought of the wonderful and mysterious ways in which God works.

We had developed this retreat thinking that the influential and powerful leaders of the country would come. Instead, the Lord in His wisdom sent fishermen who drank too much, construction men with family problems, repairmen who gambled.

I looked across the harbor at our skiffs pulled up along shore and thought of another body of water where rough men, interrupted in their work, saw a Man standing on the beach beckoning them. "Lord," I prayed, "help all of us who stumble and fall to keep following you."

The sun sank into the bay. The quiet waters mirrored an evening star and crest of moon. I looked at them, thinking of a little boy on the bank of the Maple River.

Pictures swam before me of Mother, Dad, Jesse and the love in that little yellow house, of three little girls and my lovely wife. I thought of the war, the jails, the trucks. I could almost see the presidents, kings, emperors, parliamentarians, the poor, the mentally ill, the condemned, all who had been part of my life.

"Lord," I murmured, "how You have blessed me!"

I glanced at the house. Lights were beginning to glow in the windows. I turned and walked toward it; my family would be waiting for me.

33

Miracle on 43rd Street

SOME MONTHS AFTER my announcement of not running for Senate reelection I took part in an extraordinary luncheon in New York City which has served to chart my course as Christ's disciple to all people.

An invitation had been extended to eighteen ambassadors to the United Nations for a luncheon at the Princeton Club on 43rd Street in Manhattan. I was to be the host. Members of the Senate and House prayer groups had invited the guests. The invitation stated that the luncheon would be held to discuss the implications of the message they had heard at the National Prayer Breakfast.

I felt the invitation would scare off most of the ambassadors. The day of the luncheon came at the wrong time for me and I almost missed my flight from Washington. Along with Doug Coe I arrived at LaGuardia Airport, harried and anxious, and slumped into the car of a brother, Ken White, who met us. As Ken headed into the crowded expressway toward Manhattan, he handed me the list of ambassadors who were coming to the luncheon. "You had better take a good look at your guests," he said apprehensively. At first glance I could see the reason for his concern.

Coming to the luncheon were Soviet ambassador Yakov Malik, three other Communist ambassadors from the Ukraine, Byelorussia and Poland, along with ambassadors from Pakistan, Mongolia, Lebanon, Ecuador, Panama, plus several black African nations and South Africa.

I glanced up, my head snapping as the car bounced from a pot hole in the expressway. "Most of these men are Communists, Muslims, Buddhists, or atheists," I said. "What can I say to a group like this? It's impossible!"

Ken cleared his throat. "Well, that's only half the problem, Senator. The South African ambassador said he wouldn't come if any black ambassadors are present."

"We'd better get to the club and get down and pray," I said. "This is the worst mess I've ever seen in my life. I just don't know how to handle this one."

The car was silent as we lurched along the bumpy Manhattan streets. We parked near the Princeton Club, went in, checked our coats, and hurried to the dining room where a T-shaped linen covered table sparkled with glassware and china. We met Dick Hightower there. In a corner of the room, the four of us got on our knees.

"It's Your luncheon, Lord, not ours," I prayed. "You'd better take over and run it. We're helpless and don't know what to do. Help us for the sake of Your Kingdom and Your Son, Jesus Christ."

We were just rising from our knees when the first guests began arriving. To our consternation, they all came.

Hearts beating rapidly, we greeted them, desperately voicing an air of joviality. We noticed that the black ambassadors kept far apart from the South African man. The Mongolian ambassador had written us stating he couldn't speak English but would bring an interpreter. Russian Ambassador Malik turned out to be a dominant and witty man. I noticed that when he talked, the others listened.

After a few minutes of mixing, we invited the group to sit down. Praise God—everyone sat down together! Ambassador Malik sat at the end of the table near me. After we opened our napkins, I explained that I came as a representative of the United States Senate prayer group and wanted to tell them how such groups operated in Washington.

As the waiters began ladling soup into our bowls, Ambassador Malik signaled my attention.

"Senator," he asked with a mischievous smile, "I want to ask you a naughty question."

"Go ahead."

"Why did you not seek reelection to the United States Senate?" His question caught the attention of the others and all chatter ceased.

I sensed that he thought the Watergate controversy had become too much for me. Thank you, Lord. Out of the mouth of an adversary comes the opportunity to testify.

"Well, Mr. Ambassador," I began. "I'm glad to answer that question. But I must tell you that it causes me to testify to my faith in Jesus Christ and my trust in God Almighty."

"Well, Senator," he demurred, his eyes crinkling in Slavic humour, "you know I don't believe those Hebrew myths."

"Mr. Ambassador, perhaps you don't believe the Bible is inspired by God, but I do. And I believe that its truth will eventually bring about the brotherhood of man if we learn to live by it."

His chubby face tightened slightly but his eyes sparked at the scent of combat: "You know, Senator, I'm a Marxist-Leninist. I believe that Communism will bring about the brotherhood of man." Then, as if to quickly change the subject, he asked: "*If* you had stayed in the Senate, the New York *Times* would be here reporting what you had to say today." He looked around the room, then turned back to me smiling impishly. "But who will listen to an ordinary farm boy from Iowa?"

"You're making the assumption," I answered, "that the New York *Times* is more powerful than God. I believe that God can give me any platform that He chooses at any time anywhere in the world and for the purpose He sees fit."

The burly ambassador pushed back his chair, looked at the floor, then sat up and slapped the table: "You sound just like my mother!"

I almost upset my soup bowl.

"Yes," he said, looking around the table, "my mother is a believer and she sounds just like the Senator."

The room was dead silent for a moment. Then Doug Coe cleared his throat: "How do you and your mother get along?"

"Oh," he laughed, "she thinks I'm the greatest son in the world and I think she's the greatest mother in the world and we believe in peaceful coexistence."

"Mr. Ambassador," I said, "I'd like to finish answering your question. Whether you believe it or not, I want to tell you to Whom I'm giving my life. It's to Jesus Christ and I want to make a clear distinction between Him and Christianity.

"I found out long ago that the term 'Christian' turns off more people in the world than it turns on, for one reason alone," I said, "and that's because many people who carry His name fail to live by His words. Thus they are walking, talking hypocrites who neither believe nor trust Him.

"I'm trying not to be a hypocrite," I added. "I'm willing to give my life in trying to obey Him and live by His word. My belief in Christ has led me to reject war as an answer to problems. I don't believe peace on earth will come by negotiation or treaties, alliances or balances of power. I think that peace will come when Christ enters into the hearts of men so they can love one another. To give my full time to help bring this about, Mr. Ambassador," I emphasized, "is the reason I'm not seeking relection to the Senate."

He sat back, quiet and reflective.

At this, the Pakistani ambassador sitting next to him spoke up. "I'm a Muslim," he said, "and as far as I'm concerned we are all hypocrites." He glanced around. "How many of us live by our faith?" he asked. "If we did, the world would be a better place."

Pointing to Ambassador Malik, he said, "Let me tell you about Ambassador Malik's country. I've been all over Russia and I'll tell you something he won't tell you. There are over fifty million Christians in Russia and the churches are full every Sunday."

He looked at Malik and smiled: "Isn't that right, Mr. Ambassador?"

The Russian glanced around with a sly smile and said, "I don't know whether those statistics are reliable or not. They're Christian statistics."

With the tension completely broken at the table, the mood became open and relaxed. One by one the men began talking about their faith, including some who candidly stated they had none.

An interesting little byplay took place between Ambassador Smirnov of Byelorussian Soviet Socialist Republic and his fellow diner Ambassador von Hirschberg of South Africa. Smirnov placed his hand on von Hirschberg's arm and said: "You know, Mr. Ambassador, I have seen you at the U.N. assemblies for years but have never wanted to speak to you." He smiled, adding, "I am happy you are here today and that we can become better acquainted."

Finally, we finished our dessert. I looked around and said, "Well, gentlemen, it's customary at our fellowship get-togethers that we close with prayer. Unless one of you objects, I'd like us to stand in a circle and hold hands while I pray for all of you men and your countries. I'd like to ask God that all of us learn to love one another and live in peace."

I looked around at each man in the eye. There was total silence. Just as we stood up to pray, Ambassador Malik slammed his hand down hard on the table.

My heart leaped. Now what?

"Just a minute," he said loudly, his finger pointing at those of us at the table like a gun barrel. "I want to say something to my colleagues," he turned to me, "and to *you,* Senator."

"You know," he continued, "I've been listening very carefully to the Senator and what he believes." He looked around to make sure everyone was listening. "Now I don't agree with what he believes. I don't accept those Hebrew myths. I believe Communism will bring about true brotherhood and not Jesus Christ. However," he continued, "I can understand Senator Hughes. I can relate to a man who gave up one of the most powerful positions in the world for what he believes in. And I believe he's a man who would lay down his life for his faith."

He turned to me. "I salute and applaud you because if men lived by what they believed, there would be hope for this world."

I stood staggered by his words. "You're very kind, Mr. Ambassador. I pray that I can live up to those words. Now shall we pray? I know you all have to get back to work."

I took the hands of the men next to me and almost everyone did the same. I glanced at Malik and noticed he didn't hold anyone's hand. I reached over and placed his hand into that of his neighbor. He took it and smiled at me. Then I prayed that God would lead and empower these men as they worked for peace on earth. I finished in the name of Jesus.

Finally, every ambassador left except one man, the Mongolian, who stood by the wall silently. He walked up to me without his interpreter and in perfect English said, "Mr. Senator, I'm a nonbeliever but I believe in the philosophy you express. I believe that it can help heal nations and I wonder if you would come to my country and share it with the leaders of my nation."

I told him I would consider it. After he left, I leaned against the wall in awe at what had happened during that hour. Black and white Africans had shaken hands and broken bread together, we had prayed in the name of Jesus with the most divided religions of the world. It had been a luncheon which started with a sense of defeat, yet the Holy Spirit had used the voice of the adversary to invite from me a witness for Christ.

If I had sought reelection to the Senate, I wonder if I would have had an opening to present the love of Jesus Christ to these men.

Since Then...

THE CALLS TO witness to God's message keep coming to Harold Hughes. In this he continues working with alcoholics both on an individual and group basis. In 1972 he was named President of the World Council on Alcoholism, and has been on the board of the National Council of Alcoholism since 1974. He continues to work closely as a consultant with R. Brinkley Smithers of the Smithers Foundation for the Prevention of Alcoholism, and with Maurice Shear of Mount Pleasant Hospital for the treatment of alcoholics in Lynn, Massachusetts.

In addition, he travels the world on preaching missions and as retreat leader, discussing God's love everywhere from a barrio in the Philippines to conferences at Windsor Castle in England.

He also continues his outreach to the North American Indian nations with Mark Small of the Northern Cheyenne people in Indian prayer groups in Washington, D.C. and counseling with tribal leaders throughout the country.

Again, he finds himself going back to prison, now as part of Prison Fellowship, a dynamic nationwide ministry to men behind bars. In this he works with Charles Colson whose inspiration for this outreach was born in his own prison experience.

Still involved in government affairs, Hughes visits both the United States Congress and federal agencies regularly, attending prayer groups, Bible studies and continuing his ministry as an unofficial counselor.

From 1975 through 1976 he was special consultant to the Chairman of the Judiciary Committee, also serving it as a special advisor on the Panama Canal Zone. During this same period he also chaired the Commission on the Operation of the Senate.

In January 1977 Harold's mother died at the age of 87. At the time he was leading the devotions at the National Prayer Breakfast in Washington, D.C. Her death brought him again to the wintry hill overlooking Ida Grove where, the wind whipping his coat, he looked on the snow-covered graves of his brother, daughter, father and mother.

Life continued on at Cedar Point. Hughes and local men worked through the winter of 1977–78 repairing and reroofing buildings and landscaping the grounds. In January 1978 he was called to Hollywood where he appeared before the cameras portraying himself in the filmed version of Charles Colson's book *BORN AGAIN* for which he earned the plaudits of professional film critics.

In the spring of 1978, the Canadian geese lifted from the bays and streams of the Chesapeake and winged north in great honking formations. Then another sorrow came as Connie's husband, Dennis, was killed in a traffic accident in April 1978 near their Colorado home. She and her two children came to live near Cedar Point.

Following sadness came joy when the following month Phyllis married a young writer, Mike Ewing, in a beautiful outdoor ceremony on Broad Creek.

As this book goes to press, it is autumn 1978. Through his office window Harold Hughes can watch large flocks of geese settling on the ruffled waters of the Bay, returning again in the great rhythm of God. He is glad to be part of that rhythm.

> He who, from zone to zone,
> Guides through the boundless sky thy certain flight,
> In the long way that I must tread alone,
> Will lead my steps aright.*

THE EDITOR

---

* From *To A Waterfowl* by William Cullen Bryant

Harold E. Hughes

Commerce Commission—Governor—U.S. Senator

A PARTIAL RECORD

Iowa Commerce Commission—1958–1962

Chairman
Made Commission appointive instead of elective.

Governor of Iowa—1962–1968

Active in trade and commerce—

Enacted a uniform commercial code as a guideline for commerce.

Organized "Sell Iowa" delegations to financial centers of United States and dispatched foreign trade missions to three continents.

Iowa broke all records for industrial development during his tenure as Governor.

Concern for the elderly—

Provided tax relief for elderly.

Established Iowa's first statutory commission for the aging.

Schools—

Carried through state's first realistic long-range school financing plan.

Established educational radio and TV programs.

Initiated plan for area vocational/technical schools.

Inaugurated a long-needed state scholarship program for colleges and universities.

People—

Took Iowa's first action for consumer protection.

Established equality of voting rights.

Established civil service system for state employees.

Made substantial gains in unemployment and workmen's compensation.

Established the state's first statutory civil rights commission.

Improved state programs for dependent children, mentally ill, the retarded and physically handicapped.

Built a maximum security hospital for treating the criminally disturbed.

Founded an alcoholic treatment center.

Promulgated liquor control laws.

Inaugurated comprehensive state planning, coordinating state activities and resources.

Established a state law enforcement academy.

United States Senator—1969–1975

Assistant Majority Whip

Member of Legislative Review Committee of the Senate

Active throughout Senate career in alcohol and drug abuse reform—

1969—Appointed Chairman of first congressional subcommittee on alcoholism and narcotics.

1969—Won approval of funding for alcoholism program in Office of Economic Opportunity.

1970—Author of first comprehensive Federal Alcoholism Treatment and Prevention Act.

1970—Prompted the Defense Department and other agencies to give full recognition of alcoholism and drug treatment in Vietnam and throughout armed services.

1971—Appointed Chairman of Armed Services Subcommittee on Alcoholism and Drug Abuse.

1971–72—Member of National Commission on Marijuana and Drug Abuse.

1973—Sponsored congressional action to prevent job discrimination against recovered alcoholics and drug patients.

Early and vocal opponent of Vietnam War—

1972—Added provision for SALT I approval resolution stating that the United States should not develop a nuclear first-strike capability.

1972–73—Helped end Vietnam War by exposing unauthorized bombing of North Vietnam and secret bombing of Cambodia.

1974—Author of Hughes-Ryan amendment forbidding covert operations by CIA in foreign countries unless Congress is informed.

1974—Helped bring Southeast Asian war to end by winning congressional approval of reductions of amount of military aid going to South Vietnam.

Member of following Senate committees and subcommittees:

Armed Services
   Strategic Arms Limitation Talks (SALT)
   Tactical Air Power
   Close Air Support

Banking and Currency

Labor and Public Welfare
    Alcoholism and Narcotics—Chairman
    International Health, Education & Labor—Chairman
    Aging
    Employment, Manpower and Poverty
    Migratory Labor
    Health
    Railroad Retirement
    Labor

Veterans Affairs
    Housing and Insurance—Chairman
    Health and Hospitals
    Compensation and Pensions

My Appreciation

TO THE MEN AND WOMEN ON THE FARM
AT CEDAR POINT:
> Dick and Mary Felgenhouer
> Kenny and Faye Phillips
> Charles and Shirley Parker
> Jim and Catherine Lednum
> Larry and Nancy Woolford
> Mark and Cloette Small
> Dave Faulkner
> Charles Powell

Who helped in the labor—and all the dozens of volunteers

TO MY FAMILY:
> Eva, Connie, and Phyllis and Michael Ewing
> Tracy and Jon Otto

To Dr. Wayne Shoemaker and Father Harry Dailey, my constant counselors and leaders in the faith.

To Douglas Coe, Fred Heyn, Jim Hiskey, John Staggers, Al Quie, Graham Purcell, Paul Temple, Chuck Colson, Senator Chiles, Senator Bartlett, Senator Dominici, Senator Nunn, and Senator Culver.

To William Knapp, Joe Rosenfield, Ed Campbell, Park Rinard, Dwight Jensen, Martin Jensen, Ruth Yauk, Jo Nobles, Nancy Olson, and all my staff in the Governor's and Senator's offices.

To R. Brinkley Smithers who, in the field of alcoholism, was a mainstay of encouragement and support.

To Mercedes McCambridge, Judge Ray Harrison, and all those who had the courage to stand as recovered alcoholics when it would have been easy to do otherwise.

To my many friends in Ida Grove who forgave and helped me along the way. There is no way I can express my love to the hundreds who helped me with selfless trust throughout my life.